CompTIA® CASP+
Practice Tests
EXAM CAS-003

CompTIA® CASP+
Practice Tests
EXAM CAS-003

Nadean H. Tanner

SYBEX®
A Wiley Brand

6b 65 6e 6e 65 74 68 2c 20 69 20 6c 6f 76 65 20 79 6f 75 21

Acknowledgments

To Kenneth, thank you for all the love and question suggestions and for cooking dinner when I had a deadline.

To Shelby and Gavin, thank you for your patience and encouragement and for eating the dinners Daddy cooked.

To Kenyon Brown for making the ask, to Jan Lynn for keeping me on task, and to my dearest friend, Ryan Hendricks, for making sure I was right. I couldn't have done this without such talent and dedication.

And, to those of you taking the CASP+ exam, whether you volunteered or were voluntold—this book is for you. Best of luck, you got this!

About the Author

Nadean Hutto Tanner is the senior manager of Technical Education Strategy for Puppet software. Prior to Puppet, she was the lead instructor at Rapid7 teaching Nexpose, incident detection and response, and Metasploit. For more than 20 years, she has worked in academia as the IT director at a private school and a technology instructor at the university level. Tanner holds many industry certifications including the following:

ISC^2: CISSP

CompTIA: A+, Network+, Security+, Server+, CTT+, CIOS, CNIP, CSIS, CASP+

ITIL: ITILv3

Microsoft: MCTS, MCITP, MCSA, MCT, MCP, MOS

Rapid7: IICS, IVMCA, MPCS, NACA, NCP

Tanner has trained and consulted for Fortune 50 companies in cybersecurity and security awareness, and has received hands-on experience working for the Department of Defense.

She is the author of the *Cybersecurity Blue Team Toolkit*, published by Wiley in 2019.

About the Technical Editor

Ryan Hendricks (CISSP, CEH, CASP+, Security+) has more than 15 years of cybersecurity and intelligence experience. His first venture was working on intelligence operations for the U.S. Navy; he continued in the government and private sectors as an educator, facilitator, consultant, and advisor for a multitude of information technology and cybersecurity principals.

Hendricks holds many certifications covering hardware, networking, operating systems, and cybersecurity. He worked as a trainer for the U.S. Department of Defense, educating hundreds of students on everything from military communication systems to the CompTIA CASP+ and (ISC)² CISSP certifications.

Hendricks currently supports all technical product training operations at VMware Carbon Black, including creating content, developing labs, updating materials, piloting and expanding the certification programs, mentoring and managing the training team, and educating anyone who is willing to learn. When not working, he tries to balance spending his time learning new security tools and attack techniques to feed his need for knowledge and playing video games with his kids.

Contents at a Glance

Contents

Contents

Introduction

CompTIA CASP+ (CompTIA Advanced Security Practitioner) Practice Tests is a companion volume to *CompTIA CASP+ (CompTIA Advanced Security Practitioner) Study Guide* (Wiley, 2019, Parker/Gregg). If you're looking to test your knowledge before you take the CASP+ exam, this book will help you by providing a combination of 1,000 questions that cover the five CASP+ domains and by including easy-to-understand explanations of both right and wrong answers.

If you're just starting to prepare for the CASP+ exam, we highly recommend that you use *CompTIA Advanced Security Practitioner+ (CASP+) Study Guide* to help you learn about each of the domains covered by the CASP+ exam. Once you're ready to test your knowledge, use this book to help find places where you might need to study more or to practice for the exam itself.

Because this is a companion to *CASP+ Study Guide*, this book is designed to be similar to taking the CASP+ exam. It contains multi-part scenarios as well as standard multiple-choice questions similar to those you may encounter on the certification exam.

CompTIA

CompTIA is a nonprofit trade organization that offers certification in a variety of IT areas, ranging from the skills that a PC support technician needs, which are covered on the A+ exam, to advanced skills like the CompTIA Advanced Security Practitioner (CASP+) certification. CompTIA divides its exams into four categories based on the skill level required for the exam and the topics it covers, as shown here:

Infrastructure	Core	Cybersecurity	Additional Professional
Cloud+	ITF+	CySA+	CTT+
Linux+	A+	PenTest+	Cloud Essentials+
Server+	Network+	CASP+	Project+
	Security+		

As you can see, the CompTIA Advanced Security Practitioner+ certification fits into the Cybersecurity category, which is the same place you'll find the popular A+, Network+, and Security+ credentials. The CompTIA Advanced Security Practitioner+ exam is a more advanced exam, intended for professionals with 10 years of hands-on experience who possess the knowledge covered by all of the prior exams.

CompTIA certifications are ISO and ANSI accredited, and they are used throughout multiple industries as a measure of technical skill and knowledge. In addition, CompTIA certifications, including the Security+ and the CASP+, have been approved by the U.S. government as information assurance baseline certifications and are included in the State Department's Skills Incentive Program.

The CompTIA Advanced Security Practitioner+ Exam

The CompTIA Advanced Security Practitioner+ exam, which CompTIA refers to as the CASP+, is designed to be a vendor-neutral certification for cybersecurity, threat, and vulnerability analysts. The CASP+ certification is designed for security analysts and engineers as well as security operations center (SOC) staff, vulnerability analysts, and threat intelligence analysts. It focuses on security analytics and practical use of security tools in real-world scenarios.

The CASP+ exam is conducted in a format that CompTIA calls *performance-based assessment*. This means the exam uses hands-on simulations using actual security tools and scenarios to perform tasks that match those found in the daily work of a security practitioner. Exam questions may include many types of questions such as multiple-choice, fill-in-the-blank, multiple-response, drag-and-drop, and image-based problems.

CompTIA recommends that test takers have 10 years of information security–related experience before taking this exam. The exam costs $439 in the United States, with roughly equivalent prices in other locations around the globe. You can find more details about the CASP+ exam and how to take it at certification.comptia.org/certifications/comptia-advanced-security-practitioner.

Study and Exam Preparation Tips

We recommend you use this book in conjunction with *CompTIA Advanced Security Practitioner+ (CASP+) Study Guide*. Read through chapters in the study guide and then try your hand at the practice questions associated with each domain in this book.

You should also keep in mind that the CASP+ certification is designed to test practical experience, so you should also make sure you get some hands-on time with the security tools covered on the exam. CompTIA recommends the use of NetWars-style simulations, penetration testing and defensive cybersecurity simulations, and incident response training to prepare for the CASP+.

Additional resources for hands-on exercises include the following:

- Exploit-Exercises.com provides virtual machines, documentation, and challenges covering a wide range of security issues at exploit-exercises.com/.

- Hacking-Lab provides capture-the-flag (CTF) exercises in a variety of fields at www
  .hacking-lab.com/index.html.
- The OWASP Hacking Lab provides excellent web application–focused exercises at
  www.owasp.org/index.php/OWASP_Hacking_Lab.
- PentesterLab provides subscription-based access to penetration testing exercises at
  www.pentesterlab.com/exercises/.

Because the exam uses scenario-based learning, expect the questions to involve analysis and thought, rather than relying on simple memorization. The questions in this book are intended to help you be confident that you know the topic well enough to think through hands-on exercises.

Taking the Exam

Once you are fully prepared to take the exam, you can visit the CompTIA website to purchase your exam voucher.

www.comptiastore.com/Articles.asp?ID=265&category=vouchers

CompTIA partners with Pearson VUE's testing centers, so your next step will be to locate a testing center near you. In the United States, you can do this based on your address or your ZIP code, while non-U.S. test takers may find it easier to enter their city and country. You can search for a test center near you at the Pearson Vue website, where you will need to navigate to "Find a test center."

www.pearsonvue.com/comptia/

Now that you know where you'd like to take the exam, simply set up a Pearson VUE testing account and schedule an exam.

certification.comptia.org/testing/schedule-exam

On the day of the test, bring *two* forms of identification, and make sure to show up with plenty of time before the exam starts. Remember that you will not be able to take your notes, electronic devices (including smartphones and watches), or other materials in with you.

After the CompTIA Advanced Security Practitioner+ Exam

Once you have taken the exam, you will be notified of your score immediately, so you'll know if you passed the test right away. You should keep track of your score report with your exam registration records and the email address you used to register for the exam.

Maintaining Your Certification

CompTIA certifications must be renewed on a periodic basis. To renew your certification, you can either pass the most current version of the exam, earn a qualifying higher-level CompTIA or industry certification, or complete sufficient continuing education activities to earn enough continuing education units (CEUs) to renew it. CompTIA provides information on renewals via its website.

certification.comptia.org/continuing-education/how-to-renew

When you sign up to renew your certification, you will be asked to agree to the CE program's Code of Ethics, to pay a renewal fee, and to submit the materials required for your chosen renewal method.

You can find a full list of the industry certifications you can use to acquire CEUs toward renewing the CASP+ here:

certification.comptia.org/continuing-education/renewothers/renewing-casp

Using This Book to Practice

This book is composed of five domain-based chapters and two randomized test chapters to emulate the real test experience.

As you work through questions in this book, you will encounter tools and technology that you may not be familiar with. If you find that you are facing a consistent gap or that a domain is particularly challenging, we recommend spending some time with books and materials that tackle that domain in depth. This can help you fill in gaps and help you be more prepared for the exam.

CASP+ Domains

The following table shows how much weight is given to an objective on the exam.

Domain	Percentage of Exam
1.0 Risk Management	19%
2.0 Enterprise Security Architecture	25%
3.0 Enterprise Security Operations	20%
4.0 Technical Integration of Enterprise Security	23%
5.0 Research, Development, and Collaboration	13%
Total	100%

Objectives Map

The following table shows where you can find an objective covered in this book.

Objective	Chapter
1.0 Risk Management	
1.1 Summarize business and industry influences and associated security risks.	Chapter 1
Risk Management of new products, technology, and users. Business models including partnerships, outsourcing, cloud, and strategies around mergers, divestiture, and acquisitions. Data ownership and reclassification. Rules, policies, regulations. Competitors, auditors, regulations.	
1.2 Compare and contrast security, privacy policies, and procedures based on organizational requirements.	Chapter 1
Policy and process life cycles. Legal compliance and advocacy by partnering with human resources, legal, and management. Common business documents supporting security including risk assessments, business impact analysis, interoperability agreement, interconnection security agreements, memorandum of understanding, service level and operating level agreements, as well as non-disclosure, business partnership, and master service agreements. Research security requirements such as requests for proposals, for quotes, and for information. Privacy requirements and development of policies containing standard security practices.	
1.3 Given a scenario, execute risk mitigation strategies and controls.	Chapter 1
CIA and security controls. Scenario planning and risk analysis. Risk determination using metrics, such as annual loss and single loss expectancy. Recommending a strategy based on risk avoidance, transference, mitigation, and acceptance. Risk management processes, including exemptions, deterrence, inherent, and residual. Business continuity planning.	
1.4 Analyze risk metric scenarios to secure the enterprise.	Chapter 1
Review effectiveness of security controls with gap analysis, lessons learned, and after-action reports. Reverse engineer existing solutions and analyze metrics. Prototype solutions, benchmarks, and baselines, and interpretation of data to anticipate cyber defense needs. Analyze possible solutions based on performance, latency, scalability, capability, usability, maintainability, availability, and recoverability.	

Objective	Chapter
2.0 Enterprise Security Architecture	
2.1 Analyze a scenario and integrate network and security components, concepts, and architectures to meet security requirements.	Chapter 2
Physical and virtual network security devices as well as application and protocol-aware technologies. Advanced network design and complex network security for data in transit. Secure configuration, baselining, and monitoring of assets. Security zones, network access control, and critical infrastructure.	
2.2 Analyze a scenario to integrate security controls for host devices to meet security requirements.	Chapter 2
Trusted operating systems, endpoint security software, host hardening, and hardware vulnerabilities. Terminal services and application delivery services.	
2.3 Analyze a scenario to integrate security controls for mobile and small-form-factor devices to meet security requirements.	Chapter 2
Enterprise mobility management, including containers, remote assistance and wiping, VPN, and mobile payment systems. Security implications and privacy concerns of data storage. Wearable technology and security implications.	
2.4 Given software vulnerability scenarios, select the appropriate security controls.	Chapter 2
Application security design considerations and application issues, including XSS, CSRF, SQLi, session management, input validation, buffer overflow, memory leaks, race conditions, and privilege escalation. Application sandboxing, secure encrypted enclaves, database monitoring, web application firewalls, and client-side versus server-side processing. Operating system and firmware vulnerabilities.	
3.0 Enterprise Security Operations	
3.1 Given a scenario, conduct a security assessment using the appropriate methods.	Chapter 3
Malware, debugging, reconnaissance, fingerprinting, code review, social engineering, OSINT, and pivoting. Type of penetration testing, including black, white, and gray box. Vulnerability assessments, audits, and team exercises.	

Objective	Chapter
3.2 Analyze a scenario or output, and select the appropriate tool for a security assessment.	Chapter 3

Network tools, such as port scanners, vulnerability scanners, protocol analyzers, fuzzers, and logging-analysis tools. Host tool types, such as password crackers, command line tools, SCAP, FIM, antivirus, and reverse-engineering tools. Physical security tools, such as lock picks, RFID tools, and IR camera.

3.3 Given a scenario, implement incident response and recovery procedures.	Chapter 3

E-discovery, data retention, recovery, ownership, and handling. Data breach response, detection, mitigation, recovery, response, and disclosure. Incident detection and response, incident response tools to help determine the severity of the incident or breach, and posting incident response.

4.0 Technical Integration of Enterprise Security

4.1 Given a scenario, integrate hosts, storage, networks, and applications into a secure enterprise architecture.	Chapter 4

Data flow security. Open, competing, adherence, and de facto standards. Interoperability issues, including software types, legacy systems, application requirements, protocols, and standard data formats. Resilience issues, provisioning, and deprovisioning resources, including users, servers, virtual systems, and applications. Network segmentation, security and privacy considerations, and enterprise applications.

4.2 Given a scenario, integrate cloud and virtualization technologies into a secure enterprise architecture.	Chapter 4

Technical deployment models (outsourcing/insourcing/managed services/partnerships), cloud and virtualization considerations, security advantages, and disadvantages of virtualization. Cloud-augmented security services, and vulnerabilities associated with hosts with different security requirements.

4.3 Given a scenario, integrate and troubleshoot advanced authentication and authorization technologies to support enterprise security objectives.	Chapter 4

Authentication, authorization, attestation, identity proofing, identity propagation, federation, and trust models.

Objective	Chapter
4.4 Given a scenario, implement cryptographic techniques.	Chapter 4

Cryptographic techniques, such as hashing, digital signatures, code signing, data-in-transit encryption, data-in-memory processing, data-at-rest encryption, and steganography. Implementing encryption in an enterprise, such as DRM, SSH, SSL, S/MIME, and PKI.

4.5 Given a scenario, select the appropriate control to secure communications and collaboration solutions.	Chapter 4

Remote access, resources and services, and remote assistance. Unified collaboration tools for video/audio/web conferencing, instant messaging, email, VoIP, and collaboration sites.

5.0 Research, Development, and Collaboration

5.1 Given a scenario, apply research methods to determine industry trends and their impact on the enterprise.	Chapter 5

Ongoing research in best practices, new technologies, security systems, and services. Threat intelligence of latest attacks, current vulnerabilities, and threats; zero-day mitigation controls; and threat modeling. Research security implications of emerging business tools and the global IA industry/community.

5.2 Given a scenario, implement security activities across the technology life cycle.	Chapter 5

Systems/software development lifecycles. Application frameworks, development approaches, secure coding standards, and documentation. Validation and acceptance testing. Adapting solutions to address emerging threats, security trends, and disruptive technology. Asset management and inventory control.

5.3 Explain the importance of interaction across diverse business units to achieve security goals.	Chapter 5

Interpreting security requirements and goals to communicate with stakeholders, such as sales, programmers, DBA, network administrators, human resources, and legal counsel. Provide guidance and recommendations to staff and management on processes and security controls. Governance, risk, and compliance committees.

CompTIA® CASP+
Practice Tests
EXAM CAS-003

Chapter

1

Risk Management

THE CASP+ EXAM TOPICS COVERED IN THIS CHAPTER INCLUDE:

✓ **Domain 1: Risk Management**

- 1.1 Summarize business and industry influences and associated security risks.

  - Risk management of new products, new technologies, and user behaviors

  - New or changing business models/strategies

    - Partnerships

    - Outsourcing

    - Cloud

    - Acquisition/merger—divestiture/demerger

    - Data ownership

    - Data reclassification

  - Security concerns of integrating diverse industries

    - Rules

    - Policies

    - Regulations

    - Export controls

    - Legal requirements

    - Geography

    - Data sovereignty

    - Jurisdictions

  - Internal and external influences

    - Competitors

    - Auditors/audit findings

    - Regulatory entities

    - Internal and external client requirements

    - Top-level management

- Impact of de-perimeterization (e.g., constantly changing network boundary)

  - Telecommuting
  - Cloud
  - Mobile
  - BYOD
  - Outsourcing
  - Ensuring third-party providers have requisite levels of information security

- 1.2 Compare and contrast security, privacy policies, and procedures based on organizational requirements.

  - Policy and process life cycle management

    - New business
    - New technologies
    - Environmental changes
    - Regulatory requirements
    - Emerging risks

  - Support legal compliance and advocacy by partnering with human resources, legal, management, and other entities.

  - Understand common business documents to support security.

    - Risk Assessment (RA)
    - Business Impact Analysis (BIA)
    - Interoperability Agreement (IA)
    - Interconnection Security Agreement (ISA)
    - Memorandum of Understanding (MOU)
    - Service-Level Agreement (SLA)
    - Operating-Level Agreement (OLA)
    - Non-Disclosure Agreement (NDA)
    - Business Partnership Agreement (BPA)
    - Master Service Agreement (MSA)

- Research security requirements for contracts.
  - Request for Proposal (RFP)
  - Request for Quote (RFQ)
  - Request for Information (RFI)
- Understand general privacy principles for sensitive information.
- Support the development of policies containing standard security practices.
  - Separation of duties
  - Job rotation
  - Mandatory vacation
  - Least privilege
  - Incident response
  - Forensic tasks
  - Employment and termination procedures
  - Continuous monitoring
  - Training and awareness for users
  - Auditing requirements and frequency
  - Information classification
- 1.3 Given a scenario, execute risk mitigation strategies and controls.
  - Categorize data types by impact levels based on CIA.
  - Incorporate stakeholder input into CIA impact-level decisions.
  - Determine minimum-required security controls based on aggregate score.
  - Select and implement controls based on CIA requirements and organizational policies.
  - Extreme scenario planning/worst-case scenario
  - Conduct system-specific risk analysis.
  - Make a risk determination based upon known metrics.

- Magnitude of impact based on ALE and SLE
- Likelihood of threat
  - Motivation
  - Source
  - ARO
  - Trend analysis
- Return on Investment (ROI)
- Total cost of ownership
- Translate technical risks in business terms.
- Recommend which strategy should be applied based on risk appetite.
  - Avoid
  - Transfer
  - Mitigate
  - Accept
- Risk management processes
- Exemptions—Deterrence—Inherent—Residual
- Continuous improvement/monitoring
- Business continuity planning
  - RTO
  - RPO
  - MTTR
  - MTBF
- IT governance
  - Adherence to risk management frameworks
  - Enterprise resilience
- 1.4 Analyze risk metric scenarios to secure the enterprise.
  - Review effectiveness of existing security controls.
    - Gap analysis
    - Lessons learned
    - After-action reports

- Reverse engineer/deconstruct existing solutions.
- Creation, collection, and analysis of metrics
  - KPIs
  - KRIs
- Prototype and test multiple solutions.
- Create benchmarks and compare to baselines.
- Analyze and interpret trend data to anticipate cyber defense needs.
- Analyze security solution metrics and attributes to ensure they meet business needs.
  - Performance
  - Latency
  - Scalability
  - Capability
  - Usability
  - Maintainability
  - Availability
  - Recoverability
  - ROI
  - TCO
- Use judgment to solve problems where the most secure solution is not feasible.

1. One of the biggest tasks as a security professional is identifying vulnerabilities. What is the difference between a vulnerability and a threat?

   A. A vulnerability is a weakness in system design, procedure, or code. A threat is the circumstance or likelihood of a vulnerability being exploited.

   B. A vulnerability is the driving force behind the activity. A threat is the probability of an attack.

   C. A vulnerability is the value to an institution where a threat is the source of the risk, internal or external.

   D. A vulnerability is the probability of the realization of a threat. A threat is the driving force behind the activity.

2. Which of the following BEST defines risk in IT?

   A. You have a vulnerability with a known active threat.

   B. You have a threat with a known vulnerability.

   C. You have a risk with a known threat.

   D. You have a threat with a known exploit.

3. A situation that affects the CIA triad of an IT asset can include an internal and external risk source. A breach of physical security can be instigated by_____.

   A. untrusted insiders or trusted outsiders

   B. trusted insiders or untrusted outsiders

   C. hidden costs

   D. service deterioration

4. Your organization provides cloud computing for a highly classified project. You implemented a virtual data center with multifactor authentication. Using the SIEM, you discovered a breach affecting confidential data. Sensitive information was found within the hypervisor. What has most probably occurred?

   A. You found a token and a RAM exploit that was used to move data.

   B. You found a local admin who could move data to their hard drive.

   C. A vulnerable server was unpatched, and the attacker was able to use VMEscape for access.

   D. A guest account used privilege escalation to move data from one virtual token to another.

5. An internal auditor has completed the annual audit of the company's financial records. The report has found several lapses in security policies and procedures, including proper disposal and sanitation of financial transactions. What would be their recommendation?

   A. You should wait for an external audit.

   B. You should recommend a separation of duties.

   C. You should institute job rotation.

   D. You should implement mandatory training.

6. An analyst has been attempting to acquire a budget for a new security tool. Which of the following should the analyst give to management to support the request?

   A. Threat reports and a trend analysis

   B. Interconnection security agreement (ISA)

   C. Master service agreement (MSA)

   D. Request for information (RFI)

7. An audit found a lack of security controls regarding employee termination. The current company policy states that the terminated employee's account is disabled within one hour of termination. The audit found that more than 10 percent of terminated employees still have active accounts. What is the BEST course of action?

   A. Review the termination requirements.

   B. Implement a monthly review of terminated employees.

   C. Update the policy to accommodate the delay.

   D. Review the termination policy with managers.

8. Several servers went offline since an update was pushed out. Other servers without that patch are still operational but vulnerable to attack. As the security administrator, you must ensure that critical servers are patched while minimizing downtime. What is the best strategy to minimize risk?

   A. All updates are tested in a lab before deployment.

   B. All systems in production are patched automatically.

   C. Production servers are patched only when updates are released.

   D. All updates are tested after being installed in a live environment.

9. Your organization is in the middle of a risk assessment for a new network infrastructure upgrade. All planning is complete, and your plan must include which security controls are to be put in place during each stage of the upgrade. What risk response is most likely being considered while creating an SLA contract with a third party?

   A. Accepting risk

   B. Identifying risk

   C. Transferring risk

   D. Mitigating risk

10. Your company hired a new CISO, and the first order of business is to perform a risk assessment on a new mobile device that is to be given to all employees. The device is commercially available and runs a popular operating system. What are the most important security factors that you should consider while conducting this risk assessment?

   A. Remote wipe and controls, encryption, and vendor track record

   B. Encryption, IPV6, cost, and color

   C. Remote wipe, maintenance, and inventory management

   D. Remote monitoring, cost, SSD, and vendor track record

11. Your CISO wants you to conduct a risk assessment for a vital new healthcare system that needs to be in place in a month. As you conduct the assessment, you find a vulnerability report that details the low likelihood of exploitation. Why does your CISO still have reservations about making an exemption for this risk?

    A. The CISO has concerns about government regulations and compliance.

    B. The CISO feels rushed to make a decision.

    C. Competitors have elected not to use this system.

    D. Even one attack would be devastating to the organization, both financially and to its reputation.

12. Your company is looking at a new strategy to reach customers that includes social media. The marketing director would like to share news, updates, and promotions on all social websites. What are the major security risks to be aware of when this new program goes into effect?

    A. Malware, phishing, and social engineering

    B. DDOS, brute force, and SQLi

    C. Mergers and data ownership

    D. Regulatory requirements and environmental changes

13. Your CEO purchased the latest and greatest mobile device (BYOD) and now wants you to connect it to the company's intranet. You have been told to research this process. What BEST security recommendation do you recommend to make the biggest impact on risk?

    A. Making this a new corporate policy available for everyone

    B. Adding a PIN to access the device

    C. Encrypting nonvolatile memory

    D. Auditing requirements

14. Your organization wants to move a vital company process to the cloud. You are tasked with conducting a risk analysis to minimize the risk of hosting email in the cloud. What is the best path forward?

    A. All logins must be done over an encrypted channel and obtain an NDA and SLA from the cloud provider.

    B. Remind all users not to write down their passwords.

    C. Make sure that the OLA covers more than just operations.

    D. Require data classification.

15. A web developer builds a web form for customers to fill out and respond to the company via a web page. What is the first thing that a developer should do to avoid this page becoming a security risk?

    A. SQLi

    B. Input validation

    C. Cross-site request forgery

    D. Fuzzing

16. Your organization is pressured by both the company board and employees to allow personal devices on the network. They asked for email and calendar items to be synced between the company ecosystem and their BYOD. Which of the following BEST balances security and usability?

    A. Allowing access for the management team only, because they have a need for convenient access

    B. Not allowing any access between a BYOD device and the corporate network, only cloud applications

    C. Only allowing certain types of devices that can be centrally managed

    D. Reviewing security policy and performing a risk evaluation focused on central management, including the remote wipe and encryption of sensitive data

17. Your organization decided to outsource systems that are not mission critical. You have been tasked with calculating the risk of outsourcing these systems because a recent review indicates that core business functions are dependent on these outsourced systems. What is the BEST tool to use?

    A. Business impact analysis

    B. Annual loss expectancy

    C. Total cost of ownership

    D. Gap analysis

18. The retail division of your organization purchased touchscreen tablets and wireless mice and keyboards for all their representatives to increase productivity. You communicated the risk of nonstandard devices and wireless devices, but the deployment continued. What is the BEST method for evaluating and presenting potential threats to upper management?

    A. Conducting a vulnerability assessment

    B. Developing a standard image for these assets

    C. Making new recommendations for security policies

    D. Working with the management team to understand the processes these devices will interface with, and to classify the risk connected with the hardware/software deployment life cycle

19. Your organization experiences a security incident that costs $20,000 in downtime each time it occurs. It's happened twice this fiscal year. The device causing the issue is scheduled to be upgraded next year. The cost of implementing a fix is more than $250,000 and also requires maintenance contracts. What is the *most* cost-effective way to deal with this risk?

    A. Mitigate the risk.

    B. Avoid the risk.

    C. Accept the risk.

    D. Transfer the risk.

20. You have an asset that is valued at $1,000. The EF for this asset is 10 percent. The ARO is 2. What is the ALE?

    A. The ALE is $200.

    B. The ALE is $100.

    C. The ALE is $400.

    D. ALE cannot be calculated with the numbers provided.

21. A security administrator is reviewing an audit and finds that two users in human resources also have access to finance data. One of these users is a recruiter, while the other is an intern. What security measure is being violated?

    A. Job rotation

    B. Disclosure

    C. Mandatory vacation

    D. Least privilege

22. Your organization experienced a security event that led to the loss and disruption of services. You were chosen to investigate the disruption to prevent the risk of it happening again. What is this process called?

    A. Incident management

    B. Forensic tasks

    C. Mandatory vacation

    D. Job rotation

23. Your new role with a law enforcement agency is to support the development of policies and to implement standard IT security practices. You will be writing the procedures for _____ such as collecting digital evidence, recording observations, and taking photographs.

    A. least privilege

    B. incident responses

    C. master service agreements

    D. forensic tasks

24. Your company is working with a new ISP and wants to find out technical details, such as system numbers, port numbers, IP addressing, and the protocols used. What document will you find this information in?

    A. Memorandum of understanding

    B. Disclosure of assets

    C. Operation level agreement

    D. Interconnection security agreements

25. Your new line of business is selling directly to the public. Two major risks are your lack of experience with establishing and managing credit card processing and the additional compliance requirements. What is the BEST risk strategy?

    A. Transferring the initial risk by outsourcing

    B. Transferring the risk to another internal department

    C. Mitigating the risks by hiring additional IT staff

    D. Accepting the risks and log acceptance

26. A large enterprise is expanding through the acquisition of a second corporation. What should be done first before connecting the networks?

    A. System and network vulnerability scan

    B. Implementation of a firewall system

    C. Development of a risk analysis for the two networks

    D. Complete review of the new corporation

27. The CISO is researching ways to reduce risk associated with the separation of duties. In the case where one person is not available, another needs to be able to perform all the duties of their co-workers. What should the CISO implement to reduce risk?

    A. Mandatory requirement of a shared account for administrative purposes

    B. Audit of all ongoing administration activities

    C. Separation of duties to ensure no single administrator has access

    D. Role-based security on the primary role and provisional access to the secondary role on a case-by-case basis

28. How can you secure third-party applications and introduce only acceptable risk into your environment?

    A. Code review and simulation

    B. Roundtable discussions

    C. Parallel trials

    D. Full deployment

29. Your company policy states that only authorized software is allowed on the corporate network, and BYOD needs to be configured by IT for the proper software and security controls to adhere to company policy. The marketing manager plugs in a USB received at a conference into their laptop and it auto-launches. What is the greatest risk?

    A. Employee transferring the customer database and IP

    B. Employee using non-approved accounting applications

    C. Infecting the network with malware

    D. File corruption by the USB exiting out improperly

30. What risks and mitigations are associated with BYOD?

    A. Risk: Data exfiltration
        Mitigation: Remote wipe

    B. Risk: Confidentiality leaks
        Mitigation: Corporate policy

    C. Risk: Theft
        Mitigation: Minimal storage

    D. Risk: GPS tracking
        Mitigation: Minimal cost

31. Your software company is acquiring a new program from a competitor. All the people working with that company will become your employees. They will retain all access to their former network and resources for two weeks to ease the transition. For productivity, the decision was made to join the two networks. Which of the following threats is the highest risk for your company?

    A. IP filters

    B. Loss of code

    C. Malware

    D. Comingling the networks

32. Your bank outsourced the security department to an outside firm. The CISO just learned that this third-party outside firm subcontracted security operations to another organization. The board of directors is now pressuring the CISO to ensure that the bank is protected legally. What is the BEST course of action for the CISO to take?

    A. Creating another NDA directly with the subcontractor

    B. Confirming that the current outside firm has an SLA with the subcontractor

    C. Performing a risk analysis on the subcontractor

    D. Terminating the contract immediately and looking for another outside firm

33. The CIO created a goal for the security team to reduce vulnerabilities. They are not high profile, but they still exist. Many of these vulnerabilities have compensating controls in place for security reasons. At this point in time, the budget has been exhausted. What is the BEST risk strategy to use?

    A. Accepting risk

    B. Mitigating risk

    C. Transferring risk

    D. Avoiding risk

34. Your database team would like to use a service-oriented architecture (SOA). The CISO suggested you investigate the risk for adopting this type of architecture. What is the biggest security risk to adopting an SOA?

    A. SOA available only over the enterprise network

    B. Lack of understanding from stakeholders

C. Risk of legacy networks and system vulnerabilities

D. Source code

35. With traditional network architecture, one best practice is to limit network access points. This limitation allowed for a concentration of network security resources and a protected attack surface. With the introduction of 802.1x into enterprise network architecture, what was introduced into the network?

    A. Increased capability and increased risk and higher TCO

    B. Decreased capability and increased risk and higher TCO

    C. Increased capability and decreased risk and lower TCO

    D. Decreased capability and decreased risk and lower TCO

36. Marketing asked for web-based meeting software with a third-party vendor. The software you reviewed requires user registration and installation, and the user has to share their desktop. To ensure that information is secure, which of the following controls is BEST?

    A. Disallow. Avoid the risk.

    B. Hire a third-party organization to perform the risk analysis, and based on outcomes, allow or disallow the software.

    C. Log and record every single web-based meeting.

    D. After evaluating several providers, ensure acceptable risk and that the read-write desktop mode can be prevented.

37. You are tasked with writing the security viewpoint of a new program that your organization is starting. Which of the following techniques make this a repeatable process and can be used for creating the best security architecture?

    A. Data classification, CIA triad, minimum security required, and risk analysis

    B. Historical documentation, continuous monitoring, and mitigation of high risks

    C. Implementation of proper controls, performance of qualitative analysis, and continuous monitoring

    D. Risk analysis; avoidance of critical risks, threats, and vulnerabilities; and the transference of medium risk

38. Because of time constraints and budget, your organization has opted to hire a third-party organization to begin working on an important new project. From a security point of view, what BEST balances the needs of the organization and managing the risk of a third-party vendor?

    A. Outsourcing is a valid option and not much of a concern for security because any damage is the responsibility of the third party.

    B. If the company has an acceptable security record, then it makes perfect sense to outsource.

    C. You should never outsource. It leads to legal and compliance issues.

    D. The third party should have the proper NDA, SLA, and OLA in place and should be obligated to perform adequate security activities.

39. Your organization must perform vast amounts of computations of big data overnight. To minimize TCO, you rely on elastic cloud services. The virtual machines and containers are created and destroyed nightly. What is the biggest risk to confidentiality?

   A. Data center distribution

   B. Encryption

   C. Physical loss of control of assets

   D. Data scraping

40. You work for a SOHO and replace servers whenever there is money readily available for expenditure. Over the past few tech-refresh cycles, you have received many servers and workstations from several different vendors. What is the challenge and risk of this style of asset management?

   A. OS and asset EOL issues and updates

   B. OS complexities and OS patch version dependencies

   C. Failure rate of legacy equipment, replacement parts, and firmware updates and management

   D. Poor security posture, inability to manage performance on old OS

41. You are brought in as a consultant to improve the security of business processes. You improve security by applying the proper controls, including transport encryption, interface restrictions, and code review. What else can you do to improve business processes now that you've already done all the technical improvements?

   A. Modify the company security policies and procedures.

   B. Meet with upper management to approve new company standards and a mission statement.

   C. Conduct another technical quantitative risk analysis on all current controls.

   D. Conduct a gap analysis and give a recommendation on nontechnical controls to be incorporated into company documentation.

42. Your bank's board of directors want to perform monthly security testing. As CISO, you must form a plan specifically for its development. This test must have a low risk of impacting system stability because the company is in production. The suggestion was made to outsource this to a third party. The board of directors argue that a third party will not be as knowledgeable as the development team. What will satisfy the board of directors?

   A. Gray-box testing by a major consulting firm

   B. Black-box testing by a major external consulting firm

   C. Gray-box testing by the development and security assurance teams

   D. White-box testing by the development and security assurance teams

43. A vendor of software deployed across your corporate network announced that an update is needed for a specific vulnerability. Your CIO wants to know the vulnerability time (Vt). When can you give them that information?

   A. After the patch is downloaded and installed in the affected system or device

   B. After the patch is released and available to the public

C. After the patch is created by the vendor

D. After the vulnerability is discovered

44. You have an accountant who refuses to take their required time off. You must institute a policy that will force people in critical financial areas of the organization to take time off. Which of the following standard security practices do you institute?

   A. Separation of duties

   B. Mandatory vacation

   C. Forensic tasks

   D. Termination procedures

45. A small insurance business implemented least privilege. Management is concerned that staff might accidentally aid in fraud with the customers. Which of the following addresses security concerns with this risk?

   A. Policy

   B. Job rotation

   C. Separation of duties

   D. Security awareness training

46. A corporation expanded their business by acquiring several similar businesses. What should the security team first undertake?

   A. Development of an ISA and a risk analysis

   B. Installation of firewalls between the businesses

   C. Removal of unneeded assets and Internet access

   D. Scan of the new networks for vulnerabilities

47. Your company began the process of evaluating different technologies for a technical security-focused project. You narrowed down the selection to three organizations from which you received RFIs. What is the next request that you will make of those three vendors?

   A. RFQ

   B. RFP

   C. RFC

   D. RFI

48. Your security team is small and must work economically to reduce risk. You do not have a lot of time to spend on reducing your attack surface. Which of the following might help reduce the time you spend on patching internal applications?

   A. VPN

   B. PaaS

   C. IaaS

   D. Terminal server

49. A competitor of your company was hacked, and the forensics show it was a social engineering phishing attack. What is the first thing you do to prevent this from happening at your company?

    A. Educate all employees about social engineering risks and countermeasures.

    B. Publish a new mission statement.

    C. Implement IPSec on all critical systems.

    D. Use encryption.

50. Many organizations prepare for highly technical attacks and forget about the simple low-tech means of gathering information. Dumpster diving can be useful in gaining access to unauthorized information. How should you reduce your company's dumpster-diving risk?

    A. Data classification and printer restrictions of intellectual property.

    B. Purchase shredders for the copy rooms.

    C. Create policies and procedures for document shredding.

    D. Employ an intern to shred all printed documentation.

51. Qualitative risk assessment is explained by which of the following?

    A. Can be completed by someone with a limited understanding of risk assessment and is easy to implement

    B. Must be completed by someone with expert understanding and uses detailed analysis for calculation

    C. Is completed by subject-matter experts and is difficult to implement

    D. Brings together SME with detailed metrics to handle a difficult implementation

52. What is the customary practice of responsible protection of an asset that affects an organization or community?

    A. Due diligence

    B. Risk mitigation

    C. Insurance

    D. Due care

53. Your global banking organization is acquiring a smaller local bank. As part of the security team, what will your risk assessment evaluate?

    A. Threats to assets, vulnerabilities present, the likelihood of an active threat, the impact of exposure, and residual risk

    B. Threats to assets, vulnerabilities present, the likelihood of a passive threat, the impact of exposure, and total risk

    C. Threats to assets, vulnerabilities present, the likelihood of a passive threat, the impact of exposure on the acquired bank, and total risk

    D. Threats to assets, vulnerabilities present, the likelihood of an active threat, the impact of exposure, and total inherent risk

54. During the risk analysis phase of planning, what would BEST mitigate and manage the effects of an incident?

    A. Modifying the scenario the risk is based on

    B. Developing an agenda for recovery

    C. Choosing the members of the recovery team

    D. Implementing procedural controls

55. You have been added to the team to conduct a business impact analysis (BIA). This BIA will identify:

    A. The impact of vulnerabilities to your organization

    B. How to best efficiently reduce threats

    C. The exposure to loss within your organization

    D. How to bring about change based on the impact on operations

56. You live and work in an area plagued by hurricanes. What BEST describes the effort you made to determine the consequence of a disruption due to this natural disaster?

    A. Business impact analysis

    B. Risk assessment

    C. Table-top exercises

    D. Mitigating control analysis

57. You are a consultant for a cybersecurity firm and have been tasked with quantifying risks associated with information technology when validating the abilities of new security controls and countermeasures. What is the BEST way to identify the risks?

    A. Vulnerability management

    B. Pentesting

    C. Threat and risk assessment

    D. Data reclassification

58. You are employed in a high-risk, geographically diverse production environment. Which of these options would be the BEST reason to deploy link encryption to reduce risk?

    A. Link encryption provides better flow confidentiality and routing.

    B. Link encryption encrypts routing information and is often used with satellite communication.

    C. Link encryption is used for message confidentiality.

    D. Link encryption is implemented for better traffic integrity.

59. Your manufacturing organization implemented a new vulnerability management tool. As the security analyst, you are tasked with creating a successful process for vulnerability assessment. What do you have to fully understand before assuming this task?

    A. Threat definitions and identification

    B. CVE and CVSS

    C. Risk assessments and threat identification

    D. Vulnerability appraisal and access review

60. Bob is conducting a risk assessment and wants to assign an asset value to the servers in the data center. The concern of his organization is to ensure there is a budget to rebuild in case of a natural disaster. What method should Bob use to evaluate the assets?

    A. Depreciated cost

    B. Purchase cost

    C. Replacement cost

    D. Conditional cost

61. Alice is responsible for PCI compliance for her organization. The policy requires she remove information from a database, but she cannot due to technical restrictions. She is pursuing a compensating control to mitigate the risk. What is her best option?

    A. Insurance

    B. Encryption

    C. Deletion

    D. Exceptions

62. Bob is a security risk manager with a global organization. The organization recently evaluated the risk of flash floods on its operations in several regions and determined that the cost of responding is expensive. The organization chooses to take no action currently. What was the risk management strategy deployed?

    A. Risk mitigation

    B. Risk acceptance

    C. Risk avoidance

    D. Risk transference

63. Greg is a security researcher for a cybersecurity company. He is currently examining a third-party vendor and finds a way to use SQLi to deface their web server due to a missing patch in the company's web application. What is the threat of doing business with this organization?

    A. Web defacement

    B. Unpatched applications

    C. Hackers

    D. Education awareness

64. Your organization's primary network backup server went down at midnight. Your RPO is nine hours. At what time will you exceed the business process recovery tolerably, given the volume of data that has been lost in that time frame?

    A. 6 A.M.

    B. 9 A.M.

C. Noon

D. 3 P.M.

65. Your company needs to decide on a data backup plan strategy. You established your RPO as 8 hours, and your RTO after any disaster, man-made or natural, as 48 hours. These RTOs were established by the business owner while developing the BIA. The RTO includes which of the following?

A. Recovery, testing, and communications

B. Decision time

C. Parallel processing

D. Only the time for trying to fix the problem without a recovery

66. Your organization has a new policy to implement security based on least privilege and separation of duties. A key component is making a decision on data access. They decided it is BEST made by which of the following roles?

A. Data steward

B. Data owner

C. User/manager

D. Senior management

67. You are hired by an insurance company as their new data custodian. Which of the following best describes your new responsibilities?

A. Writing and proofing administrative documentation

B. Ensuring accessibility and appropriate access using policy and data ownership guidelines

C. Conducting an audit of the data's strategic, tactical, and operation (STO) controls

D. Improving the data consistency and increasing data integration

68. Your healthcare organization decided to begin outsourcing some IT systems. Which of the following statements is true?

A. All outsourcing frees your organization from any rules or requirements.

B. All compliance and regulatory requirements are passed on to the provider.

C. The IT systems are no longer configured, maintained, or evaluated by your organization.

D. The outsourcing organization is free from any rules or regulations.

69. You work as a security analyst for a large banking organization that is about to disclose to the public that a substantial breach occurred. You are called into a meeting with the CISO and CEO to discuss how to ensure proper forensic action took place and that the incident response team responded appropriately. Which of these should you ensure happens after the incident?

A. Avoid conflict of interest by hiring outside counsel

B. Creation of forensic images of all mission-critical servers

    C. Formal investigation performed by yourself without law enforcement

    D. Incident treated as though a crime had been committed

70. Bob is the owner of a website that provides information to healthcare providers. He is concerned that the PHI data he is storing falls under the jurisdiction of HIPAA. How does he ensure that he removes the data correctly?

    A. By deleting the suspected PHI data on the drive

    B. By degaussing the drives that hold suspected PHI data

    C. By determining how long to keep the healthcare data securely encrypted and then using a drive-wipe utility

    D. By adding SSDs to the web server and storing used drives in a physically secured location

71. Your U.S.-based company manufactures children's clothing and is contemplating expanding their business into the European Union. You are concerned about regulation and compliance. What should your organization examine first?

    A. Payment Card Industry

    B. General Data Protection Regulation

    C. Children's Online Privacy Protection

    D. Family Educational Rights and Privacy Act

72. A company outsourced payroll and is concerned about whether the right technical and legal agreements are in place. Data is viewed and stored by a third party, and an agreement needs to be set in place about that data. Which type of interoperability agreement can you use to make sure the data is encrypted while in transit and at rest?

    A. BPA

    B. MOU

    C. ISA

    D. NDA

73. You decided to start a new consulting business. You began the risk analysis process and developed employee policies and researched and tested third-party security. What is the next riskiest problem for SOHO?

    A. Mobile devices

    B. Email

    C. Training

    D. Guidelines

74. You need an agreement that lets your business implement a comprehensive risk allocation strategy and provides indemnification, the method that holds one party harmless against existing or future losses. What contract should you negotiate?

    A. Master service agreement

    B. Business impact agreement

C. Interconnection security agreement

D. Memorandum of understanding

75. Which of the following security programs is designed to provide employees with the knowledge they need to fulfill their job requirements and protect the organization?

A. Awareness

B. Training

C. Indoctrination

D. Development

76. You have a well-configured firewall and IDS. Which of the following can BEST steal intellectual property or trade secrets because there is no system auditing?

A. Hacktivist

B. Auditors

C. Malware

D. Employees

77. Bob needs your professional opinion on encryption capabilities. You explained to him that cryptography supports all the core principles of information security with an exception. What is that exception?

A. Authenticity

B. Integrity

C. Confidentiality

D. Availability

78. Alice discovered a meterpreter shell running a keylogger on the CFO's laptop. What security tenet is the keylogger mostly likely to break?

A. Availability

B. Threats

C. Integrity

D. Confidentiality

79. You were hired for a role in healthcare as a system architect. You need to factor in CIA requirements for a new SAN. Which of the following CIA requirements is best for multipathing?

A. Confidentiality

B. Threat

C. Integrity

D. Availability

80. As a technical project manager on a VoIP/teleconference project, the customer shared their requirements with your department. Availability must be at least five nines (99.999 percent), and all devices must support collaboration. Which controls are the BEST to apply to this ecosystem?

   A. All images must be standardized and double redundant.

   B. Security policies of network access controls and high-speed processing.

   C. RAID 0 and hot sites.

   D. Enforced security policies, standard images/configurations, and backup on all storage devices.

81. A software startup hired you to provide expertise on data security. Clients are concerned about confidentiality. If confidentiality is stressed more than availability and integrity, which of the following scenarios is BEST suited for the client?

   A. Virtual servers in a highly available environment. Clients will use redundant virtual storage and terminal services to access software.

   B. Virtual servers in a highly available environment. Clients will use single virtual storage and terminal services to access software.

   C. Clients are assigned virtual hosts running on shared hardware. Physical storage is partitioned with block cipher encryption.

   D. Clients are assigned virtual hosts running shared hardware. Virtual storage is partitioned with streaming cipher encryption.

82. Your company is considering adding a new host to a computer cluster. The cluster will be connected to a single storage solution. What are you most likely trying to accomplish?

   A. Availability

   B. Provisioning

   C. Integrity

   D. Confidentiality

83. You work as a security analyst for a healthcare organization. A small legacy cluster of computers was acquired from a small hospital clinic. All virtual machines use the same NIC to connect to the network. Some of these machines have patient data, while others have financial data. One of these VMs is hosting an externally facing web application. What is the biggest problem you see with this scenario?

   A. Confidentiality

   B. Threats

   C. Integrity

   D. Utilization

84. You are a security administrator for a network that uses Fibre Channel over Ethernet (FCoE). The network administrator would like to access raw data from the storage array and restore it to yet another host. Which of the following might be an issue for availability?

   A. The new host might not be compatible with FCoE.

   B. The data may not be in a usable format.

C. The process could cause bottlenecks.

D. Deduplication will cause errors in the data.

85. A senior security architect for a hospital is creating a hardened version of the newest GUI OS. The testing will focus on the CIA triad as well as on compliance and reporting. Which of these is the BEST life cycle for the architect to deploy in the final image?

A. Employing proper disposal protocols for existing equipment and ensuring compliance with corporate data retention policies

B. Updating whole disk encryption and testing operational models

C. Employing interoperability, integrity of the data at rest, network availability, and compliance with all government regulations

D. Creating a plan to decommission the existing OS infrastructure, implementing test and operational procedures for the new components in advance, and ensuring compliance with applicable regulations

86. As a network administrator, you are asked to connect a server to a storage-attached network. If availability and access control are the most important, which of the following fulfills the requirements?

A. Installing a NIC in the server, enabling deduplication

B. Installing a NIC in the server, disabling deduplication

C. Installing an HBA in the server, creating a LUN on the SAN

D. Installing a clustered HBA in the server, creating two LUNS on a NAS

87. One of the requirements for a new device you're adding to the network is an availability of 99.9 percent. According to the vendor, the newly acquired device has been rated with an MTBF of 20,000 hours and an MTTR of 3 hours. What is the most accurate statement?

A. The device will meet availability because it will be at 99.985 percent.

B. The device will not meet availability because it will be at 99.89 percent.

C. The device will not meet availability because it will be at 99.85 percent.

D. The device will meet availability because it will be at 99.958 percent.

88. Good data management includes which of the following?

A. Data quality procedures, verification and validation, adherence to agreed-upon data management, and an ongoing data audit to monitor the use and the integrity of existing data

B. Cost, due care and due diligence, privacy, liability, and existing law

C. Determining the impact the information has on the mission of the organization, understanding the cost of information, and determining who in the organization or outside of it has a need for the information

D. Ensuring the longevity of data and their reuse for multiple purposes, facilitating the interoperability of datasets, and increasing data sharing

89. Which of the following confidentiality security models ensures that a subject with clearance level of Secret can write only to objects classified as Secret or Top Secret?

A. Biba

B. Clark–Wilson

C. Brewer–Nash

D. Bell–LaPadula

90. Your organization needs a security model for integrity where the subject cannot send messages to objects of higher integrity. Which of the following is unique to the Biba model and will accommodate that need?

A. Simple

B. Star

C. Invocation

D. Strong

91. You had an incident and need to verify that chain of custody, due diligence, and processes were followed. You are told to verify the forensic bit stream. What will you do?

A. Employ encryption.

B. Instigate containment.

C. Compare hashes.

D. Begin documentation.

92. As a new CISO, you are evaluating controls for availability. Which set of controls should you choose?

A. RAID 1, classification of data, and load balancing

B. Digital signatures, encryption, and hashes

C. Steganography, ACL, and vulnerability management

D. Checksum, DOS attacks, and RAID 0

93. As a new CISO, you are evaluating controls for integrity. Which set of controls should you choose?

A. RAID 1, classification of data, and load balancing

B. Digital signatures, encryption, and hashes

C. Steganography, ACL, and vulnerability management

D. Checksum, DOS attacks, and RAID 0

94. As a new CISO, you are evaluating controls for confidentiality. Which set of controls should you choose?

A. RAID 1, classification of data, and load balancing

B. Digital signatures, encryption, and hashes

C. Steganography, ACL, and vulnerability management

D. Checksum, DOS attacks, and RAID 0

95. You have a web server in your network that is the target of a distributed denial-of-service attack. Multiple systems are flooding the bandwidth of that system. Which information security goal is impacted by this type of an attack?

   A. Availability

   B. Baselines

   C. Integrity

   D. Emergency response

96. Bob is implementing a new RAID configuration needed for redundancy in the event of disk failure. He has compared standard hardware benchmarks with a week-long baseline of the server to find the assets used the most. What security goal is Bob trying to accomplish?

   A. Availability

   B. Integrity

   C. Confidentiality

   D. Disclosure

97. Because of your facility's geolocation and its propensity for hurricanes, you are tasked with finding another data processing facility to provide you with a location in case of a natural disaster. You are negotiating a contract with an organization with HVAC, power, water, and communication but no hardware. What kind of facility are you building?

   A. Hot site

   B. Warm site

   C. Mobile site

   D. Cold site

98. You are a project manager for an organization that just acquired another company. Your company uses mostly in-house tools, whereas the company you just acquired uses mostly outside vendors. As the project manager, you need to merge these two organizations quickly, have an immediate return on investment (ROI), and retain the ability to customize systems. Each organization thinks their way is the best way. What do you do?

   A. Raise the issue with the CEO and board of directors to escalate the decision to outsource all services.

   B. Arrange a meeting between all department heads, project managers, and a representative from the board of directors to review requirements and calculate critical functions.

   C. Perform a cost-benefit analysis of in-house versus outsourcing and the ROI in-house.

   D. Calculate the time to deploy and support the new systems and compare the cost to outsourcing costs. Present the document to upper management for their final decision.

99. Your company experienced a natural disaster, used your hot site for three months, and now is returning to the primary site. What processes should be restored first at the primary site?

   A. Finance department

   B. External communication

   C. Mission critical

   D. Least business critical

100. Your organization is in an area susceptible to wildfires. Within the last 30 days, your employees were evacuated twice from the primary location. During the second evacuation, damage occurred to several floors of the building, including the data center. When should the team return to start recovery?

    A. In 72 hours.

    B. You should not return to the primary location.

    C. Immediately after the disaster.

    D. Only after it is deemed safe to return to the primary location.

101. Your cyber company has officially grown out of its startup phase and tasked your team with creating a pre-disaster preparation plan that will sustain the business should a disaster, natural or man-made, occur. Which of the following is the most important?

    A. Off-site backups

    B. Copies of the BDR

    C. Maintaining a warm site

    D. Chain of command

102. You are tasked with conducting a risk analysis based on how it affects business processes. What activity are you performing?

    A. Gap analysis

    B. Business disaster recovery

    C. Intrusion detection

    D. Business impact analysis

103. Your organization is attempting to make the best use of all the resources allocated to a security project. If your organization is not making the best use of currently held resources, the project may not perform as planned. What type of analysis needs to be done?

    A. BDR

    B. BIA

    C. Gap

    D. Risk

104. When you look at the business impact analysis given to your office for approval, you notice it is less narrative and more mathematical calculations. What will make this BIA more balanced?

    A. More qualitative analysis

    B. More quantitative analysis

    C. More gap analysis

    D. More risk analysis

105. While developing your business continuity plan, your business impact analysis statement should include all but which of the following?

  A. Critical areas and dependencies

  B. All business units

  C. Financial losses due to disaster or disruption

  D. Recovery methods and responses

106. You examined your company's disaster recovery plans and are working on the proper response. If your mission-critical processes have an RTO of 36 hours, what would be the best recovery site to have?

  A. Service

  B. Warm

  C. Hot

  D. Cold

107. Your company just experienced an emergency and needs to initiate a business continuity plan (BCP). Who is responsible for initiating the BCP?

  A. Senior management

  B. Security personnel

  C. Recovery team

  D. Database admins

108. In the past, your global organization tasked individual locations and departments with creating their own separate disaster recovery plans because those employees know best how their organization works. Your new CISO tasked your team with creating a viable plan should your company experience a disaster. What is your mission?

  A. Record as many separate plans as necessary.

  B. Create one fully integrated business continuity plan.

  C. Create separate plans for each geographic location.

  D. Keep separate plans for each logical department, regardless of the physical location.

109. As a security architect, you implemented dual firewalls, an IPS, and ACLs. All the files on this network are copied to a tape backup every 24 hours. This backup solution addresses which security tenet?

  A. Availability

  B. Distribution

  C. Integrity

  D. Confidentiality

110. You need to perform a test where a BCP is tested but no actions take place. It needs to be scheduled periodically. Which of the following is the BEST type of test to perform?

    A. Full interruption test

    B. Parallel test

    C. Structured walk-through

    D. Simulation test

111. You completed a structured walk-through of your disaster recovery plan. Senior management would like you to use the absolute best way to verify that the DRP is sufficient and has no deficiencies. What test do you choose next?

    A. Roundtable exercises

    B. Dry-run exercises

    C. Full interruption test

    D. External audit

112. Over the last month, you reviewed security reports that state there was a significant increase in the number of inappropriate activities on the network by employees. What is the first step in improving the security level in your organization?

    A. Awareness sessions

    B. Stronger auditing

    C. Reduce employee permissions

    D. Termination

113. You have been contacted by senior management to conduct an investigation. They suspect that malicious activities are caused by internal personnel and need to know if it is intentional or unintentional. After investigating, you believe it is unintentional and that the most likely cause is which of the following?

    A. Fraud

    B. Espionage

    C. Embezzlement

    D. Social engineering

114. A white-hat penetration test showed your organization to be susceptible to social engineering attacks. One victim in your organization was phished successfully, while another clicked a link in an email and downloaded possible malware. What steps do you take to prevent social engineering in the future?

    A. Use IPSec on critical systems

    B. Publish a policy and educate users on risks

    C. Use encryption

    D. Establish KPIs

115. With the rise of malware spread with removable media, your company wrote an amendment to include a ban of all flashcards and memory drives. They pose a threat due to all but which of the following?

   A. Physical size

   B. Transportability

   C. Storage capacity

   D. Being cheap and easy to use

116. You received final documentation from your compliance audit. They suggested you implement a complementary security tool to work with your firewall to detect any attempt at scanning. Which device do you choose?

   A. RAS

   B. PBX

   C. IDS

   D. DDT

117. Your company is using a traditional signature-based IDS system, and it seems to have some problems. You and your fellow analysts are seeing more and more false positives. What might be the issue?

   A. Anomaly detection requires vast amounts of resources.

   B. FIM.

   C. Excessive FTP traffic.

   D. Poorly written signatures.

118. One of your end users contacted the security administrator because the mouse on his computer seems to be moving all by itself. If your company's focus is confidentiality, which of the following is the best action to take?

   A. Delay the intruder.

   B. Disconnect the intruder.

   C. Record the intruder.

   D. Monitor the intruder.

119. You disconnected a computer from the network because of a suspected breach. Which of the following should you do next?

   A. Back up all security and audit logs on that computer.

   B. Update the security policy.

   C. Reimage the machine.

   D. Deploy new countermeasures.

120. You are developing a security policy regarding password management. Which of these is not important?

   A. Account lockout

   B. Training users to create complex, easy-to-remember passwords

C. Preventing users from using personal information in a password, such as their birthday or spouse's name

D. Storing passwords securely

121. As a hospital, you rely on some assets running high-end customized legacy software. What precaution should you implement to protect yourself if this developer goes out of business?

A. Access control

B. Service level agreement

C. Code escrow

D. Outsourcing

122. A security analyst on your team was written up for a multitude of offenses. The latest transgression left you no choice but to terminate this employee. Which of the following is most important to do when informing the employee of their separation from the company?

A. Allowing them to complete their project

B. Giving them two weeks' severance

C. Allowing them to collect their personal belongings

D. Disabling network access and changing the passwords to devices to which they had access

123. As a CISO, you built a team of developers, managers, educators, architects, and administrators. Some of the people in these roles are finding they are duplicating efforts and not utilizing their time well. What can you use to initiate solid administrative control over the situation?

A. AUP

B. TCO

C. Mandatory vacation

D. Job descriptions

124. You have an amazing developer on staff. They are a great problem-solver and work very well with others. However, this developer continues to perform risky behavior on the network even after security awareness sessions and several warnings. What should you do next?

A. Begin a separation of duties.

B. Terminate them and perform an exit interview.

C. Employ mandatory vacation.

D. Decrease permissions.

125. Your vulnerability manager contacted you because of an operating system issue. There are a few security-related issues due to patches and upgrades needed for an application on the systems in question. When is the BEST time to complete this task?

A. As quickly as possible after testing.

B. After experiencing the issue the vulnerability manager described.

C. After other organizations have tested the patch or upgrade.

D. During the usual monthly maintenance.

126. You need to assign permissions so that users can access only the resources they need to complete specific tasks. Which security tenet should you utilize to meet the need?

A. Separation of duties

B. Need to know

C. Job rotation

D. Least privilege

127. You recorded data that includes security logs, object access, FIM, and other activities that your SIEM often uses to detect unwanted activity. Which of the following BEST describes this collection of data?

A. Due diligence

B. Syslog

C. IDR

D. Audit trail

128. You are tasked with hiring a third party to perform a security assessment of your manufacturing plant. What type of testing gives the most neutral review of your security profile?

A. White hat

B. Gray hat

C. Black hat

D. Blue hat

129. You work in law enforcement supporting a network with HA. High availability is mandatory, as you also support emergency 911 services. Which of the following would hinder your HA ecosystem?

A. Clustered servers

B. Primary firewall

C. Switched networks

D. Redundant communication links

130. You are tasked to with creating a security plan for your point-of-sale systems. What is the BEST methodology when you begin architecting?

A. Outside in

B. Assets out

C. No write up

D. No write down

131. Alice needs some help developing security policy documentation. She turns to you for help in developing a document that contains instructions or information on how to remain in compliance with regulations. What document do you need to develop?

   A. Procedures

   B. Standards

   C. Policy

   D. Guidelines

132. You are the security administrator for a large governmental agency. You implemented port security, restricted network traffic, and installed NIDS, firewalls, and spam filters. You think the network is secure. Now you want to focus on endpoint security. What is the most comprehensive plan to follow?

   A. Anti-malware/virus/spyware, host-based firewall, and MFA

   B. Antivirus/spam, host-based IDS, and TFA

   C. Anti-malware/virus, host-based IDS, and biometrics

   D. Antivirus/spam, host-based IDS, and SSO

133. You oversee hardware distribution for your global enterprise. You conduct a data analysis to figure out failure rates of a certain brand and model of laptop. You need to calculate the average number of times that specific model is likely to break in a year. Which of the following BEST describes your calculation?

   A. Annualized rate of occurrence

   B. Exposure factor

   C. Single loss expectancy

   D. Annualized loss expectancy

134. Prioritization is an important part of your job as a security analyst. You are trying to calculate the ALE for all assets and risks. What purpose will this serve?

   A. To estimate insurance

   B. To arrive at a budget and head count

   C. To prioritize countermeasures

   D. To inform design

135. You need to calculate the ALE for an asset. Which of these is the proper formula?

   A. ARO × EF × AV

   B. ARO × AV

   C. EF × SLE

   D. EF × SLE × AV

136. As a software developer, you are frustrated with your customer who keeps calling you on the phone and leaving messages to make changes. What should you do to make the development process easier?

   A. Change control.

   B. Increase security.

    C. Apprise senior management.

    D. Provide detailed documentation.

137. One of the software developers made a change in code that unintentionally diminishes security. Which of the following change control processes will be most effective in this situation?

    A. Rollback

    B. Logging

    C. Compiling

    D. Patching

138. A newly certified administrator makes a change to Group Policy for 12,000 users. The box is checked on the operating systems to not allow the overwriting of security logs. After 48 hours, no users can log into their domain accounts because the security logs have filled up. What change control process step was skipped?

    A. Approval

    B. Testing

    C. Implementation

    D. Deployment

139. Your organization finds it difficult to distinguish what data can be shared with a customer and what should remain internal. They assigned you the task of data classification. What is the primary purpose of this task?

    A. Justification of expenses

    B. Assigning value to data

    C. Defining necessary security protections

    D. Controlling user access

140. The security awareness training informed employees that within their operating systems an auditing feature was enabled. What form of control is used when end users are informed that their actions are monitored on the network?

    A. Directive

    B. Corrective

    C. Detective

    D. Preventative

141. Your external auditor submitted the final report to the board of directors and upper management. Who is responsible for implementing the recommendations in this report?

    A. End users

    B. Internal auditors

    C. Security administrators

    D. Senior management

142. A security vulnerability was discovered while a system went through the accreditation process. What action should come next?

  A. Start the accreditation process over again once the issue is fixed.

  B. Restart the accreditation process from when the issue was discovered.

  C. Reimage the system and start the accreditation from the beginning.

  D. Reimage the system and start from the current point.

143. Your organization was breached, but you have been able to prove that sufficient due care was taken. What burden is eliminated?

  A. Liability

  B. Investigation

  C. Financial loss

  D. Negligence

144. You are a security administrator and were notified by your IPS that there is an issue. You quickly solve the problem. What needs to be done once the problem has been fixed?

  A. After-action report

  B. MOA

  C. Incident report

  D. Update to security policy

145. Your department was tasked with implementing Bluetooth connectivity controls to mitigate risk. Which of these BEST describes the network you will create?

  A. PAN

  B. LAN

  C. WAN

  D. WLAN

146. You are planning the site security for a new building. The network administrators would like the server room door to be secured with RFID. The security team would like to use a cipher lock. Loss of the data on these servers is high risk. What should your plan start with?

  A. A meeting to discuss security options

  B. Smartcards

  C. TFA, both cipher lock and RFID

  D. A keyed lock only

147. You are a systems analyst conducting a vulnerability assessment. Which of the following is not a requirement for you to know?

  A. Access controls

  B. Understanding of the systems to be evaluated

   C. Potential threats

   D. Passwords

148. You are made aware of a threat that involves a hacking group holding large amounts of information about your company. What BEST describes the threat you face from this hacking group?

   A. DoS

   B. TCO

   C. Latency

   D. Data mining

149. Your CISO has asked you to evaluate an antivirus tool for all company-issued laptops. The cost is $3,000 for all 90 laptops. From historical data you anticipate that 12 computers will be affected with a SLE of $1,500. What do you recommend to the CISO?

   A. Accept the risk.

   B. Mitigate the risk.

   C. Transfer the risk.

   D. Avoid the risk.

150. You are evaluating the risk for your data center. You assigned threat, vulnerability, and impact a score from 1 to 10. The data center scores are as follows: Threat: 4, Vulnerability: 2, Impact: 6. What is the risk?

   A. 12

   B. 16

   C. 48

   D. 35

151. You are tasked with creating a grouping of subjects and objects with the same security requirements. What should you build?

   A. Matrix

   B. Domain

   C. LLC

   D. Meshed network

152. You have a new security policy that requires backing up critical data off-site. This data must be backed up hourly. Cost is important. What method are you most likely to deploy?

   A. Remote accounting

   B. Electronic vaulting

   C. Active clustering

   D. Database shadow copies

153. Your customer-facing website experiences some failures. The security engineer analyzed the situation and believes it is the web application firewall. Syslog shows that the WAF was down twice for a total of 3 hours in the past 72 hours. Which of the following is your mean time to repair (MTTR)?

A. 2.5 hours

B. 1.5 hours

C. 34.5 hours

D. 3 hours

154. Your financial institution decided to purchase costly custom computer systems. The vendor supplying the custom systems is experiencing a few minor legal issues. What should the CISO recommend to limit exposure?

A. Source code escrow

B. Penalty clause

C. SLA

D. Proof of insurance in the RFP

155. Your department started to plan for next year. You need to gain clarity about what your key performance indicators are for the current year. Which of the following is not found in a KPI?

A. Measurement

B. Target

C. Investment

D. Data source

156. Your senior management wants to measure how risky an activity will be. This metric is used to provide a signal of increasing risk exposure. You need to identify which of the following?

A. Key risk indicators

B. Key performance indicators

C. Total cost of ownership

D. Risk assessment

157. Capturing lessons learned is an ongoing effort you have implemented in your technical project management. You will use this data in the future for process improvements. Not learning from project failures can lead to which of the following?

A. Repeating the failure

B. Missing opportunities

C. Implementing good processes

D. Preparing for current projects

Chapter

2

Enterprise Security Architecture

THE CASP+ EXAM TOPICS COVERED IN THIS CHAPTER INCLUDE:

✓ **Domain 2: Enterprise Security Architecture**

- 2.1 Analyze a scenario and integrate network and security components, concepts, and architectures to meet security requirements.
  - Physical and virtual network and security devices
    - UTM
    - IDS/IPS
    - NIDS/NIPS
    - INE
    - NAC
    - SIEM
    - Switch
    - Firewall
    - Wireless controller
    - Router
    - Proxy
    - Load balancer
    - HSM
    - MicroSD HSM
  - Application and protocol-aware technologies
    - WAF
    - Firewall
    - Passive vulnerability scanners
    - DAM

- Advanced network design (wired/wireless)
  - Remote access
  - VPN
    - IPSec
    - SSL/TLS
  - SSH
  - RDP
  - VNC
  - VDI
  - Reverse proxy
  - IPv4 and IPv6 transitional technologies
  - Network authentication methods
  - 802.1x
  - Mesh networks
  - Placement of fixed/mobile devices
  - Placement of hardware and applications
- Complex network security solutions for data flow
  - DLP
  - Deep packet inspection
  - Data flow enforcement
  - Network flow (S/flow)
  - Data flow diagram
- Secure configuration and baselining of networking and security components
- Software-defined networking
- Network management and monitoring tools
  - Alert definitions and rule writing
  - Tuning alert thresholds
  - Alert fatigue
- Advanced configuration of routers, switches, and other network devices

- Transport security
- Trunking security
- Port security
- Route protection
- DDos protection
- Remotely triggered black hole
  - Security zones
    - DMZ
    - Separation of critical assets
    - Network segmentation
  - Network access control
    - Quarantine/remediation
    - Persistent/volatile or non-persistent agent
    - Agent versus agentless
  - Network enabled devices
    - System on a chip (SoC)
    - Building/home automation systems
    - IP video
    - HVAC controllers
    - Sensors
    - Physical access control systems
    - A/V systems
    - Scientific/industrial equipment
  - Critical infrastructure
    - Supervisory control and data acquisition (SCADA)
    - Industrial Control Systems (ICS)
- 2.2 Analyze a scenario to integrate security controls for host devices to meet security requirements.
  - Trusted OS (e.g., how and when to use it)

- SE Linux
- SE Android
- Trusted Solaris
- Least functionality
- Endpoint security software
  - Anti-malware
  - Antivirus
  - Antispyware
  - Spam filters
  - Patch management
  - HIPS/HIDS
  - Data loss prevention
  - Host-based firewalls
  - Log monitoring
  - Endpoint detection response
- Host hardening
  - Standard operating environment/configuration baselining
    - Application whitelisting and blacklisting
  - Security/group policy implementation
  - Command shell restrictions
  - Patch management
    - Manual
    - Automated
      - Scripting and replication
  - Configuring dedicated interfaces
    - Out-of-band management
    - ACLs
    - Management interface
    - Data interface
  - External I/O restrictions

- USB
- Wireless
  - Bluetooth
  - NFC
  - IrDA
  - RF
  - 802.11
  - RFID
- Drive mounting
  - Drive mapping
  - Webcam
  - Recording mic
  - Audio output
  - SD port
  - HDMI port
- File and disk encryption
- Firmware updates
- Boot loader protections
  - Secure boot
  - Measured launch
  - Integrity measurement architecture
  - BIOS/UEFI
    - Attestation services
    - TPM
- Vulnerabilities associated with hardware
- Terminal services/application delivery services
- 2.3 Analyze a scenario to integrate security controls for mobile and small-form factor devices to meet security requirements.
  - Enterprise mobility management
    - Containerization

- Configuration profiles and payloads
- Personally owned, corporate-enabled
- Application wrapping
- Remote assistance access
  - VNC
  - Screen mirroring
- Application, content, and data management
- Over-the-air updates (software/firmware)
- Remote wiping
- SCEP
- BYOD
- COPE
- VPN
- Application permissions
- Side loading
- Unsigned apps/system apps
- Context-aware management
  - Geolocation/geofencing
  - User behavior
  - Security restrictions
  - Time-based restrictions
- Security implications/privacy concerns
  - Data storage
  - Device loss/theft
  - Hardware anti-tamper
    - efuse
  - TPM
  - Rooting/jailbreaking
  - Push notification services
  - Geotagging

- Encrypted instant messaging apps
- Tokenization
- OEM/carrier Android fragmentation
- Mobile payment
  - NFC enabled
  - Inductance-enabled
  - Mobile wallet
  - Peripheral-enabled payments (credit card reader)
- Tethering
  - USB
  - Spectrum management
  - Bluetooth 3.0 versus 4.1
- Authentication
  - Swipe pattern
  - Gesture
  - Pin code
  - Biometric
    - Facial
    - Fingerprint
    - Iris scan
- Malware
- Unauthorized domain bridging
- Baseband radio/SOC
- Augmented reality
- SMS/MMS/messaging
- Wearable technology
  - Devices
    - Cameras
    - Watches
    - Fitness devices

- Glasses
- Medical sensors/devices
- Headsets
- Security implications
  - Unauthorized remote activation/deactivation of devices or features
  - Encrypted and unencrypted communication concerns
  - Physical reconnaissance
  - Personal data theft
  - Health privacy
  - Digital forensics of collected data
- 2.4 Given software vulnerability scenarios, select the appropriate security controls.
  - Application security design considerations
    - Secure by design, by default, by deployment
  - Specific application issues
    - Unsecure direct object references
    - XSS
    - Cross-Site Request Forgery (CSRF)
    - Click-jacking
    - Session management
    - Input validation
    - SQL injection
    - Improper error and exception handling
    - Privilege escalation
    - Improper storage of sensitive data
    - Fussing/fault injection
    - Secure cookie storage and transmission
    - Buffer overflow
    - Memory leaks

- Integer overflows
- Race conditions
  - Time of check
  - Time of use
- Resource exhaustion
- Geotagging
- Data remnants
- Use of third-party libraries
- Code reuse
- Application sandboxing
- Secure encrypted enclaves
- Database Activity monitor
- Web application firewalls
- Client-side processing versus server-side processing
- JSON/REST
- Browser extensions
  - ActiveX
  - Java applets
- HTML5
- AJAX
- SOAP
- State management
- JavaScript
- Operating system vulnerabilities
- Firmware vulnerabilities

1. Intrusions are usually detected in one of three basic ways. Which detection method can reassemble packets and look at higher-layer activity?

    A. Signature recognition

    B. Heuristic detection

    C. Anomaly detection

    D. Protocol decoding

2. Sally's CISO asked her to recommend an intrusion system to recognize intrusions traversing the network and send email alerts to the IT staff when one is detected. What type of intrusion system does the CISO want?

    A. HIDS

    B. NIDS

    C. HIPS

    D. NIPS

3. The CISO of an organization asked the security department to recommend a system to be placed on business-critical servers to detect and stop intrusions. Which of the following will meet the CISO's requirement?

    A. HIPS

    B. NIDS

    C. HIDS

    D. NIPS

4. The IT security department was tasked with recommending a single security device that can perform various security functions. The security functions include antivirus protection, antispyware, a firewall, and an IDP. What device should the IT security department recommend?

    A. Next-generation firewall

    B. Unified threat management system

    C. Quantum proxy

    D. Next-generation IDP

5. The military wants to encrypt data on mounted drives between its headquarters and a military unit. Which of the following devices could the military use to accomplish this task?

    A. Firewall

    B. Unified threat management system

    C. Proxy

    D. Inline network encryptors

6. A pentester has been hired to do physical reconnaissance on your building. An organization installed various Ethernet ports in its facility. Anyone can walk up to a port and plug their computer into the network unabated, gaining network access. A security audit found this situation to be a security risk. What technology should be implemented to ensure only authorized computer equipment can connect to the network using these Ethernet ports?

   A. Network access control

   B. Proxy

   C. Next-generation firewall

   D. Security information and event management system

7. What system is used to collect and analyze data logs from various network devices and to report detected security events?

   A. Syslog server

   B. NIPS

   C. HIPS

   D. SIEM system

8. What is the lookup table used to store MAC addresses on a switch called?

   A. Content addressable memory

   B. Random access memory

   C. Read-only memory

   D. Nonvolatile memory

9. Which of the following BEST describes how a frame is forwarded through a switch?

   A. The destination MAC address of an incoming frame and the CAM table are used to find the destination port out of which the frame is to be forwarded.

   B. All frames entering a switch are forwarded out of all ports except the port on which it came in.

   C. All frames entering a switch are forwarded out of all ports including the port on which it came in.

   D. The destination IP address of an incoming frame and the CAM table are used to find the destination port from which the frame is to be forwarded out.

10. What address type does a switch use to forward frames?

   A. IP address

   B. Frame address

   C. TCP/IP address

   D. MAC address

11. Which is an example of a routable protocol and a routing protocol?

   A. Frames and OSPF

   B. Frames and RIP

    C. IP and OSPF

    D. Segments and RIP

12. Sally needs to implement a network security device at the border of her corporate network and the Internet. This device filters network traffic based on source and destination IP addresses, source and destination port numbers, and protocols. Which network security device BEST suits her needs?

    A. Packet filter firewall

    B. Proxy

    C. HSM

    D. DMZ

13. Your company has grown to a point where a screened host firewall solution is no longer viable. IT wants to move to a screened subnet solution. Which of the following is considered a type of screened subnet?

    A. LAN

    B. DMZ

    C. Intranet

    D. WAN

14. The IT department decided to implement a security appliance in front of their web servers to inspect HTTP/HTTPS/SOAP traffic for malicious activity. Which of the following is the BEST solution to use?

    A. Screened host firewall

    B. Packet filter firewall

    C. DMZ

    D. WAF

15. After analyzing traffic flows diagrams on the network, your department noticed that many internal users access the same resources on the Internet. This activity utilizes a lot of Internet bandwidth. Your department decides to implement a solution that can cache this type of traffic the first time it is requested and serve it to the internal users as requested, thereby reducing the Internet bandwidth used for accessing this traffic. Which solution BEST accomplishes this task?

    A. Proxy

    B. Packet filter firewall

    C. WAF

    D. IPS

16. You were asked to recommend a technology that will lessen the impact of a DDoS attack on your server farm. Which of the following is the BEST technology?

    A. HIDS

    B. Packet filter firewall

C. Proxy

D. Load balancing

17. Your company currently has a software-based cryptography and a security processing system that has significantly slowed down over the years. You are tasked with recommending a new solution to speed up the processes. What is the BEST option for completing this task?

A. PCI

B. TrueCrypt

C. EFS

D. HSM

18. You are asked to recommend a lightweight and mobile key management solution for your company's users. Which of the following provides this function?

A. EFS

B. TPM

C. microSD HSM

D. NTFS

19. What is the concern with using the C language commands `scanf ()`, `strcpy ()`, `bcopy ()`, `vsprintf ()`, and `gets ()`?

A. These commands are no longer supported in C.

B. These commands don't check buffer size and lend themselves to buffer overflow attacks.

C. These commands don't perform input validation and, therefore, lend themselves to injection attacks.

D. There is no concern with using these commands.

20. You were asked to recommend a solution to intercept network traffic and analyze its content for malicious activity while not interacting with the host computer. Of the following, which is the BEST solution?

A. System scanner

B. Application scanner

C. Active vulnerability scanner

D. Passive vulnerability scanner

21. Your company deployed various databases throughout its network with PHI and PII on them. A solution is needed to monitor the databases and to analyze the type of activity occurring on them to prevent data theft. Which of the following provides the BEST solution?

A. DAM

B. SIEM

C. XSS

D. WAF

22. Your organization experienced some network failures over the past year within the core part of its network. These failures cost the company a lot of money in lost productivity. Upper management wants to stop the failures. The IT department explained to upper management that these failures can't be avoided, but the network can be reconfigured and tuning alerts configured at a cost so that the impact of such failures is greatly reduced. Which network configuration is the IT department likely to propose?

A. Hub and spoke

B. Full mesh

C. Point-to-point

D. Partial mesh

23. A security audit was conducted for your organization. It found that a computer plugged into any Ethernet port in its shipping facility was able to remotely access network resources without authentication. You are directed to fix this security issue. Which standard, if implemented, could resolve this issue?

A. 802.1x

B. 802.3

C. 802.1q

D. 802.11

24. Instead of having salespeople travel back to the corporate office to upload customer information and to download new electronic marketing materials, upper management tasked the IT department with recommending a secure but simple-to-use solution. This solution should enable the salespeople to remain in the field but utilize Internet access to transfer the necessary information to and from the corporate office. All salespeople are familiar with using a web browser. What solution BEST suits this need?

A. A VPN solution using SSL/TLS via a web browser

B. A VPN solution using an application solution with IPSec

C. A VPN solution using a web browser with WAF

D. A VPN solution using an application solution with HIDS

25. Your company opened a remote office and needs secure communications between the corporate office and the remote office. To save money, upper management wants to utilize the Internet access each location has to provide this secure link. Secure communication on the individual LANs is not required. Which solution provides the BEST option for this situation?

A. VPN via SSL/TLS using a web browser.

B. VPN via IPSec in transport mode.

C. VPN via IPSec in tunnel mode.

D. No additional configuration is needed because IPv4 includes IPSec.

26. A network engineer must configure a router on the network remotely. What protocol should be used to ensure a secure connection?

   A. Telnet

   B. FTP

   C. HTTP

   D. SSH

27. You were asked to secure the Ethernet ports on the company's switches used to connect to host systems to prevent a VLAN hopping attack. Which of the following actions helps prevent this issue?

   A. Ensuring the Ethernet ports are statically defined as trunk ports

   B. Ensuring the Ethernet ports have DPT turned off

   C. Ensuring the Ethernet ports have DTP turned on

   D. Ensuring the Ethernet ports are configured as access ports

28. Your company has a fence around the perimeter of its data center. A sensor is connected to the fence and trips an alarm whenever something impacts the fence. The data center is located in an area with tumbleweeds that often impact the fence in the fall, causing alarm fatigue. In this scenario, what alert type is causing alarm fatigue?

   A. True positive

   B. True negative

   C. False positive

   D. False negative

29. The company discovered that some of your organization's employees are copying corporate documents to cloud drives outside the control of the company. Your CISO wants to stop this practice from occurring. Which of the following can stop this practice from happening?

   A. DLP

   B. NIDS

   C. NIPS

   D. Firewall

30. Which of the following is a protocol that provides a graphical interface to a Windows system over a network?

   A. RDP

   B. VNC

   C. VDI

   D. DLP

31. An attacker scanned your network and discovered a host system running a vulnerable version of VNC. Which of the following can an attacker perform if they can access VNC on the host?

   A. Remotely access the BIOS of the host system.

   B. Remotely view and control the desktop of the host system.

   C. Remotely view critical failures, causing a stop error or the blue screen of death on the host system.

   D. All of the above.

32. The firewall administrator implemented the following rules. Which statement is true concerning these rules?

Rule #	Rule	Protocol	Source	Destination	Port
1	Permit	IP	10.1.2.25	10.1.0.224	80
2	Permit	TCP	10.2.45.123	10.1.0.235	23
3	Deny	TCP	Any	10.1.0.130	22
4	Deny	TCP	10.2.45.123	10.1.0.235	23
5	Deny	IP	Any	Any	Any

   A. TCP traffic from source IP 10.2.45.123 will be allowed to destination IP 10.1.0.235 port 23 because rule 2 will be performed.

   B. TCP traffic from source IP 10.2.45.123 will not be allowed to destination IP 10.1.0.235 port 23 because rule 4 will be performed.

   C. TCP traffic from source IP 10.2.45.123 will be allowed to destination IP 10.1.0.235 port 23 because rule 5 will be performed.

   D. TCP traffic from source IP 10.2.45.123 will not be allowed to destination IP 10.1.0.235 port 23 because of the implicit deny at the end of the firewall list.

33. As a security analyst, you look for a method that can examine network traffic and filter its payload based on rules. What is this method called?

   A. Network flow

   B. DLP

   C. Data flow enforcement

   D. Deep packet inspection

34. You set the following command on a switch port, and a host sends frames to it. Assuming defaults for all other settings, which of the following statements is correct?

```
Switch(config-if)#switchport port-security mac-address 00:0E:08:34:7C:9B
```

   A. When a frame enters the port with a source MAC address other than 00:0E:08:34:7C:9B, the port will be placed in restricted mode.

    B. Nothing. The command format is incorrect.

    C. Enables only frames without source MAC address 00:0E:08:34:7C:9B into the port.

    D. Enables only frames with source MAC address 00:0E:08:34:7C:9B into the port.

35. If a Cisco switch port is in an "error-disabled state," what is the procedure to reenable it after you enter privilege exec mode?

    A. Issue the `no shutdown` command on the error-disabled interface.

    B. Issue the `shutdown` and then the `no shutdown` command on the error-disabled interface.

    C. Issue the `no error` command on the error-disabled interface.

    D. Issue the `no error-disable` command on the error-disabled interface.

36. Understanding normal traffic patterns of personally owned, corporate-enabled devices for your organization can help identify which of the following?

    A. Malware

    B. DDoS attack

    C. Ransomware

    D. Spoofing attack

37. Your organization decided to move away from dedicated computers on the desktop for controlling HVAC and A/V systems and move to a virtual desktop environment. The desktop image resides on a server within a virtual machine and is accessed via a desktop client over the network. Which of the following is being described?

    A. VPN

    B. VDI

    C. VNC

    D. RDP

38. The IT group within your organization wants to filter requests between clients and their servers. They want to place a device in front of the servers that acts as a middleman between the clients and the servers. This device receives the request from the clients and forwards the request to the servers. The server will reply to the request by sending the reply to the device; then the device will forward the reply onward to the clients. What device best meets this description?

    A. Firewall

    B. NIDS

    C. Reverse proxy

    D. Proxy

39. Your CISO wants to put in place a technique that helps mitigate a DDoS attack, should one be launched against the company. The CISO tasks you with identifying a technique that would drop malicious DDoS traffic destined for an IP address, or range of IP addresses, under attack. What technique performs this task?

A. Remotely triggered black hole

B. Transport security

C. Trunking security

D. Port security

40. Your corporate network is configured such that all network devices reach each other without going through a routing device. Your CISO wants the network reconfigured so that the network is segmented based on departments. In addition, the servers must be on their own subnetwork. What is a benefit of subdividing the network in this way?

A. No benefit at all.

B. By subdividing the network, the port numbers can be better distributed among assets.

C. By subdividing the network, rules can be placed to control the flow of traffic from one subnetwork to another.

D. Ease of deployment.

41. The corporate network grew to a point where the management of individual routers and switches is problematic. Your CISO wants to move to a solution where the control function of the routers and switches is centralized, leaving the routers and switches to perform the basic forwarding of traffic. Which technology BEST performs this function?

A. CDC

B. NAS

C. SAN

D. SDN

42. You work as a security consultant for a petroleum chemical company. The company uses SCADA to monitor sensors and control valves throughout their facility. Of the answers provided, which BEST secures the company's SCADA system?

A. Installing HIDS on the devices that make up the SCADA system

B. Implementing defense in depth in front of the SCADA system

C. Ensuring devices within the SCADA system have implicit allow rules on the firewall

D. Installing antivirus software on the devices that make up the SCADA system

43. You perform a security audit to find out whether any IoT devices on your network are publicly accessible. What website would you use to find this type of information?

A. Shodan

B. OWASP

    C. VirusTotal

    D. Maltego

44. What did the Mirai botnet used to launch a massive DDoS attack in 2016 consist primarily of?

    A. IoT

    B. Servers

    C. Laptop computers

    D. Switches

45. What is a major security concern associated with IoT?

    A. Lack of encryption

    B. Use of hard-coded passwords

    C. Lack of firmware support

    D. All of the above

46. Your CISO is concerned with unauthorized network access to the corporate wireless network. You want to set a mechanism in place that not only authenticates the wireless devices but also requires them to meet a predefined corporate policy before allowing them on the network. What technology BEST performs this function?

    A. HIDS

    B. NAC

    C. Agent

    D. NIPS

47. Your security team is implementing NAC for authentication as well as corporate policy enforcement. The team wants to install software on the devices to perform these tasks. In the context of NAC, what is this software called?

    A. Program

    B. Process

    C. Agent

    D. Thread

48. Your security team implemented NAC for authentication as well as corporate policy enforcement. Originally, the team installed software on the devices to perform these tasks. However, the security team decided this method is no longer desirable. They want to implement a solution that performs the same function but doesn't require software to be installed on the devices. In the context of NAC, what is this configuration called?

    A. Agent

    B. Agentless

    C. Volatile

    D. Persistent

49. Your IT group decided to do limited filtering of known malicious traffic entering the border router from the Internet. Which traffic with the following source IP addresses should NOT be filtered inbound from the Internet?

   A. 127.0.0.0/8

   B. RFC 1918 addresses

   C. 172.32.0.0/16

   D. 0.0.0.0/8

50. A firewall administrator added new rules to the corporate border firewall. What should the firewall administrator do next to ensure that the rules are functioning properly?

   A. All firewall rules should be tested with traffic matching the rules.

   B. Only the new firewall rules should be tested with traffic matching the rules.

   C. No testing is required. Firewalls rules are checked for validity within the firewall.

   D. Because of time constraints, only firewall rules considered to be the most important should be tested.

51. Your organization has currently deployed some standard Linux systems in its network. The system admin for these Linux systems wants to secure these systems by using SELinux. Which of the following is a benefit of using SELinux?

   A. Moves from a discretionary access control system to a system where the file creator controls the permissions of the file

   B. Moves from a discretionary access control system to a mandatory access control system

   C. Moves from a mandatory access control system to a system where the file creator controls the permissions of the file

   D. Moves from a mandatory access control system to a discretionary access control system

52. What NSA project promoted the use of SELinux in Android devices?

   A. SEinAndroid

   B. SEAndroid

   C. SELinAndroid

   D. SAndroid

53. Your organization has endpoints that are considered low-priority systems. Even though they are considered low priority, they still must be protected from malicious code capable of destroying data and corrupting systems. Malicious code is capable of infecting files but generally needs help moving from one system to another. What type of security product protects systems from this type of malicious code only?

   A. Anti-malware

   B. Antispyware

   C. Antivirus

   D. Anti-adware

54. Your CISO wants to install a security product capable of detecting and removing most malicious programs such as viruses, Trojans, ransomware, spyware, adware, and the like from high-value hosts within the organization. Which of the following is BEST suited to meet the criteria?

    A. Antivirus

    B. Anti-malware

    C. Anti-adware

    D. Antispyware

55. As a security analyst, you analyzed suspicious traffic flowing from a host on your network. After further examination, it appears that the data consists of website addresses, items downloaded, emails sent and received, and other data. You suspect malicious software is on the host. You want to install a product on the host to discover and remove the expected software. Which of the following products will likely discover the program performing this malicious activity?

    A. Anti-adware

    B. Antivirus

    C. Antispyware

    D. Anti-malware

56. Many users within your organization clicked on emails that, while looking legitimate, are malicious. Malicious code executes once the email is opened, infecting the user's system with malware. What could be implemented on the email server to help prevent such emails from reaching the end user?

    A. Firewall

    B. Spam filters

    C. WAF

    D. Proxy

57. As a security analyst, you ran a vulnerability scan on your network. While examining the scan results, you notice various servers are missing patches. You decide to look for an automated process of installing patches on systems. Which of the following automates this process?

    A. Security assessment

    B. Vulnerability management

    C. Vulnerability scanner

    D. Patch management system

58. Your CISO asked you to implement a solution on the servers in your DMZ that can detect and stop malicious activity. Which solution accomplishes this task?

    A. HIDS

    B. NIDS

    C. HIPS

    D. NIPS

59. Your CISO asked you to implement a solution on the servers in your data center that can detect malicious activity and send alerts to IT staff once they are detected. Which solution accomplishes this task?

    A. HIDS

    B. NIDS

    C. HIPS

    D. NIPS

60. Many of your corporate users are using mobile laptop computers to perform their work. Security is concerned that confidential data residing on these laptops may be disclosed. What technology helps prevent the loss of such data?

    A. DLP

    B. DPS

    C. HIDS

    D. HIPS

61. Your organization has a problem with users downloading programs from untrusted Internet sites. Some of these programs included malware that has infected the systems. Your CISO wants to stop users from doing this. What technique permits only approved programs to be downloaded to an end user's system?

    A. Blacklisting

    B. Pinklisting

    C. Whitelisting

    D. Graylisting

62. To curtail end-user visits to known malicious websites, the security team decided to block users from accessing them. Which of the following solutions performs this task?

    A. Pinklisting

    B. Graylisting

    C. Whitelisting

    D. Blacklisting

63. You're installing an antivirus product on computers within your corporate domain. Installing the product manually on each computer will take a long time to complete. Noting that your company uses Microsoft Active Directory in your environment, which technique listed is more efficient?

    A. Providing a copy of the antivirus product to the end users and allowing them to install the product themselves

    B. Using Group Policy to push out the antivirus product to all computers

C. Creating a master image of the computers with the antivirus product installed and then reimaging all the computers

D. Contracting out the installation of the antivirus product to a third party who manually installs the product on all the computers

64. A network engineer enters the following commands on an Ethernet port of a router. The port is currently in its default configuration. What command must be entered after the following commands to bring up the interface?

```
Router>enable
Router# configure terminal
Router(config)#interface fastethernet 0/1
Router(config-if)#ip address 192.168.1.23 255.255.255.0
```

A. no shutdown

B. up

C. restart

D. start

65. If loaded into a router, which set of commands allows a network engineer to log into it if he knows the correct password?

A. Router>enable
Router# configure terminal
Router(config)#line vty 0 4
Router(config-line)#password secret

B. Router>enable
Router# configure terminal
Router(config)#line vty 0 4
Router(config-line)#password secret
Router(config-line)#login

C. Router>enable
Router# configure terminal
Router(config)#line vty 0 4
Router(config-line)#password
Router(config-line-password)# secret
Router(config-line)#log in

D. Router>enable
Router# configure terminal
Router(config)#line vty 0 4
Router(config-line)#password secret
Router(config-line)#log in

66. A network engineer wants to configure a router so that remote connections to it via SSH are possible. Which of the following commands must be entered after the `line vty 0 4` command to ensure that only SSH connections are allowed?

   A. `transport secure`

   B. `transport ssh`

   C. `transport input secure`

   D. `transport input ssh`

67. A network engineer configures a router to block inbound traffic from a computer with IP address 192.168.1.25 on Ethernet port 0. Which ACL performs the action of blocking this computer?

   A. `!`
```
interface ethernet0
ip access-group 1 in
!
access-list 1 permit any
access-list 1 deny host 192.168.1.25
```

   B. `!`
```
interface ethernet0
ip access-group 1 in
!
access-list 1 deny host 192.168.1.25
access-list 1 permit any
```

   C. `!`
```
interface ethernet0
ip access-group 1 in
!
```

   D. `!`
```
interface ethernet0
ip access-group 1 in
!
access-list 1 deny any
access-list 1 deny host 192.168.1.25
access-list 1 permit any
```

68. If a packet received by a router is examined by an ACL and no statement in the ACL matches the packet, what happens to the packet?

   A. The packet is dropped.

   B. The packet is forwarded.

   C. The packet is sent to another queue for further examination.

   D. The packet is returned to the sender.

69. A network engineer wants to prevent people outside of the corporate network from pinging systems within the network but allow all other traffic. The router's Ethernet 0 interface is connected to the Internet. Which ACL prevents this type of traffic?

A.
```
!
interface ethernet0
ip access-group 101 in
!
access-list 101 deny icmp any any
access-list 101 permit ip any any
```

B.
```
!
interface ethernet0
ip access-group 1 in
!
access-list 1 deny icmp any any
access-list 1 permit ip any any
```

C.
```
!
interface ethernet0
ip access-group 101 in
!
access-list 101 permit ip any any
access-list 101 deny icmp any any
```

D.
```
!
interface ethernet0
ip access-group 1 in
!
access-list 1 permit ip any any
access-list 1 deny icmp any any
```

70. A network engineer is working on a router at a remote office. She connects a telephone line and modem to the router so that she can access the router if the single network circuit fails. What is this type of connection referred to as?

   A. Failover management

   B. Redundant management

   C. Out-of-band management

   D. Standby management

71. Your CISO is concerned that all employees can use personal USB storage devices on the company's computers. She is concerned about malware introduction into the corporate environment and that data loss is possible if this practice continues. She is also concerned that a USB could be used for tethering a corporate system to the Internet and experience data loss. She wants to manage who can use USB storage devices on the company's computers. Which of the following actions should be used to implement this constraint?

   A. Replacing all computers with those that do not have USB ports

   B. Placing glue in the computers' USB ports

   C. Cutting the computers' USB cables

   D. Configuring a Group Policy within Microsoft Active Directory to manage USB storage device use on those computers

72. A home user wants to secure his new wireless router through the management interface. He has done spectrum analysis to find the best frequency for his home network. Which of the following should he NOT do?

   A. Change the default administrator name and use a strong password.

   B. Set SSID broadcast to nonbroadcast.

   C. Use WEP.

   D. Use MAC filtering.

73. A security engineer is concerned that logs may be lost on networked devices if the devices should fail or become compromised by an attacker. What solution ensures that logs are not lost on these devices?

   A. Configuring a firewall on the local machine

   B. Archiving the logs on the local machine

   C. Sending the logs to a syslog

   D. Installing a NIPS

74. A network engineer is concerned that the logs retrieved from various networked devices have inaccurate timestamps, making it difficult to correctly sequence the logs. What could the network engineer do to ensure the timestamps are current?

   A. Configure NTP on all devices.

   B. Manually set the date/time on all devices.

   C. Reverse engineer the correct date/time by using the current date/time and the original date/time of the device at boot.

   D. Outsource the correction process to a third party.

75. An attacker who compromised your network was caught and is being prosecuted. The logs from various pieces of equipment showing the attacker's actions are one of the key pieces of evidence. Upon examining the logs, it is determined that the timestamps are inaccurate and off by years. What is likely to happen to the logs as related to the prosecution of the attacker?

   A. The defense attorney will likely be given an opportunity to correct the timestamps.

   B. The judge will likely enable a third party to correct the timestamps.

C. The company will likely be given an opportunity to correct the timestamps, making them admissible in court.

D. The logs will likely not be allowed in court because the timestamps are incorrect.

76. As a security professional, you were asked to provide tips on how to best protect Bluetooth-enabled devices. Of the following answers, which is NOT a recommended way to protect your device?

A. Turn Bluetooth off when not needed.

B. Ensure Bluetooth is in hidden mode.

C. Turn Bluetooth pairing off unless needed.

D. Ensure Wi-Fi is off when not needed.

77. You are explaining the differences between various IEEE standards to a colleague. The colleague asks which IEEE standard concerns Wi-Fi. Which IEEE standard is the umbrella standard for Wi-Fi networks?

A. 802.11

B. 802.2

C. 802.3

D. 802.5

78. Your organization deployed various IoT devices throughout the network. Unfortunately, many of these devices have few security mechanisms in place to protect them. What is one measure that can be taken to secure these IoT devices?

A. Loading antivirus product on them

B. Keeping the firmware up to date

C. Installing a HIDS on them

D. Installing a HIPS on them

79. A security engineer is concerned that an attacker could bypass OS authentication on a computer if the attacker has physical access to the SD or HDMI ports on the device. The concern is that the attacker could access the BIOS and have the computer boot from a removable drive. How could you prevent this from happening?

A. Install a HIDS on the system.

B. Disable all removable drives using Group Policy.

C. Password protect the BIOS.

D. Install anti-malware on the system.

80. As security engineer, you were asked to recommend a file encryption technology that your end users can use to secure individual files. All the end users have Windows 10 systems. Which of the following is the BEST option available?

A. FAT32

B. EFS

    C. BitLocker

    D. FAT64

81. As security engineer, you were asked to recommend a disk encryption technology that your end users can use to secure an entire disk or partition. Management is very concerned about encrypted communication on the device including any files captured with the webcam or microphone. All the end users have Windows 10 systems. Which of the following is the BEST option available?

    A. EFS

    B. FAT32

    C. NTFS

    D. BitLocker

82. You have Ubuntu servers within your organization. You are looking for an economical software package that can be installed on these systems and provide file and communication encryption. Of the following options, which option can provide this functionality?

    A. GNU Privacy Guard

    B. BitLocker

    C. EXT4

    D. EFS

83. You work for a company that has the Microsoft Windows OS deployed on its computers. Various versions of Windows are being used within your organization. You want to take advantage of EFS to secure individual files on these systems. Which file system supports EFS?

    A. FAT16

    B. EXT4

    C. FAT32

    D. NTFS

84. Your organization is upgrading computers. The new computers include a chipset on the motherboard that is used to store encryption keys. What is this chipset called?

    A. EKC

    B. TPM

    C. ESM

    D. RSA

85. You are bidding on a military contract that requires the validation of hardware components for security reasons. What is the validation process from a third party called?

    A. Authorization

    B. Authentication

    C. Isolation

    D. Attestation

86. What security mechanism does UEFI include that prevents the boot process from being hijacked by malware?

- **A.** Secure Boot
- **B.** Secure Bootup
- **C.** Secure Start
- **D.** Secure Run

87. A governmental agency purchases new computers for its employees and wants to ensure that the computers' boot loader process is protected from rootkits and bootkits loading during startup. What protection mechanism requires UEFI's Secure Boot process and TPM to work together to ensure that an OS is allowed to load and which parts of the process are allowed to execute?

- **A.** Early Launch Anti-Malware
- **B.** Integrity Measurement Architecture
- **C.** Measured Launch
- **D.** Attestation Services

88. A governmental agency is purchasing new Windows-based computers for some departments. The agency wants to ensure these computers have a security mechanism in place to detect whether files have been accidentally or maliciously altered. What mechanism provides this function?

- **A.** Secure Boot
- **B.** Attestation Services
- **C.** Integrity Measurement Architecture
- **D.** Early Launch Anti-Malware

89. A system administrator has a bash script that doesn't need many commands available in bash. For security reasons, he wants to run the bash script in restricted mode. Which of the following commands does NOT provide a restricted shell?

- **A.** `bash /r`
- **B.** `rbash`
- **C.** `bash --restricted`
- **D.** `bash -r`

90. Your security vulnerability management team has a specific timeline for patching all systems in your organization. Which of the following will automate this process?

- **A.** Patch management system
- **B.** Automated patching system
- **C.** Update management system
- **D.** Automated update system

91. As a security engineer, you discovered that some of your computers are still using BIOS for hardware initialization. What security feature is missing from BIOS that is available using UEFI?

    A. Loads boot loader

    B. Setting system clock

    C. Secure Boot

    D. Initializes system hardware components

92. Your IT department discovered that some of your legacy computers and servers don't have a TPM chipset in them but they do have eFUSE, an IBM technology that allows a chip to be rewritten in real time. What security feature is missing from these computers?

    A. Time synchronization of logs

    B. Program sandboxing

    C. Throttling of bandwidth protection

    D. Storage of cryptographic keys

93. Some employees were issued NFC-capable corporate phones. As part of the security department, you are tasked with recommending how to use these devices securely. Which answer should be included in your recommendation?

    A. Keeping patches up to date

    B. Turning off pairing mode

    C. Turning off discovery mode

    D. Turning on NFC when not in use

94. Your IT staff is seeking a wireless solution to transmit data in a manufacturing area with lots of electrical motors. The technology must transmit approximately 1 Mbps of data approximately 1 meter using line of sight. No obstacles are between the devices using this technology. Because of the environment, using RF is not a viable solution. What technology is BEST suited for this situation?

    A. Wi-Fi

    B. Bluetooth

    C. IrDA

    D. RF

95. Your company started upgrading the computers in your organization. As a security professional, you recommend creating a standard image for all computers with a set level of security configured. What is this process called?

    A. Configuration baselining

    B. Imaging

    C. Duplication

    D. Ghosting

96. Your company purchased new computers and wants consistent reliability and performance out of them. You recommend that an operating system and software application configuration be installed on these systems prior to the addition of programs. What is this process called?

A. Base configuration

B. Production operating environment

C. Standard operating environment

D. Standard configuration

97. Employees at your company want Bluetooth 4.1 enabled for their mobile devices including any device that can use audio because of the low energy usage benefits. What is your primary security concern?

A. Bluetooth can be overused.

B. Bluetooth sends data as clear text.

C. Bluetooth uses weak encryption.

D. Bluetooth is a lower-power wireless technology.

98. Your staff wants to use Bluetooth on their networked mobile devices, and you were asked to be the Bluetooth administrator. What type of network are you implementing?

A. MAN

B. LAN

C. WLAN

D. PAN

99. An employee uses a smartphone for both business and personal use. You think the phone is compromised, but you do not suspect the employee has malicious intent. What should you do?

A. Confiscate the phone.

B. Get a subpoena to access the phone.

C. Ask the user to surrender the phone for testing.

D. Get a warrant for the phone.

100. You are investigating the encryption of data at rest and data in transit and trying to determine which algorithm is best in each situation. Which of the following does not contain data at rest?

A. SAN

B. NAS

C. SSD

D. VPN

101. You have privacy concerns regarding the WLAN. You decide to disable SSID, enable MAC filtering, and enable a security method adhering to IEEE 802.11i standards. Which of the following do you enable?

    A. WPA

    B. PEAP

    C. WPA2

    D. WEP

102. Your hospital's security policy states that wearable technology and IoT devices are not allowed in secure areas where patient information is discussed. Wearable devices are designed to be worn by one individual, but some are quite powerful with artificial intelligence. Why is this a concern?

    A. Danger of eavesdropping and compliance violations

    B. Insurance premiums going up

    C. Malpractice and litigation

    D. Chain of custody of evidence

103. An employee downloads an IP video of someone stealing a package off their porch from their smart doorbell. How do you mitigate the risk of storing that type of data on your business network?

    A. Implementing a security policy and awareness

    B. Performing audits

    C. Monitoring networks for certain file types

    D. Using third-party threat intelligence reports

104. Your DevOps team decided to use containers because they allow running applications on any hardware. What is the first thing your team should do to have a secure container environment?

    A. Install IPS.

    B. Lock down Kubernetes and monitor registries.

    C. Configure anti-malware and traffic filtering.

    D. Disable services that are not required and install monitoring tools.

105. Unnecessary services are disabled on the container host, and monitoring tools are installed. You want to monitor the intercontainer traffic so that attackers cannot move laterally through the environment. What should you install on the host?

    A. Malwarebytes

    B. IPS

    C. SIEM

    D. TPM

106. You deployed containers to bundle and run applications in your production environment. You need a way to manage the containers and to ensure that there is no downtime. If one container goes down, another one needs to spin up. Which technology will allow you to NOT spin up machines manually in case of a failure?

- **A.** Kubernetes
- **B.** Instantiation
- **C.** Rollback
- **D.** Tiagra

107. Your organization's container ecosystem handles extremely sensitive data. You want to scan and validate the configuration of each container as it is added to the container registry. Which of these is most important when securely locking down and monitoring the container registry?

- **A.** It can cost a lot of money to spin up containers that your team is not utilizing.
- **B.** It ensures that only containers meeting with the team's development processes and security policies are added to the environment.
- **C.** There is a limit to how many containers can operate in one single deployment.
- **D.** The hypervisor on the container image could have vulnerabilities that are now cloud-based and easier to take advantage of.

108. The containers you built are running, and software is currently undergoing a patch. These changes must be integrated into the application to reduce risk. What tool can you use to ensure that changes are not causing security issues on the containers in production?

- **A.** Container image scanner
- **B.** Container vulnerability scanner
- **C.** Container port scanner
- **D.** Container antivirus

109. As a security specialist for your organization, you are increasingly concerned about strong endpoint controls of developers' workstations as well as access control of servers running developer tools. Which of these is NOT a benefit of an access control scheme?

- **A.** Helping meet security goals and standards
- **B.** Ensuring only authorized users have access to code repositories
- **C.** Having runtime self-protection controls
- **D.** Safeguarding system integrity

110. Your mobile devices need configuring just like desktop and server systems. You were told to standardize all mobile devices, both iOS and tvOS. What do you deploy to these devices?

- **A.** Mobile device configuration profile.
- **B.** Group Policy.
- **C.** Root the devices and install a golden mobile image.
- **D.** Containerization.

111. Several payload variables can be configured in a mobile device configuration profile. Meaning, you can configure each mobile device and user to which you are giving the profile. If you want to include a unique identifier in the profile, which of these would you choose to populate?

    A. $DEVICENAME

    B. $SITENAME

    C. $USERNAME

    D. $UDID

112. As a mobile application management administrator, you want specific policy elements to be applied to your company's mobile devices. You do not want to change the underlying application. Which of the following should you implement?

    A. Sandboxing

    B. App wrapping

    C. Risk analysis

    D. USB OTG

113. In the next fiscal year, all your company's salespeople will get a company-issued cell phone. As you develop a security policy to address lost or stolen data, malware, and malicious applications, one major risk to address is a lost or stolen device. How do you approach this risk?

    A. MDM

    B. MAM

    C. BYOD

    D. TPM

114. An employee's company-issued cell phone was left in the back of a ride-sharing vehicle and has not been returned in a timely manner. Per the security policy, they contacted the IT department, and now you must perform a remote wipe on that asset. What type of server allows remote wiping of the device?

    A. MAM

    B. MDM

    C. RDP

    D. DNS

115. Your CISO decided to implement an overarching enterprise mobility management (EMM) strategy. She wants to ensure that sensitive corporate data isn't compromised by the employees' apps on their mobile devices. Which of these will implement that BEST?

    A. App config through IDC

    B. App wrapping through SDK

C. Open source through API

D. Platform DevOps

116. Your global organization has tech support offices that "follow the sun." Meaning, tech support is open 24 hours a day, 7 days a week, and some of those support offices are located in other countries. Depending on the time of day, it may be necessary for tech support personnel to access systems remotely over the Internet, managing your own server without using a centralized service. What is the BEST choice in this list to accomplish the support personnel's need?

A. MRA

B. VNC

C. RDP

D. TeamViewer

117. Your CISO wants to wirelessly share his phone or other mobile device screen with a larger screen in a conference room. He wants to give presentations and directly share feedback from applications. Which of the following is his BEST option?

A. Screen mirroring

B. Video conferencing

C. IMS

D. TPM

118. Your mobile device wirelessly receives its over-the-air (OTA) update. The company determined it is not a security risk for your mobile device to receive new software or data this way. You do not want to lose access to your mobile device during business hours, so what type of OTA do you configure?

A. Manual

B. Instinctive

C. Responsive

D. Automatic

119. You are in a large-scale enterprise organization, and your IT administrators do not have time to manually distribute certificates to mobile devices. What is the BEST protocol to use?

A. MDM

B. ICMP

C. RDP

D. SCEP

120. You have implemented a Simple Certificate Enrollment Protocol (SCEP) in your organizations. SCEP is designed to support the issuing of certificates in a scalable way. How does SCEP work in an enterprise environment?

A. The SCEP server CA issues and approves the certificate.

B. The SCEP server RA issues pending certificates automatically, and the IAM admin approves them.

    C. A certificate is requested from the SCEP server and is issued automatically.

    D. The SCEP issues the certificate, the CA approves and issues the certificate.

121. Your new CISO wants to implement a mobile device strategy. All staff have mobile devices, and you need something quickly implemented that is not very expensive. Which of the following strategies is the BEST one for your organization?

    A. BYOD

    B. CYOD

    C. COPE

    D. IDEA

122. Your organization is revisiting its mobile device strategies due to security's need to have vetted hardware on corporate networks. You want to give employees a choice, but you need to keep costs down. What is the BEST strategy to deploy?

    A. BYOD

    B. CYOD

    C. COPE

    D. TPM

123. Your global banking organization wants to use mobile devices in their main offices as well as remote branches. Employees handle sensitive financial documents, including bank statements, loan applications, and mortgage documents. Given that your organization is very risk averse, what type of mobile strategy would work BEST for them?

    A. BYOD

    B. CYOD

    C. COPE

    D. OSPF

124. Your employees need internal access while traveling to remote locations. You need a service that enables them to securely connect back to a private corporate network from a public network to log into a centralized portal. You want the traffic to be encrypted. Which of the following is the BEST tool?

    A. Wi-Fi

    B. VPN

    C. RDP

    D. NIC

125. Your VPN needs the strongest authentication possible. Your network is comprised of Microsoft servers. Which of the following protocols provides the most secure authentication?

    A. EAP-TLS with smart cards

    B. SPAP

C. CHAP

D. LEAP

126. Your employees complain that when they connect to the network through the VPN, they cannot view their social media posts and pictures. What mostly likely has been implemented?

A. Split tunnels

B. DNS tunnels

C. ARP cache

D. Full tunnels

127. Your marketing team wants to share files between local devices without using the network or a physical memory card at the next conference. Which of these terms is BEST suited for the preceding situation?

A. Uploading

B. Downloading

C. Sideloading

D. P2TP

128. An audit for your mobile device policies found that your COPE devices are allowing unsigned applications. The default value on these assets is set to $true. After developing an app, the developer must sign it in or make it traceable and publish it to the Play store. Is there a valid business need for installing unsigned applications on a company device?

A. If a developer wants to test and troubleshoot an app.

B. To validate the keystore: debug and release.

C. To remove the app's digitally signed certificates.

D. No, there is never a reason to use unsigned apps.

129. You want to use a USB drive with your phone to read data from the USB device without a PC. What type of cable do you need?

A. USB to USB

B. Paraflex Matrix

C. MicroUSB to C

D. USB OTG

130. You are traveling for work, and no Wi-Fi is available. You are in a public space and need to use your laptop to go online. If supported, you could tether through a mobile device to the Internet. What are the drawbacks of tethering?

A. Your mobile connection will be slow, and the battery will draw down quickly on your mobile device.

B. You must have an app to tether your phone to your laptop.

    C. Your phone calls will go straight to voicemail.

    D. Security will be an issue.

131. You want to evaluate the most secure authentication method on a mobile device, primarily your phone. Authentication includes many options and could possibly use multiple methods for secure access excluding gestures. Which of the following is not something you know?

    A. Password

    B. Pattern lock or swipe patterns

    C. Fingerprint

    D. PIN

132. Your company wants to begin using biometrics for authentication using Apple products. Apple products use a secure enclave to store the device passcode and biometric data, for Face ID or Touch ID. Which of the following are not biometrics that can be verified by a system to give an individual access?

    A. Facial recognition

    B. Iris recognition

    C. Retina recognition

    D. PIN recognition

133. Your new program using biometrics for authentication is going well. Biometrics are hard to fake and increase convenience. Which of these is not an advantage of using biometrics for authentication?

    A. Servers require less database memory.

    B. Ease of use.

    C. Stable and enduring with little variation.

    D. Technical accuracy, partial capture of data.

134. While presenting the business plan to migrate to a biometric solution, many questions arise regarding privacy, accuracy, and, most importantly, what else?

    A. Cost

    B. Acceptance

    C. Rejection

    D. Time

135. Augmented reality Mobile apps in your environment are causing concern because of the unintentional data leakage. "Riskware" applications pose the biggest problem for mobile users who give all permissions asked for without checking the need or security. These apps are usually the free fun apps and can be found in official app stores. What should you advise mobile device users about data leakage?

    A. Make sure that your network is fast.

    B. Instruct users to check for upgrades often.

C. Only give apps permissions they must have, and delete any app that asks for more than is necessary.

D. Give apps all the permissions they ask for.

136. You believe attackers set up fake access points in high-traffic public locations near your hospital campus. These access points have common names like Hospital Guest. What is this type of attack called?

A. Network hacking

B. Network spoofing

C. Phishing

D. Whaling

137. As a security analyst, you received a phone call from your CFO. He received the same email three times this week asking for approval of a bank transfer. You investigate the email and find it is not legitimate. What type of attack is this?

A. Phishing

B. Introspection

C. Ransomware

D. Buffer overflow

138. Your app developers focus on the speed of app development more than security for their instant messaging application. Because of this, they use easier-to-implement encryption algorithms with known vulnerabilities. What is the result of using this type of encryption algorithm?

A. Malware infection

B. Modification

C. Attacker cracks the passwords

D. Remote code execution

139. To facilitate ease of access for mobile device users, many apps use tokens. These tokens enable users to perform multiple actions without requiring users to reauthenticate their identity. Which of the following is a best practice in using this methodology?

A. Generating new tokens with each access attempt.

B. Keeping old tokens for a specific amount of time.

C. Using token until the app or page is closed.

D. Tokens should never expire.

140. Your terminated IT network administrator turned in his company iPhone. You found that he was able to remove the limitations put in place by the device's manufacturer. Third-party software is installed on the device. What did the IT network administrator do?

A. Locking

B. Rooting

C. Jailbreaking

D. Recompiling

141. Your system administrator attempted to gain access to low-level systems on her phone. She wants to uninstall system applications and revoke permissions on installed apps. What is this type of access called?

A. Malware

B. Unlocking

C. Rooting

D. Jailbreaking

142. Your software developer has a custom ROM for Android and wants to further customize it for mobile device use in your healthcare network. Android is an open source operating system, but your developer experiences difficulties uploading the new ROM to a test device. What does he need to unlock before uploading the new ROM?

A. Bootloader

B. BIOS

C. FIFO

D. TPM

143. The corporate contract with your current mobile device provider is nearly over, and you are considering moving to a new provider. Many phones, particularly ones that are subsidized with a contract, come locked into a specific carrier. The phone is configured to operate only with that carrier. What action must you provide to move your mobile phone fleet to a new carrier?

A. Jailbreak

B. Root

C. Lock

D. Unlock

144. You want to find a way for your shop's new mobile app to notify people when there is a sale without the user opening the application. What do you need to create?

A. Push notification

B. Text message

C. Email

D. SMS

145. Privacy is of utmost importance to your organization. As a security architect, you are tasked with protecting instant messages. Which of the following is the BEST choice for protecting these messages?

A. SMS

B. Encryption

C. Surveillance

D. Transmission

146. Your MDM allows for the use of mobile payments using virtual smartphone wallets. Paying with your smartphone replaces swiping a card. Your end users are skeptical, but your security analyst supports it. What is the security analyst's argument for using this technology?

A. Mobile wallets use encryption to mask payment card numbers.

B. Mobile wallets use encryption to mask the phone's number.

C. Mobile payment methods are not more secure than cards or cash.

D. Loss of a smartphone is like losing a credit card.

147. You are investigating a method to send information over radio waves that is fast and secure while sending data, primarily for taking payments. What is the BEST option in this list?

A. Bluetooth

B. Infrared

C. RFID

D. NFC

148. You use a process that substitutes a sensitive data element with something that is not sensitive. You use this process to map back to the sensitive data. What is this called?

A. Masking

B. Encryption

C. Tokenization

D. Authorization

149. Your organization creates a business case for purchasing company-owned, personally enabled (COPE) mobile devices. One specific issue with mobile device open source operating systems is increased disparity. Which BEST describes the problem with manufacturers creating their own version and updates?

A. Morphism

B. Instantiation

C. Fragmentation

D. Mutation

150. Your organization includes employees who travel internationally and who occasionally post on their social media their business travel locations. In some social media platforms, physical location is shared or attached to a post or picture. What do employees need to be most aware of with these digital posts on the Internet?

A. Credit card theft

B. Phishing

    C. RFID cloners

    D. Geotagging

151. Your risk audit for mobile devices shows the best way to deal with data lost in a breach is coverage from financial losses. Which of the following is the BEST choice to accomplish this?

    A. Cyber liability insurance

    B. Risk acceptance

    C. Risk avoidance

    D. Encryption

152. You created an addendum to your corporate security policy. This policy states that whenever a device is lost or stolen, the enterprise has the ability to protect its data on that device. What should this policy recommend?

    A. Incident detection and response

    B. Remote lock and data wipe

    C. Replacement of a device and destruction of old one

    D. Termination of the employee

153. Your role as an IT administrator includes providing new hardware to different departments within your organization. The company decided that all servers need dual NICs, so you are compiling a summary from public RFPs. Upper management wants to select the lowest bidder, but you have never heard of this overseas manufacturer. What do you recommend in this decision-making process?

    A. Requiring well-known and trusted hardware manufacturers

    B. Going with the lowest bidder if it makes upper management happy

    C. Requesting samples from all the bidders and vetting the hardware yourself

    D. Buying all new servers because there aren't that many new ones

154. You finished a penetration test that identified a web server with a critical vulnerability. The web server's role is mission critical to your organization and has an uptime requirement of 99.9 percent. If you patch the vulnerability, it may break the application running on this server. How do you secure the web server until another solution is found?

    A. Using a stateful inspection firewall

    B. Installing antivirus protection

    C. Using a circuit-level gateway

    D. Via a HIDS/HIPS

155. You attempt to fix a problem with a workstation and discover that the end user installed unauthorized software. The workstation now conflicts with security policy. You uninstall the software and make sure the system is compliant. What do you do next?

    A. Report the user to human resources.

    B. If the user is a direct report, document the problem and confiscate all the installation media.

    C. Have the end user request the software be placed on the approved list.

    D. Give the end user a list of all the approved software.

156. Your role in developing secure software requires that you follow a methodology for defense in depth called SD3. What type of strategy is this?

    A. Secure by design, default, and deployment.

    B. Secure review code three times.

    C. An outside SD3 audit as recommended by NIST.

    D. No methodology is called SD3.

157. The application you are building handles sensitive data, specifically PII. You want to encrypt the data and protect it from being stolen or altered. You consider cryptography in your application process. What is this an example of?

    A. Secure by design

    B. Secure by default

    C. Secure by deployment

    D. Secure by download

158. A subset of programmers in your organization tested the beta of your application. During the testing phase, you asked that they install the software by selecting optional components during the setup procedure. For any changes they want to make in the future, they will need to rerun the installation process. What is this called?

    A. Secure by design

    B. Secure by default

    C. Secure by deployment

    D. Secure by download

159. In the event of application failure or error, a system should be set in place so that your end users have a general error indicator but the events are logged for future reference. What is this called in production?

    A. Secure by design

    B. Secure by default

    C. Secure by deployment

    D. Secure by download

160. You test an application by mapping out all areas where a user's input is used to reference objects. This input accesses a file on a mapped drive, and you try to change the value, bypassing all authorization. What type of attack is this?

    A. CSRF

    B. DDoS

    C. Insecure direct object reference

    D. Click-jacking

161. You are a penetration tester, searching for unlinked content on a web server. What type of an attack is this?

   A. CSRF

   B. Forced browsing

   C. SQLi

   D. Click-jacking

162. You run a security verification process on a web server. You attempt to replace the decimal encoding of ../ with %2E%2E%2F. What type of attack are you attempting?

   A. Phishing

   B. Input validation

   C. Ransomware

   D. Double encoding

163. You implement a CAPTCHA system on your corporate web server to prevent spam. Which of the following other attacks are most likely to be prevented?

   A. XSRF

   B. XSS

   C. Two-factor authentication

   D. XMLi

164. You are the senior security analyst for a large online news organization. You were briefed that your organization fell victim to an XSS attack that executed malicious web-scripting code in a trusted web page. How can you prevent this from happening in the future?

   A. Make sure the web application can validate and sanitize input.

   B. Implement patch management immediately.

   C. Request an external penetration test.

   D. You cannot prevent this from happening on a publicly facing web server.

165. Your company's HR department alerted IT that an end user is complaining of a suspicious web page on the intranet. The user said they clicked a button to download software updates, and instead, it opened their personal bank account homepage. What type of attack was most likely perpetrated against your organization?

   A. CSRF

   B. Phishing

   C. Social engineering

   D. Click-jacking

166. You are a consultant for a software developer working for a bank. You need to build the rule set that governs the interaction between your end users and the web application linking authentication and access. What type of rule set is this?

   A. Session management

   B. Secure cookies

    C. Java flags

    D. Stateless firewall

167. You were hired to perform a white-hat penetration test and instructed to concentrate on a specific web server. You run the following command: `nmap -sV -p80 192.168.1.6`. This is the response: `80/tcp open http Apache httpd 1.3.30`. What is this an example of?

    A. XSS

    B. Information leakage

    C. Request/response

    D. Error handling

168. Your penetration test of several SQL databases returned the following: `ERROR: unterminated quoted string at or near " '" "`. What should you call this in your report?

    A. Improper error handling

    B. Proper error handling

    C. Vulnerability

    D. XSS

169. You logged into your bank account at `http://mycreditunion.com`. You open another tab and search for the best Italian restaurants. One of those sites is owned by a bad actor. This website has the following: `<img>` tag: `<img src="http://mycreditunion.com/transfer.asp?to_acct123456&amp;amount=500">`. What type of attack is this?

    A. CSRF

    B. XSS

    C. SQLi

    D. XMLi

170. You are examining SQL server logs and are seeing `userid: 101 or 1=1`. What is most likely happening on that SQL server?

    A. XMLi

    B. XSS

    C. SQLi

    D. Buffer overflow

171. Your penetration testers' report shows that they obtained the credentials of specific user accounts through social engineering and phishing campaigns. Once on the organization's network, the penetration testers used these credentials to bypass access controls and to gain access to remote systems. In one case, they were able to switch from a user-level account to an administrator-level account. What is this type of attack called?

    A. XSRF

    B. Password mitigation

    C. Token theft

    D. Privilege escalation

172. Your web application stores sensitive information, including credit card numbers and account records. Which of the following is an encryption mistake and can possibly lead to insecure storage in your website?

    A. Strong algorithm

    B. Initialization vectors

    C. Support for key changes

    D. Storage of certificates on USB

173. Your company hired a third party to conduct an application assessment. The tool they use can provide results with little effort and remain running for weeks. However, it might not find all the bugs depending on how it is configured. What type of tool do they use?

    A. Vulnerability scanner

    B. Fuzzer

    C. Data validator

    D. HIPS

174. Which of the following attacks is a form of software exploitation that transmits a stream of input larger than what the software is designed to handle?

    A. Buffer overflow

    B. SQLi

    C. XSS

    D. TOC

175. You build a web application for your new retail organization. Your developer failed to check the length of input before processing his code. What is this code susceptible to?

    A. Session management

    B. XSS

    C. Privilege escalation

    D. Buffer overflow

176. You conduct a privacy audit for your organization and are concerned about possible violations. Which of the following is most concerning?

    A. FTP

    B. VPN

    C. Rogue access points

    D. Cookies

177. The performance on the server running SQL is degrading and occasionally fails when running replication scripts. You ran diagnostics, and despite having adequate RAM, your OS is not correctly managing the resources. What is most likely happening?

A. Memory leak

B. Dysfunctional dependency

C. SQLi

D. Virus

178. Your program is designed to handle certain tasks in a sequence. Unfortunately, this program seems to be locking up. Upon further review, it seems the program is performing these operations simultaneously. What is this called?

A. Sequencing

B. Thread blocking

C. Race condition

D. Circular addressing

179. In software development, a timing problem can occur when time to check (ToC) is misaligned with time of use (ToU). This time gap can be exploited by an attacker when they are scheduled for execution after each operation by the victim. To prevent ToCToU (pronounced Toctoo), which of the following is most effective?

A. Do not perform a check before use.

B. Alter the file owned by the current user.

C. Request the timing gap be closed.

D. Limit multiple processes and operations.

180. As a marketing analyst for a large retail enterprise organization, you want to deploy a technology that will responsibly personalize the in-person shopping experience for those shoppers using cell phones, cameras, smart watches or other fitness devices. What technology do you explore using with your retail app?

A. Home delivery

B. Personal shoppers

C. Geotagging

D. Customer feedback

181. GPS is built into cell phones and cameras as well as some medical and fitness devices, enabling coordinated longitude and latitude to be embedded in a machine-readable format as part of a picture or in apps and games. Besides physical coordinates of longitude and latitude, which of these will not be embedded in the metadata of a photo taken with a cell phone?

A. Names of businesses that are near your location

B. Elevation

C. Bearing

D. Phone number

182. Your OKR for the upcoming year is to modernize your IT strategy by adopting cloud-based features and storage for industrial control systems (ICS). You understand that once your intellectual property is in the cloud, you have less visibility and control as a consumer. What else is a security concern for important data stored in the cloud?

A. Cost effectiveness

B. Elastic use

C. Being on demand

D. Data remnants

183. You evaluate cloud storage providers and give each a product evaluation form. Which of these is not the best practice for a cloud service provider?

A. Strict initial registration and validation

B. System event and network traffic monitoring

C. Utilization of weak encryption algorithms

D. Incident response processes that help BCP

184. You need an authorization framework that gives a third-party application access to resources without providing the owners' credentials to the application. Which of these is your BEST option?

A. MAC

B. Biometrics

C. SAML

D. OAuth

185. Your CTO believes in the adage "Security through obscurity." Which of the following types of obfuscation makes a program obscure to other computers?

A. Prevention

B. Saturation

C. Control flow

D. Data Forensics

186. You develop an application and want to prevent the reuse of information in memory when a user quits the program. Which of these is your BEST option to accomplish this task?

A. Garbage collection

B. Data validation

C. SDLC

D. OOP

187. The application you are developing has a vulnerability that can be mitigated by using SSL and TLS. Which of these attacks can be prevented by using cryptographic protocols?

A. Buffer overflow

B. SQLi

    C. MiTM

    D. Malware

188. As a security analyst, you are tasked with analyzing the logs from your web server. What kind of analysis is this?

    A. Network analysis

    B. Hardware analysis

    C. User analysis

    D. Data analysis

189. Which of the following is a threat to application security mitigated by using garbage collection?

    A. Object reuse

    B. XSS

    C. Ransomware

    D. Sandboxing

190. Which of these helps prevent accidental data loss by making sure a class defines the data it needs?

    A. Modules

    B. Classes

    C. Segmentation

    D. Encapsulation

191. Your database administrator (DBA) reached out to you because the relational database that the security department uses has modified data, so secret projects are being referred to by an identification number instead of a name. What is the security control implemented?

    A. Encryption

    B. Randomization

    C. Pseudonymization

    D. Tokenization

192. Legacy applications in your environment are running a Java applet written in Pascal. This applet was created as a supplemental tool that displays data in 3D. Because Java applets were phased out in 2017 according to JEP 289 in the OpenJDK, what should you consider doing in the near future?

    A. Coding business logic in Java and rendering in HTML5

    B. Building the program in Silverfrost

    C. Requesting an extension to maintain Java SE10—the last Java to use Java applets

    D. No need to deprecate the legacy equipment

193. Your end users utilize Internet Explorer and Microsoft Office. A few users have reached out for approval to install ActiveX. How do you advise those end users to use ActiveX securely?

    A. If you are browsing the Web and a site wants you to install an ActiveX control, decline it.

    B. If you are browsing the Web and the site wants you to install an ActiveX control, accept it.

    C. Request the vetting of the software to be downloaded.

    D. You cannot use ActiveX securely.

194. You need a web server to process requests sent by XML. What is the BEST technology to use for this?

    A. REST

    B. SOAP

    C. Ajax

    D. XSS

195. You configure the applied programming interface (API) connection between your web application that manages retail transactions and your bank. This connection must be as secure as possible. Because the API connection will handle financial transactions, what is the BEST choice for securing the API if it is well designed?

    A. SOAP

    B. HTTPS

    C. REST

    D. XML

196. Your home automation web application is going through a user experience (UX) review. The application grew to the point that issues have developed because of the complexity of the text fields, radio buttons, and other input fields impacted by the state of other text fields and radio buttons. What type of issue are you experiencing?

    A. State management

    B. Redundant libraries

    C. Request frameworks

    D. Centralized data store

197. You are a web developer who needs to secure API keys in a client-side JavaScript application created for your hospital. What is the BEST way to accomplish this task quickly and efficiently?

    A. Disable API access and use a hash of the key.

    B. Set API access and a secret key pair.

    C. Curl a request with a -H -o option.

    D. Set a RESTful request with access pairs.

198. The website you developed in JavaScript must be secured. What is the BEST way for you to encrypt the data being sent over the Internet while using your website?

A. TLS/HTTPS

B. SSL/FTP

C. OTP

D. MD5/SHA1

199. You have JavaScript installed as the foundation of most of your web applications because it is fast and interactive. You attempt to harden systems found with JavaScript vulnerabilities. Which of the following are the most commonly exploited JavaScript attacks?

A. Click-jacking

B. DNS and ARP

C. XSS and CSRF

D. SQLi and XMLi

200. After a vulnerability scan, you found critical vulnerabilities in some installed services on a device with a System on a chip (SOC). These could lead to a server-side attack. Which one of the following mitigation techniques is the *least* effective?

A. Patching

B. System hardening that is automated

C. Firewalls

D. Identity management

201. You are a security administrator reviewing network logs. You notice a UDP trend where traffic increased more than 30 percent in the past 48 hours. You use Wireshark to capture the packets and see the following: UDP 192.168.1.1:123->46.110.10.5:123. What attack scenario is most likely occurring?

A. You are being attacked via the NTP client side and successfully exploited on 192.168.1.1.

B. You are being attacked via the NTP server side and unsuccessfully exploited on 192.168.1.1.

C. You are being attacked via the DNS client side and successfully exploited on 192.168.1.1.

D. You are being attacked via the DNS server side and successfully exploited on 192.168.1.1.

202. Your company undergoes a three-year cycle of tech refreshes on mobile devices and a five-year cycle on servers and workstations. You look at the newest version operating systems including TrustedSolaris and try to decide which operating system is the safest with the most functionality for your mission-critical assets. What do you do first?

A. Build a threat model

B. Conduct developer interviews

    C. Write a report

    D. Triage results

203. As a new security administrator in a global organization, you discovered that no one at this company has addressed CVE 2017-5689, a critical firmware flaw in the Intel Management Engine that is more than a decade old and contains an undocumented kill switch. What do you implement immediately?

    A. Nothing. Most companies who bought the chip affected were notified directly by the company.

    B. Update the Intel ME firmware immediately and then block ports 16992–16995 on endpoints and firewalls.

    C. Request more input from upper management about prioritization.

    D. Ignore it because there is no real effect from this CVE.

Chapter

3

Enterprise Security Operations

THE CASP+ EXAM TOPICS COVERED IN THIS CHAPTER INCLUDE:

✓ **Domain 3: Enterprise Security Operations**

- 3.1 Given a scenario, conduct a security assessment using the appropriate methods.

  - Methods

    - Malware sandboxing

    - Memory dumping, runtime debugging

    - Reconnaissance

    - Fingerprinting

    - Code review

    - Social engineering

    - Pivoting

    - Open-source intelligence

      - Social media

      - Whois

      - Routing tables

      - DNS records

      - Search engines

  - Types

    - Penetration testing

      - Black box

      - White box

      - Gray box

- Vulnerability assessment
- Self-assessment
  - Tabletop exercises
- Internal and external audits
- Color team exercises
  - Red team
  - Blue team
  - White team
- 3.2 Analyze a scenario or output, then select the appropriate tool for a security assessment.
  - Network tool types
    - Port scanners
    - Vulnerability scanners
    - Protocol analyzer
      - Wired
      - Wireless
    - SCAP scanner
    - Network enumerator
    - Fuzzer
    - HTTP intercepter
    - Exploitation tools/frameworks
    - Visualization tools
    - Log reduction and analysis tools
  - Host tool types
    - Password cracker
    - Vulnerability scanner
    - Command line tools
    - Local exploitation tools/frameworks
    - SCAP tool

- File integrity monitoring
- Log analysis tools
- Antivirus
- Reverse engineering tools
- Physical security tools
  - Lock picks
  - RFID tools
  - IR camera
- 3.3 Given a scenario, implement incident response and recovery procedures.
  - E-discovery
    - Electronic inventory and asset control
    - Data retention policies
    - Data recovery and storage
    - Data ownership
    - Data handling
    - Legal holds
  - Data breach
    - Detection and collection
      - Data analytics
    - Mitigation
      - Minimize
      - isolate
    - Recovery/reconstitution
    - Response
    - Disclosure
  - Facilitate incident detection and response.
    - Hunt teaming
    - Heuristics/behavioral analytics
    - Establish and review system, audit, and security logs.

- Incident and emergency response
  - Chain of custody
  - Forensic analysis of compromised system
  - Continuity of operations
  - Disaster recovery
  - Incident response team
  - Order of volatility
- Incident response support tools
  - dd
  - tcpdump
  - nbtstat
  - nc(netcat)
  - memdump
  - tshark
  - foremost
- Severity of incident or breach
  - Scope
  - Impact
  - Cost
  - Downtime
  - Legal ramifications
- Post-incident response
  - Root-cause analysis
  - Lessons learned
  - After-action report

1. You contracted with a company to develop a new web application for your retail outlets to process credit cards. Which of the following assessments gives you the best level of assurance for the web application they create?

   A. Penetration testing

   B. Vulnerability assessment

   C. Implementation

   D. Code review

2. After severe budget cuts, a company decided to conduct internal assessments rather than hire a third party. They conduct these assessments on specific production servers. Which of the following tests is most likely to be used?

   A. Vulnerability scan

   B. Tabletop exercises

   C. Malware sandboxing

   D. Social engineering

3. You are a security analyst for a financial organization and are conducting a review of its data management policies. After a complete review, you found settings disabled, permitting developers to download supporting but trusted software. You submitted the recommendation that developers have a separate process to manually download software that should be vetted before use. What process supports this recommendation?

   A. NIPS

   B. Digitally signed applications

   C. Sandboxing

   D. PCI compliance

4. You are a developer for a research organization and are tasked with testing a new team member's code. You must gather as much diagnostic information as possible to troubleshoot any problems. Which of the following options is your BEST option?

   A. Memory dump

   B. Pivoting

   C. DNS records

   D. Internal audit

5. One of your teammates is struggling with understanding why a program is not responding the way she expects when it runs. What would you suggest she try next to troubleshoot?

   A. Kernel dumping

   B. Checking internal data flow

   C. Runtime debugging

   D. Automation

6. Your team was asked to do a penetration test of a large pharma corporation. The proper documentation was signed by both organizations. Because this is a black-box penetration test, where should your team start?

   A. Vulnerability scanning

   B. Social engineering

   C. Reconnaissance

   D. Malware distribution

7. As a pentester, you are conducting the type of reconnaissance that is concerned with being as untraceable as possible. What type of reconnaissance are you performing?

   A. Active reconnaissance

   B. Passive reconnaissance

   C. Geological reconnaissance

   D. Zone reconnaissance

8. While conducting a penetration test, you engaged with the systems outlined in your documentation. You started a port scan to determine accessible ports. What kind of reconnaissance did you perform?

   A. Active

   B. Passive

   C. Zero

   D. Area

9. You are a forensic analyst for a financial company with a robust security program. You were told to perform analysis of a tool that may contain a malicious payload and were given this to research:

   ```
   Text2 += "Win32DiskImager_0_9_5_install.exe"; File.WriteAllBytes(text2,
   Resources.Win32DiskImager) Process.Start);
   ```

   What process do you use to find the location of the payload?

   A. Reverse engineering

   B. Fuzzing

   C. Containerization

   D. External auditing

10. You are a security engineer. While testing an application during a regular assessment to make sure it's configured securely, you see a REQUEST containing method, resources, and headers, and a RESPONSE containing status code and headers. What technique did you most likely use to generate that type of output?

    A. Fingerprinting

    B. Fuzzing

    C. Vulnerability scanning

    D. HTTP intercepting

11. During a web application security assessment, you need to grab the basic architecture to identify the framework used. You grabbed the HTTP header banner using Netcat, which gave you the application name, software version, and web server information. What activity did you just perform?

  A. Fingerprinting

  B. Authentication

  C. Authorization

  D. Code review

12. You are on the development team testing an in-house application for vulnerabilities. During the test, the application fails repeatedly. Which of the following tools do you suggest the development team deploy to identify these bugs?

  A. Code escrow

  B. Fuzzing

  C. Pivoting

  D. OSINT

13. Your company's CISO hired an external security consultant to perform a review of the organization's physical security. In the contract, the CISO noted a concern of unauthorized access to physical offices that result in a digital compromise. How should the consultant evaluate the potential risk?

  A. Automatically grant access to physical control systems and review logs.

  B. Conduct internal audits of access logs and social media feeds.

  C. Install CCTV on all entrances and exits to detect access.

  D. Gain access to offices using social engineering techniques and then attempt to compromise the network.

14. In a social engineering campaign, you were provided the birthday of your victim. You invent a scenario to engage the victim using this information. What is this type of social engineering called?

  A. Pretexting

  B. Phishing

  C. Baiting

  D. Diversion

15. Your CFO received an email from a vendor requesting payment for services rendered. The CFO reached out to your team because the vendor's name is spelled with an extra vowel. What type of social engineering technique was being used?

  A. Spear phishing

  B. Water holing

   C. Pretext

   D. Bait and switch

16. Your office manager received a voicemail from a vendor wanting to confirm a delivery time and address. The delivery time is correct, but the address is not. What possibly happened?

   A. Baiting

   B. Water holing

   C. Phishing

   D. Diversion

17. As a network security analyst, you notice web traffic increasing from your organization to a specific shopping site. What social engineering attack can take advantage of this type of traffic?

   A. Tailgating

   B. Baiting

   C. Phishing

   D. Water holing

18. As part of your security audit, your CISO suggested leaving an infected USB in the break-room with "wedding pics" written on it. By the time you drop the USB next to the refriger-ator in the breakroom and make it back to your desk, the malicious file left on the USB had been installed. What is this type of social engineering technique called?

   A. Mantrap

   B. Quid pro quo

   C. Water holing

   D. Baiting

19. You walk into your secured office building and scan your RFID badge. Someone behind you yells at you to hold the door for them. What type of attack is that person attempt-ing to use?

   A. Tailgating

   B. Baiting

   C. Water holing

   D. Man in the middle

20. IT support called you and told you to disable your antivirus software because they have a patch that needs to run on your machine to keep you safe. What social engineering technique did this attacker use?

   A. Tailgating

   B. Honeytrap

   C. Quid pro quo

   D. Rogue access point

21. Your company hired a professional organization to conduct a penetration test. The penetration tester slowly increases the number of attacks over an extended period of time, creating multilayered attacks. What technique did this penetration tester use to compromise your network?

A. Threats

B. Pivoting

C. Exploit

D. Tailgating

22. As a security analyst, you conducted a security assessment that was divided into internal and external exploitation. The external activities have a time limit set by the statement of work. Which of the following methods would you attempt after the time limitation expired?

A. Social engineering

B. OSINT

C. Vulnerability scan

D. Pivoting

23. Your company planned to develop custom IDS/IPS rules this quarter to stay ahead of new rules released by IDS/IPS manufacturers. How should you prepare for this shift in methodology?

A. Penetration test results

B. Network monitoring

C. OSINT and threat databases

D. Vulnerability scans

24. Your CEO watched the news and saw reports of the type of attacks affecting healthcare. He asks you, as a security analyst, to gather information about controls to put into place to stop these attacks from affecting your organization. How do you begin this process?

A. Get the latest IOCs from OSINT sources.

B. Research best practices.

C. Use AI and SIEM.

D. Perform a sweep of your network using threat modeling.

25. You work for a security organization that performs penetration tests for large corporations. A corporation asks for a black-box test. You begin the process of passive reconnaissance. What should you access first?

A. DNS

B. Nmap

C. Netcat

D. Social media

26. Human resources is advertising on websites for a new position in IT. The applicant for this role needs to be familiar with specific networking and security products. Since the advertisement, you have seen targeted external scans looking for open default ports on the networking and security products you utilize. What has most likely occurred?

    A. Auditors have done their due diligence on your organization.

    B. Attackers have used job boards to find information about your company.

    C. Regulators are responding to requirements.

    D. Self-assessment using tabletop exercises is being performed.

27. Your company is concerned about Internet-facing servers. They hired a security organization to conduct a black-box test of www.yourcompany.edu to make sure it is secure. Which of the following commands helps the tester determine which servers are externally facing before they take any additional actions?

    A. Whois

    B. Whatis

    C. SMTP

    D. IPConfig

28. You are a network security administrator on a network of more than 50,000 nodes. In the past week, your end users have complained that specific pages on the Internet are not loading. You test the pages from your tablet with cellular service and access them just fine. What do you expect to find in the router logs after you have verified firewall rules?

    A. Route poisoning

    B. Device fingerprinting

    C. Gray-box testing

    D. PKI

29. Your company learned that an attacker obtained highly classified information by querying the external DNS server. You are told to not let this happen again. What do you do?

    A. Implement a split DNS. Create an internal and external zone to resolve all domain queries.

    B. Implement a split DNS. Create an internal zone for an internal DNS for resolution and an external zone to be used by the Internet.

    C. Create DNS parking for round-robin DNSBL.

    D. Create DNS parking for cloud users.

30. Your company is merging with another healthcare organization. The stakeholders are discussing the security aspects of combining digital communications. The main agreed-upon criterion is encryption on email servers/clients. What is the best option for this organization?

    A. DNSSEC

    B. TLS

C. PGP/GPG

D. Keeping both entities separate

31. You are a network security administrator for a SOHO. Your staff tends to work from coffee shops without understanding the need for a VPN. You must show them why this can be dangerous. What network traffic packets are commonly captured and used in a replay attack?

   A. Authorization

   B. Authentication

   C. FTP

   D. DNS

32. Your network administrator reaches out to you to investigate why your e-commerce site went down twice in the past three days. Everything looks good on your network, so you reach out to your ISP. You suspect an attacker set up botnets that flood your DNS server with invalid requests. You find this out by examining your external logging service. What is this type of attack called?

   A. DDoS

   B. Spamming

   C. IP spoofing

   D. Containerization

33. You are a security analyst and were tasked by your company with finding all external Internet-connected devices, webcams, routers, servers, and IoT devices on your corporate network. What is the best search engine to use to accomplish this task in the least amount of time?

   A. Yahoo

   B. Shodan

   C. Google

   D. Bing

34. Your compliance auditor requires an inventory of all wireless devices. What is the best search engine to use?

   A. Shodan

   B. WiGLE

   C. WireShark

   D. BurpSuite

35. Your organization must comply with PCI-DSS and regulations that mandate annual and ongoing penetration testing after any system changes at both the network and application layers. What is the primary purpose of penetration testing?

   A. Creates security awareness

   B. Evaluates IDS

    C. Tests the security perimeter

    D. Accesses the internal guidelines

36. A company must comply with a new HIPAA regulation that requires the company to determine whether an external attacker is able to gain access to systems from outside the network perimeter. What should the company do to meet this new regulation?

    A. Code review

    B. Black-box penetration test

    C. Inventory of hardware and software

    D. Vulnerability scan

37. Your new CTO is concerned that the IT staff is not able to secure and remediate new vulnerabilities found in the latest financial software adopted by the company. The CTO is focused on reliability and performance of the cloud software. Which of the following is the BEST way to meet the CTO's testing requirements?

    A. A small firm does a black-box test.

    B. A large firm does a white-box test.

    C. An internal team does a black-box test.

    D. An internal team does a white-box test.

38. A member of your development team was fired for harassment. The company is concerned with the security of the project to which this developer had access. What is the BEST way to ensure the integrity of this project?

    A. Peer review

    B. Red-box test

    C. Gray-box test

    D. Black-box test

39. You were informed of an upcoming external PCI-DSS audit and need to find a way to remediate thousands of vulnerabilities on production servers that will cause you to fail the audit. You want to prioritize which vulnerability is the most dangerous in your environment, not just the rating by CVSS. What type of test is BEST to conduct prioritizing vulnerability remediation?

    A. Black-box

    B. Gray-box

    C. White-box

    D. Clear-box

40. You are a developer for a security software company. Your CISO tasks you with conducting a white-box test. The advantages include optimization and thoroughness, given the fact that the developer has full knowledge of the code. Which of the following should be considered a disadvantage to a white-box test?

    A. Complexity and duration

    B. Simplicity and impartiality

C.   Redundancy and simplicity

D.   Accuracy and superficiality

41.   As a security architect, you are responsible for making all systems come together and work properly and securely. Your tester is logged into the system as a user, testing the internal mechanisms of the application. This enables an exhaustive test very similar to what an attacker might accomplish. What type of test is this?

A.   A gray-box

B.   A black-box

C.   A red-box

D.   A clear-box

42.   Your internal auditor completed the quarterly PCI-DSS audit of the financial systems and found that accounts payable has not followed proper procedures during a tabletop exercise. What is your recommendation?

A.   Review procedures and retrain employees.

B.   Wait until the external auditor completes their annual review.

C.   Delete all unnecessary financial transactions.

D.   Do a complete parallel test of accounts payable systems.

43.   An internal security audit of your organization shows consistent security configurations are needed. Your department implements a golden standard image to all servers and workstations. How can you detect unauthorized changes?

A.   Vulnerability assessments

B.   Compliance reports

C.   Audit logs continuously

D.   Scan computers against the baseline

44.   Given recent high-profile cyberattacks, your CISO asks for your input on cybersecurity control frameworks to better define what the internal auditors should use for information security management systems (ISMS) guidance. Which internal auditing framework do you recommend?

A.   SEC

B.   CISM

C.   ISO/IEC 27001

D.   CIS

45.   You are hired by a burgeoning retail startup that needs to mature its IT operations. Which of the following frameworks is BEST to use while doing the first internal audit of the organization?

A.   ITIL

B.   CISA

   C. COBIT

   D. ISO 27001

46. An external audit is a formal process involving an accredited third party. It can be expensive and time intensive. What is most important when conducting an external audit?

   A. An independent authority against a recognized standard

   B. An internal agent and a security framework

   C. A global internal assessment with gap analysis

   D. A validated outcome and scheduled future audits

47. You need a security assessment that imitates real-world attacks. What type of team should you hire to conduct this test outside of the organization that has limited or no knowledge of your company?

   A. Red team

   B. Blue team

   C. Yellow team

   D. White team

48. You are a member of the blue team for your company. This team is tasked to with engaging with a red team of mock attackers. What team referees this engagement?

   A. White team

   B. Stakeholders

   C. CISO

   D. Yellow team

49. You consider yourself to be a white-hat hacker with expertise in social engineering. Are you a good candidate for a red team black-box engagement?

   A. No, the skill set is exactly the same.

   B. Yes, the skill set is not the same.

   C. No, the skill set needed is completely opposite.

   D. Yes, the skill set is similar.

50. One of your network administrators reports that they cannot connect to a device on the local network using its IP address. The device is up and running with an IP address of 10.0.0.5. Other hosts can communicate with the device. The default gateway is 10.0.0.1, and your local IP address is 10.0.0.3. What is the BEST type of scan to run to find the MAC of the offending machine?

   A. ARP

   B. PING

   C. IPConfig

   D. IFConfig

51. You conduct a physical penetration test for a jewelry store chain. The organization wants to prevent drivers from using a vehicle to smash through the front of the store and grab valuable merchandise. What type of defense do you suggest?

   A. Security guards

   B. Iron gate

   C. Motion detector

   D. Bollards

52. A member of your board of directors asks your CEO about their proactive defense measures. In turn, the CEO asks the CISO about proactive defense strategies. Which of these tools is an example of proactive defense measures?

   A. Running Nexpose/Nessus

   B. Installing botnets

   C. War chalking

   D. Rootkits

53. You test a form on a school's website by using some odd information in a given field. A ZIP code is supposed to be five numerical characters, but you used the numerical characters 1234, in addition to the ZIP code. What type of testing did you conduct?

   A. PDCA

   B. Boundary

   C. White hat

   D. Form testing

54. One of your internal security tests finds it is not detecting the newest security threats. Management wants you to investigate what type of IDS is the BEST tool to implement. Which of the following is your suggestion?

   A. Protocol based

   B. Hash based

   C. Pattern matching

   D. Anomaly detection

55. Your senior architect submits budget requests to the CISO to upgrade their security landscape. One item to purchase in the new year is a security information and event management (SIEM tool). What is the primary function of a SIEM tool?

   A. Blocking malicious users and traffic

   B. Monitoring the network

   C. Automating DNS servers

   D. Monitoring servers

56. One of the tools that you are asked to evaluate is an open-source honeypot software called Deception Toolkit. What does honeypot software do?

   A. Gathers information about intruders

   B. Gathers information about external networks

   C. Gathers information about botnets

   D. Gathers information about network infections

57. You remove hard drives from old servers, workstations, and copy machines. Your security policy requires that no sensitive data remain on those drives. It is not in the budget to replace the drives, so you must be able to use them again. What type of tool do you use to accomplish this task?

   A. DeFraggler

   B. Killdisk

   C. Nmap

   D. OS .iso

58. One of your reports is on a server that you usually access by `ftp.myserver.com`. You are unable to download it from that address, but you can access the file server by the IP address 192.168.1.2. What tool do you check first?

   A. ARP cache

   B. DHCP server

   C. FTP server

   D. DNS server

59. You are a security analyst for a SOHO. Against your advice, upper management decided that BYOD for salespeople would be cost effective, citing employee churn. You now have security challenges, including duplicate IP addresses and infected systems on the company's network. Which of the following should you implement to help with these issues?

   A. NAC

   B. HIDS

   C. HIPS

   D. Port security

60. You requested help from your network engineers with a compliance audit that is in the very near future. They supplied you with the following host statistics: guest accounts disabled: 60 percent compliant; local firewall enabled: 90 percent compliant. Which of the following tools can provide that type of data?

   A. Port scanner

   B. Fuzzer

   C. Antivirus

   D. SCAP

61. You are an IT administrator needing visibility into your network. You believe you have all the tools and controls in place but no way to look for attackers who are currently exploiting your network. What tool do you choose to help with seeing the dark spots in your environment?

A. Fuzzer

B. HTTP interceptor

C. Port scanner

D. SIEM

62. You were asked to lead a project setting up a security operations center (SOC). One of the tools leveraged for compliance that your company already owns could also be used in the SOC because of the threat intelligence and data mining capabilities. Which tool can be used for both compliance and SOC?

A. Protocol analyzers

B. SIEM

C. Wired scanner

D. Password crackers

63. You are a new network security administrator. Your manager told you to start building your network topology map with a concentration on finding out what ports are open on which assets. What tool will accomplish the task?

A. Netcat

B. Nmap

C. BurpSuite

D. IPConfig

64. You are an IT administrator who has been alerted that there are connection requests across a large range of ports from a single host. You believe that an intruder is attempting to attack that single host. What is the attacker most likely doing?

A. Vulnerability scan

B. Port scan

C. SCAP scan

D. Host-to-host scan

65. You decided to ensure that your network is protected and will perform your own port scans using Nmap. To get accurate results, you must perform this port scan from a remote location using non-company equipment and another Internet service provider (ISP). What must you do first?

A. Get permission.

B. Decide what range of IPs and ports to scan.

C. Contact HR.

D. Create a scan for 10 packet attempts to non-listening ports.

66. Your organization is working on implementing controls for CIS top six controls. These controls are a prioritized list of actions aimed at reducing risk from real threats. Control 4 is "Monitor Vulnerability Risk." What tool should you use for this control?

   A. SIEM

   B. Nessus

   C. Nmap

   D. Fuzzer

67. Your company acquired a new company. As the lead security administrator, you want to start a vulnerability scan against a new network that joined your domain. You want to scan this new network from the outside looking in. What type of scan is this called?

   A. Authenticated

   B. Unauthenticated

   C. Secured

   D. Accessible

68. You completed a vulnerability scan on your network without using any type of SMB or SSH service credentials. It gives you an idea of what your network looks like to the outside world. The next step is to use credentials. What type of vulnerability scan is this called?

   A. Authenticated

   B. Unauthenticated

   C. Secured

   D. Accessible

69. Your auditor informs you that vulnerability scans for some compliance requirements will be run quarterly. Your organization's roadmap states the organization will begin weekly patch management. How often should you be scanning for vulnerabilities?

   A. Monthly

   B. Annually

   C. Weekly

   D. Bi-weekly

70. You are working on the maturity of your vulnerability management processes. You established network vulnerability testing but are concerned about the internal applications and web forms that are on the intranet. What type of tool should you use to scan for Common Weakness Enumerations (CWEs)?

   A. Application scanner

   B. Fuzzer

   C. Attack scanners

   D. CIS scanners

71. You had your internal team do a static analysis on compiled binaries to find errors in mobile and desktop applications. You would like an external agency to test them as well. Which of these tests BEST suits this need?

   A. DAST

   B. VAST

   C. IAST

   D. SAST

72. Your company contracts a security engineering consultant to perform a black-box penetration test of the client-facing web portal. Which of the following is the most appropriate?

   A. Increase protocol analyzation against the site to see if ports are being replayed from the browser.

   B. Scan the site with a port scanner to identify vulnerable services that are running on the web application server.

   C. Create network enumeration tools to see where the server is residing.

   D. Scan the site with an HTTP interceptor to identify areas for code injection.

73. Your organization is looking for a tool that will work as a proxy between server and browser. You want to be able to scan a target, grab a request, and forward a modified request. What tool are you going to use?

   A. SIEM

   B. HTTP interceptor

   C. Vulnerability scanner

   D. Fuzzer

74. Your web application designers handed the program over to your department for a Q&A review. Which of these tools is BEST to find any flaws like SQLi or CSS in the web application requiring approval?

   A. Nessus

   B. LogRhythm

   C. Acunetix WVS

   D. Autopsy

75. Your pentester is looking for an infrastructure to add their own custom tools to. You prefer to use free software. What is the top choice?

   A. Meterpreter

   B. Exploitation

   C. Metasploit

   D. BurpSuite

76. Your new CISO wants to upgrade from open source to an enterprise vulnerability management tool. Which tool satisfies your organization's need for comprehensive vulnerability management?

A. Nexpose

B. Optimi

C. Splunk

D. Security Analytics

77. Your pentester submitted a request to be allowed to use a port scanner tool internally on the network. Which port scanner do you recommend?

A. Nmap

B. Netcat

C. Tracert

D. Arp

78. You were tasked with testing your network traffic and firewall rule sets for vulnerabilities and intrusions. Which of these tools is BEST to use for this task?

A. Nmap

B. Wireshark

C. Traceroute

D. Packet Tracer

79. You want to ensure that there are no weak passwords on any mission-critical server or networking device. You also want to ensure that none of the top 100 exposed passwords (i.e., 12345678) is on any device. What is the BEST tool to crack any weak password on your assets?

A. Hashcat

B. Netcat

C. Wireshark

D. Splunk

80. Most modern attacks surprisingly begin with nontechnical techniques. You want to use an open-source tool to mine for information about your organization used to conduct a targeted phishing campaign. Which of these tools helps you create a real-world link between people, websites, and your company?

A. NIST

B. Wireshark

C. Maltego

D. Nmap

81. You are a blue teamer for a medium-sized business. You want to automate social engineering tests using a free Python-based tool. Which of these is the BEST tool for the job?

    A. SET

    B. Nmap

    C. BurpSuite

    D. Metasploit

82. You examine your blue team cybersecurity toolkit and want to add a tool that produces proof of an exploit and supports JavaScript and Ajax-based applications. Which of these is BEST to use?

    A. SET

    B. Nmap

    C. Netsparker

    D. SQLi

83. Your organization wants to start digging deeper into malware analysis and needs software to spot vulnerabilities that can be exploited. You do not have the budget for EnCase this year, so an open-source tool is best. You also need to create your own plugins. Which of these tools meet those criteria?

    A. Ghidra

    B. Immunity Debugger

    C. AngryIP

    D. Hydra

84. You must use a computer networking utility to read and write network connections using TCP and UDP. Which one of the following commands is a network debugging tool enabling you to create nearly any kind of connection?

    A. IPConfig

    B. Netcat

    C. Openbsd

    D. Traceroute

85. Your computer has a command prompt, and you need to see all the current TCP/IP network configuration values for this specific asset. What command do you enter?

    A. IPConfig

    B. Arp

    C. Rarp

    D. Dns

86. You downloaded a driver to the C: drive for a component you must install on a machine. The file is called `printer_driver.dll`. One of the first things to do is verify that the file was not corrupted during download. What is the command you used in CLI to ensure this file has not been tampered with using the 128-bit MD5 algorithm?

   A. `md5_C:printer_driver.dll`

   B. `md5 "C:printer_driver.dll"`

   C. `md5 printer_driver`

   D. `cd/ "printerdriver.dll" md5 -n`

87. Your security department is maturing and wants to represent data in digestible data points. You decide the next step beyond the pie chart in Excel will be using a business intelligence tool. What is this process called?

   A. Visualization

   B. Hypervisor

   C. Data complexity

   D. Clarity

88. Your security compliance audit failed due to the lack of data logging and analysis. You were chosen to lead a team to stand up a logging tool for proactively and reactively mitigating risk. What tool do you implement to lead this team to becoming compliant?

   A. SIEM

   B. VM

   C. DNS

   D. LASE

89. You view a command prompt and need to find if there is connectivity between you and another machine on the network. What command do you run?

   A. `Arp`

   B. `Vnstat`

   C. `IPConfig`

   D. `Ping`

90. You have a command prompt at a terminal window and need to find the path an IP packet is taking through the network. What command do you issue?

   A. `FMS`

   B. `IPConfig`

   C. `Traceroute`

   D. `Ping`

91. You must see the mappings between IP addresses and MAC addresses on a specific segment of your network. What command-line tool do you use?

A. Arp

B. Netstat

C. Wget

D. TraceRT

92. You are analyzing TCP and UDP connections open on a system. You need to look at statistics of sent, received, and possible errors and do a deeper dive on the ID of the processes making connections to determine if they're legitimate. What tool helps with this?

A. Netstat

B. Ping

C. Rarp

D. Traceroute

93. Your company underwent a merger, and you are attempting to consolidate domains. What tool do you use to find out who the owner of a domain is, when it expires, and contract details?

A. Netstat

B. Whois

C. SSH

D. TCPDump

94. To guard against threats, organizations must monitor their computer systems and applications. You need a method for using specific standards to enable vulnerability management, measurement, and policy compliance evaluation of systems, according to the NVD. What standard do you choose?

A. CMMI

B. INS

C. NIST

D. SCAP

95. You have critical files and intellectual property on several filesystems and need to be alerted if these files are altered by either trusted insiders abusing their privilege or malware. What should you implement?

A. FIM

B. PCI

C. DNS

D. TCP

96. Your business has PCI requirements that include standards and regulations. Those standards and regulations state that data must be monitored and managed to ensure its integrity. What will you institute?

A. SOX

B. FIM

C. IaaS

D. Cloud

97. Your FIM initial deployment went well but is now experiencing some issues. FIM's purpose is to detect change, and it is necessary to tune the solution carefully to minimize issues with false positives and volume. The issues revolve around performance and noise. What must you integrate with FIM to ensure the solution is holding up to your organizational needs?

A. Project management

B. Program management

C. Change management

D. Staff management

98. You must make a decision about your organization's File Integrity Monitoring (FIM). Stand-alone FIM generally means file analysis only. Another option is to integrate it with the host so that you can detect threats in other areas, such a system memory or an I/O. For the integration, which of the following do you need to use?

A. HIDS

B. ADVFIM

C. NIDS

D. Change management

99. Your FIM deployment solution leverages the ability to install on target systems for the most powerful analysis. The difficulty is that it needs regular updating. What term describes this use of FIM?

A. Agentless

B. Agent-based

C. Cloned

D. SaaS

100. Your organization is undergoing a physical penetration test. Which of these tools is most likely in the tester's toolkit?

A. Buttset

B. Toner probe

C. Amp set

D. Lock picks

101. Your facility was broken into, but the cameras did not have sufficient light to capture anything of substance. Your manager tasks you with exchanging the cameras with ones that are a better choice for night recording. What type of camera do you choose?

A. IDR

B. IR

C. CDR

D. Dome

102. Your division must maintain expensive equipment that ranges in price from several hundred dollars to several thousand dollars. You have multiple facilities monitoring these tools. You must be able to track them to decrease replacement costs and increase employee productivity. What do you choose?

A. RFID tags

B. QR codes

C. Bar codes

D. ISBNs

103. Your organization is concerned with the security of using RFID. Several issues exist with using RFID, but which of the following is not an issue?

A. Sniffing

B. Tracking

C. Counterfeiting

D. Destruction

104. RFID gained popularity in your organization because of low maintenance cost. You consider expanding the use of RFID, but your security analyst warns that the backend database is vulnerable. What could be the biggest worry of your analyst?

A. Virus attack

B. IR

C. Lockpicking

D. Credentials

105. Your organization slowly evolved from simple locking doors to RFID-enabled cards issued to employees to secure the physical environment. You want to protect these cards from cloning, because some parts of your organization host sensitive information. What should you implement?

A. Encryption

B. IDR

C. HIDS

D. NIPS

106. Your MDM for COPE devices neglected to restrict the use of NFC. What is the biggest worry for employees using NFC for transactions?

    A. No login/password

    B. Interception

    C. Breaches

    D. Legalities

107. Your company decides to shift the eDiscovery processes from external third parties to in-house. Which of the following is not a stage of eDiscovery?

    A. Identification

    B. Interpretation

    C. Collection

    D. Processing

108. During what phase of eDiscovery will you determine what digital data and documents should be collected for possible analysis and review?

    A. Processing

    B. Identification

    C. Collection

    D. Curation

109. Your organization is under investigation after a merger. Your data is placed in a legal hold, which means it cannot be destroyed. Failure to preserve this data can lead to fines. At what stage of eDiscovery is this done?

    A. Preservation

    B. Processing

    C. Collection

    D. Investigation

110. Your organization identifies and preserves data that your legal department requested due to a fraud investigation. You start transferring data to their office enabling them to research relevance. They call in a forensic specialist to preserve the data for presentation in court. In what stage of eDiscovery does this happen?

    A. Processing

    B. Inference

    C. Causation

    D. Collection

111. Your CISO mandates the security department implement the Center for Internet Security Top 20 controls, starting with the first control, Inventory and Control of Hardware Assets. This control states that an organization must actively manage all hardware devices on a network. The main function of this control is to prevent which of the following?

- **A.** Authorized access
- **B.** Indefinite access
- **C.** Unauthorized access
- **D.** Continuous access

112. You researched and conferred with your legal department as to what your data retention policy should be. Which of the following regulations place restrictions on data retention?

- **A.** GLBA
- **B.** HIPAA
- **C.** SOX
- **D.** All of the above

113. Your research determines what type of data your organization should preserve and the length of time the data should be stored. Which of the following is not another part of a good data retention policy?

- **A.** Format
- **B.** Certification
- **C.** Access control
- **D.** Destruction

114. You work in the computer lab provisioning hardware to be deployed throughout your enterprise. Your company policy states that end users are responsible for backing up their files. After an operating system upgrade, some people lost mission-critical files and are coming to your lab to salvage lost files. What is this process called?

- **A.** Data salvaging
- **B.** Data retrieving
- **C.** Data recovery
- **D.** Data destruction

115. Your CFO accidentally deleted an important folder from their computer. They brought their system to you to attempt data recovery. You know the files are still on the drive, but there is no reference to them in the directory structure. What should you do first?

- **A.** Do not save any documents or files.
- **B.** Turn off the computer.
- **C.** Restart the computer.
- **D.** Install a new program to rescue the files.

116. You are brought a computer to retrieve data from, but you're unable to boot it up by turning on the power button. You ask the employee if they have their files backed up, and the answer is no. What should you do to recover all the data possible?

A. Pull out the hard drive, place it in new machine, and attempt to boot up from the hard drive.

B. Use the data recovery wizard in the operating system and move files to the cloud.

C. Remove the power, battery, and then the hard drive. Connect to a new PC, boot, and access the hard drive, if possible.

D. If the machine will not boot up in its natural state, there is no recovery possible.

117. Your IT group is modernizing and adopting a DevSecOps approach, making everyone responsible for security. Traditionally, storage and security were separate disciplines inside IT as a whole. As a security analyst, what is your primary concern of data at rest?

A. Encryption

B. Authentication

C. Infrastructure

D. Authorization

118. Your department is examining the CIA triad and how it applies to storage. You want to maintain confidentiality, integrity, and availability for all authorized users. At the same time, you are asked to focus on strong enough systems so that attackers expend more work (i.e., work factor) than the data is worth. What does this hinge on?

A. Cost and value of data

B. Cost and value of privacy

C. Cost and value of encryption

D. Cost and value of potential breach

119. As an information security professional, you are tasked with ensuring that data remains available after an incident like a system failure or natural disaster. This falls under which of the following?

A. Data recovery

B. Data protection

C. Data security

D. Data reliability

120. Your CISO tasks you with creating an addendum to the security policies and procedures as they relate to security at rest. Which of these are not a concern to address in your high-level security policy and more granular procedures?

A. Data and cyberattack growth

B. Cost of breaches and increased data value

C. Regulation and business continuity

D. Network topology and subnets

121. Your current data storage solution has too many vulnerabilities that are proprietary to the manufacturer who created your storage devices. This, combined with a lack of encryption, is leading you to choose cloud storage over on-premise storage. You now have encryption, but what else should you have also added?

   A. Identity

   B. Infrastructure

   C. Complexity

   D. Confidentiality

122. You implement role-based access control for your secure data storage system. You change default passwords and enforce the use of strong passwords. What else should you do to make this even more secure?

   A. Multifactor authentication

   B. Multifactor authorization

   C. Identification

   D. Verification

123. Your main SCSI storage is embedded with an array controller, and redundancy is managed by hardware-level RAID. What is this type of storage called?

   A. SAN

   B. NAS

   C. DAS

   D. RAS

124. You work for an organization that subscribes to 99.99 percent network uptime. You must find a way to decrease downtime in case of an internal DAS hardware failure, which has happened twice in the past six months. What solution do you deploy?

   A. USB

   B. SSD

   C. SAN

   D. DASv2

125. Your department is looking for a new storage solution that enables a yet undetermined number of systems to connect using file-based protocols (such as NFS and SMB). This solution will also be used for file-sharing services such as data storage, access, and management services to network clients. What is the BEST storage solution for your organization?

   A. SAN

   B. NAS

   C. DAG

   D. DAS

126. You must identify a person who will have the administrative control and be accountable for a specific set of information and data set. It could be the most senior person in a department. What is their role?

   A. Data custodian

   B. Data user

   C. Data owner

   D. Data administrator

127. Your data owner must assign classifications to information assets and ensure regulation compliance. What other criterion is determined by a data owner?

   A. Authorization

   B. Authentication

   C. Verification

   D. Validation

128. You work for a university, and the registrar is the data owner for student data. This department is responsible for managing access, classification, and regulatory requirements. Who does the data owner work with to enforce the technical control?

   A. Other data owners

   B. Data user

   C. Data custodian

   D. Data classifier

129. In a healthcare organization, what data role is responsible for assigning access, producing reports, and logging access, as well as implementing physical safeguards to protect the confidentiality, availability, and integrity of a dataset?

   A. Data owner

   B. Data custodian

   C. Data user

   D. Data protector

130. As a data user, you are required to follow policies and procedures by the business unit, including ensuring the security of any sensitive data. You visited a website holding sensitive information about your organization. What should you do first?

   A. Hack the site to remove the information.

   B. Visit Whois and find out who owns the site and contact them directly.

   C. Report the suspected security/policy violation to the appropriate authority.

   D. Try to find out how the information was shared.

131. A data user reached out to the data custodian to request permission to give access to sensitive information to a third-party marketing agency. The third-party vendor has been vetted by security. Who should be contacted next before access is granted?

   A. Data owner

   B. CEO

   C. Board of directors

   D. Marketing VP

132. For a senior security architect, one of the most important principles of enterprise security is the rapid detection of a data breach. Many organizations that experience a breach won't learn about it for weeks or even months. Which of these will not help detect an actual breach before it causes widespread harm to your organization?

   A. Modern breach detection tools

   B. Global threat intelligence

   C. Security expertise on the team

   D. Periodic logging

133. Your security team needs to stay up to date and worked hard to develop a training program. They were taught to identify and report the early warning stages of an attack campaign. Which of these are not indicators of a compromise?

   A. Slow Internet and unexplained system reboots

   B. Multiple failed logins and locked-out accounts

   C. Anomalies in network traffic, especially after hours

   D. Patch management

134. Your CISO is notified by a three-letter agency that your network is compromised. The first thing your security department needs to understand is what the attackers stole. After security knows what was stolen, what is the BEST follow-up question to ask?

   A. Can the bad guys use our data?

   B. How did they get in?

   C. How do we keep it from happening again?

   D. How did the agency know we had been hacked?

135. Your agency was compromised but found no evidence of data exfiltration from the business. What is the first thing that all employees should do?

   A. Proactively change their passwords.

   B. Clone all hard drives for backups.

   C. Contact a PR firm for customer relations.

   D. Hold a meeting of the board of directors.

136. Your company is recovering from a data breach. The breach was not deep but raised the security awareness profile of upper management. Realizing they have gaps in access control, upper management approved the purchase of password manager software for the organization. What else do you suggest that they institute for end users?

    A. 2FA

    B. Password isolation

    C. Disaster recovery

    D. IDR

137. You work as an independent security consultant for a small town in the Midwest that was just breached by a foreign country. When it came time for payment to a town vendor, someone changed the transfer of monies from a physical check to an electronic payment. In response, what is the first security policy suggestion you make to prevent this from recurring?

    A. Incorporation

    B. Investigation

    C. Change management

    D. Data diddling

138. Your organization was just informed by a three-letter agency that your organization's POS systems were compromised. You avoided panicking and focused on gathering your incident team and assigning roles. Which role is not as important in a data breach incident response team immediately after a breach?

    A. Legal

    B. Public relations

    C. Technical

    D. Sales

139. After you are breached, one of the most difficult steps is to understand what actually occurred. Your technical team tells you which systems and data were violated, which vulnerabilities were used, and that the compromised systems are quarantined. What should your technical team do next?

    A. Ensure there are no backdoors or logic bombs left behind by attackers.

    B. Report directly to the board of directors.

    C. Place the CISO and CTO on administrative leave.

    D. Bring in a third party for a penetration test.

140. You are part of a legal team participating in creating a disclosure plan after an incident. Data-breach disclosure varies from state to state and from country to country. Even if you are not legally obligated to declare the incident, your company's reputation suffers if someone else discloses the attack. Who handles the hack's disclosure to concerned parties?

    A. Public relations

    B. Infrastructure

C. Legal

D. Data owner

141. Your breached organization is in the middle of an investigation, gathering evidence, performing forensics, and briefing upper management on all the proof gathered. What is the organization's next action after all the technical incident forensics are completed?

A. Notify the public.

B. Notify the authorities.

C. Notify your vendors.

D. File for cyber insurance coverage.

142. You build a team of cyber investigators who are actively seeking out threats on your network. They seek out anomalies in routing tables and attempt to find patterns in data to stay ahead of the criminals. What is this type of team called?

A. Black-box

B. Gray-box

C. Hunt team

D. Data analytics

143. Your hunt team wants to prove compliance at a glance. You want them to have a strong security posture, but you need some help mapping regulations. What should they map regulations to in order to show compliance?

A. Security metrics

B. Security standards

C. Security threats

D. Threat intelligence

144. Your security policy was based on rules until now, requiring specific conditions matching either good or bad events. While important, you need these rules to be more agile based on patterns. Which of the following BEST describes that type of correlation?

A. Threat intelligence

B. Heuristics

C. Complexity

D. Categorical

145. Chain of custody begins with a crime scene. A digital forensic investigator carefully examines the scene and takes detailed notes for each single piece of evidence found, including the location, time, and date. What may not be included in the chain of custody documentation?

A. Description

B. Condition

C. Unique attributes

D. Investigator CV

146. Digital evidence is a part of many legal proceedings litigated by your organization. This evidence includes social media posts, photographs, videos, and text messages. With physical evidence alone, you were tasked with creating a chain of digital evidence. After law enforcement collects the digital evidence, what should happen next?

   A. The original digital media should be forensically examined.

   B. Law enforcement should make a public statement.

   C. A forensics technician should analyze the data before making a copy.

   D. Your organization should immediately hash the original copy of the data.

147. Your organization terminates an employee from the IT department. After the IT employee is escorted from the building, a complete forensic investigation on all systems that IT employee had access to shows a logic bomb installed on a server. Only three IT staff members had access to that server, and the remaining IT employees did not have admin access; therefore, they could not have installed the logic bomb. Which of the following factors does not negate the evidence you have collected?

   A. Authorized people accessing evidence

   B. Improper storage of evidence

   C. Mislabeled evidence

   D. Alteration of digital evidence

148. As a new director of security, you review your organization's security policy. The current policy states if a compromise is suspected or detected, you should immediately disconnect the system from the network, power it down, and physically secure the system. This mode worked well in the past. However, with malware authors reducing the footprint on a hard drive, storing as much as possible within RAM, which is cleared when the system is powered down, it is now widely recommended in forensics to do which of the following?

   A. Include volatile memory as part of the incident evidence collection, using tools that quickly analyze RAM.

   B. Power down because advanced and persistent threats will still be evident on the hard drive.

   C. Pull the hard drive and RAM and then put them on dry ice indefinitely until they can be analyzed to store the digital evidence.

   D. Pull the plug and examine the network logs.

149. Your team is examining business continuity, incident detection, and response to determine its storage policy. One of the mitigating controls for this policy will be the hierarchy of evidence from most volatile to least volatile. For example, archival media is not volatile, while the most volatile are registers, cache, and read-access memory. What is this called?

   A. Order of volatility

   B. IETF

   C. Guidelines of storage capacity

   D. RFC 3227

150. Your incident detection team is responsible for finding intruders on the network and in your infrastructure. They try to trace intruder activity, contain the threat, and then remove it. Learning how attackers gain access and move around your network is valuable. What is this called?

A. INS

B. IDR

C. CIA

D. DNS

151. You are part of an IDR team building a team toolkit containing numerous tools from many sources—some open source and some prepacked with operating systems. Which of the following is a command-line tool that can be used to create a clone or image of any drive?

A. nbtstat

B. dd

C. tshark

D. netcat

152. Your toolkit needs an open-source utility that works on the command line and gives descriptions of packet content. What tool do you pull out of your toolkit?

A. tcpdump

B. dd

C. netcat

D. memdump

153. You look through your incident detection toolkit for a Windows tool that displays Net-BIOS over TCP/IP protocol statistics. Which tool do you choose?

A. netcat

B. memcat

C. nbtstat

D. tshark

154. You receive a phone call from one of your employees because their machine has BSOD. What happens when a Windows machine blue screens?

A. Collects all operating system data

B. Machine just needed a reboot

C. Created a tcpdump

D. Created a crash dump

155. Your incident detection toolkit has a command-line tool that captures packets over a network and displays them on the screen or saves them in a file. It is native in Linux and is installed on Windows when Wireshark is installed. What tool is this?

A. tshark

B. zenmap

    C. `wireshark`

    D. `netstat`

156. Your CEO brought you a device from which they accidentally deleted a set of folders containing sensitive information that must be recovered. You want to use a program to recover only specific files based on their headers, footers, or data structure. Which tool do you choose?

    A. `foremost`

    B. `dd`

    C. `nbtstat`

    D. `nc`

157. You need to find the true severity of an incident and accurately measure based on certain factors like scope and impact. Which of the following is not the other factor for measuring the severity of an incident for your organization?

    A. Cost

    B. Downtime

    C. Disclosure

    D. Legal ramifications

158. One of your users clicked a link in an email and downloaded malware. This malware ran successfully, and you had to measure how widespread it was. It was contained to just one machine, so what is the scope considered to be?

    A. Minimal

    B. Intermediate

    C. Maximum

    D. Epic

159. The impact of an incident or breach can be measured at several different levels. Which of the following is not included in the various levels?

    A. Critical

    B. High

    C. Low

    D. Junior

160. Your incident response team attempts to estimate the cost of a breach. This estimate is based on whether the data records were customer and employee or employee only. Another factor is the scope of the breach, such as how many people were affected. Now that you know who and how much, what else do you need to know?

    A. When

    B. Where

    C. What

    D. How long

161. You reached out to your legal department to determine whether there are repercussions after a data breach. Every state and federal definition of a data breach is based on the unlawful acquisition of personal information. What is the "safe harbor" for organizations?

    A. Encryption

    B. Divestiture

    C. Confidentiality

    D. Investigation

162. After an incident, it is important for you to create a lessons learned document. By conducting this critique, you evaluate the effectiveness of the response. With that after-incident mindset, what is the most important result you can derive from this document?

    A. Areas for improvement

    B. Magnitude of the problem

    C. Proper assessment of an incident

    D. Security assessment awareness

163. Your organization finished dealing with an incident that required an after-action report (AAR). Your goal is to improve your organization's response to an event or a critical situation. Which of the following should not be included in the AAR?

    A. Analyze the event to determine what your strengths are and areas of improvement for your future response plan.

    B. Understand the entire event from multiple strategic, tactical, and operational viewpoints.

    C. Improve the communication of your organization's critical response, disaster recovery, and business continuity plans.

    D. Use network topology diagrams.

164. A hard disk fails in a mission-critical server, and there is no redundancy. Many options exist when it comes to recovering data from a hard disk failure. Sometimes the corrective action has the potential to render the data unrecoverable. What is the first rule of recovering data?

    A. Install a recovery tool.

    B. Open the drive to examine the platters.

    C. Minimize access to the drive.

    D. Attempt to boot the drive in another machine.

165. Your security policies and procedures were reevaluated since a breach six months ago. After reviewing the AAR, you decided to make changes to communication procedures so that the organization can be more agile and have a faster recovery in the future. Why is this so important to an organization?

    A. By communicating intelligence that is actionable, informed decisions can be made to ensure that risks are managed and people are safe.

    B. The capability to respond to an event quickly is the most important way to deal with an incident.

   C. Improving responses to events is a challenge that no leaders face.

   D. The ability to process incident feedback from stakeholders is important to improving the guidelines in incident detection.

166. The after-action report (AAR) received from the incident response team contains lessons learned. It states that security policies were not sufficient when it comes to dealing with the current level of vulnerabilities found in the enterprise environment and the time-line allotted for patching. Attackers had a large window of time to take advantage of unpatched software. What should the security department do based on the AAR and lessons learned?

   A. Investigate the current patch management system and look for ways to improve or automate.

   B. There is no way to improve an already existing patch management program.

   C. Hire more IT analysts.

   D. Hire a third-party agency to conduct a review of the AAR and make suggestions of software to eliminate all vulnerabilities.

Chapter

4

Technical Integration of Enterprise Security

THE CASP+ EXAM TOPICS COVERED IN THIS CHAPTER INCLUDE:

✓ **Domain 4: Technical Integration of Enterprise Security**

- 4.1 Given a scenario, integrate hosts, storage, networks, and applications into a secure enterprise architecture.

  - Adapt data flow security to meet changing business needs.

  - Standards

    - Open standards

    - Adherence to standards

    - Competing standards

    - Lack of standards

    - De facto standards

  - Interoperability issues

    - Legacy systems and software/current systems

    - Application requirements

    - Software types

      - In-house developed

      - Commercial

      - Tailored commercial

      - Open-source

    - Standard data formats

    - Protocols and APIs

  - Resilience issues

    - Use of heterogeneous components

    - Course of action automation/orchestration

- Distribution of critical assets
- Persistence and non-persistence of data
- Redundancy/high availability
- Assumed likelihood of attack
- Data security considerations
  - Data remnants
  - Data aggregation
  - Data isolation
  - Data ownership
  - Data sovereignty
  - Data volume
- Resource provisioning and deprovisioning
  - Users
  - Servers
  - Virtual devices
  - Applications
  - Data remnants
- Design considerations during mergers, acquisitions, and demergers/divestitures
- Network-secure segmentation and delegation
- Logical deployment diagram and corresponding physical deployment diagram of all relevant devices
- Security and privacy considerations of storage integration
- Security implications of integrating enterprise applications
  - CRM
  - ERP
  - CMDB
  - CMS

- Integration enablers
  - Directory services
  - Domain Name System (DNS)
  - Service-Oriented Architecture (SOA)
  - Enterprise Service Bus (ESB)
- 4.2 Given a scenario, integrate cloud and virtualization technologies into a secure enterprise architecture.
  - Technical deployment models (outsourcing/ insourcing/managed services/partnership)
    - Cloud and virtualization consideration and hosting options
      - Public
      - Private
      - Hybrid
      - Community
      - Multi-tenancy
      - Single tenancy
    - On-premise versus hosted
    - Cloud service models
      - Software as a Service (SaaS)
      - Infrastructure as a Service (IaaS)
      - Platform as a Service (PaaS)
  - Security advantages and disadvantages of virtualization
    - Type 1 versus Type 2 hypervisors
    - Container-based
    - vTPM
    - Hyperconverged infrastructure
    - Virtual Desktop infrastructure
    - Secure enclaves and volumes

- Cloud-augmented security services
  - Anti-malware
  - Vulnerability scanning
  - Sandboxing
  - Content filtering
  - Cloud security broker
  - Security as a service (SaaS)
  - Managed security service providers
- Vulnerabilities associated with comingling of hosts with different security requirements
  - Virtual Machine Escape (VMEscape)
  - Privilege elevation
  - Live Virtual Machine (VM) migration
  - Data remnants
- Data security considerations
  - Vulnerabilities associated with a single server hosting multiple data types
  - Vulnerabilities associated with a single platform hosting multiple data types/owners on multiple virtual machines
- Resource provisioning and deprovisioning
  - Virtual devices
  - Data remnants
- 4.3 Given a scenario, integrate and troubleshoot advanced authentication and authorization technologies to support enterprise security objectives.
  - Authentication
    - Certificate-based authentication
    - Single sign-on
    - 802.1x

- Context-aware authentication
- Push-based authentication
- Authorization
  - Open Authorization (OAuth)
  - eXtensible Access Control Markup Language (XACML)
  - Service Provisioning Markup Language (SPML)
- Attestation
- Identity proofing
- Identity propagation
- Federation
  - Security Assertion Markup Language (SAML)
  - OpenID
  - Shibboleth
  - WAYF
- Trust models
  - RADIUS configurations
  - LDAP
  - AD
- 4.4 Given a scenario, implement cryptographic techniques.
  - Techniques
    - Key stretching
    - Hashing
    - Digital signature
    - Message authentication
    - Code signing
    - Pseudo-random number generation
    - Perfect forward secrecy
    - Data-in-transit encryption

- Data-in-memory/processing
- Data-at-rest encryption
  - Disk
  - Block
  - File
  - Record
  - Steganography
- Implementations
  - Crypto modules
  - Crypto processors
  - Cryptographic service providers
  - DRM
  - Watermarking
  - GNU Privacy Guard (GPG)
  - Secure Sockets Layer (SSL)/Transport Layer Security (TLS)
  - Secure Shell (SSH)
  - Secure/Multipurpose Internet Mail Extensions (S/MIME)
  - Cryptographic application and proper/improper implementations
    - Strength
    - Performance
    - Feasibility to implement
    - interoperability
  - Steam versus block
  - Public Key Infrastructure (PKI)
    - Wild card
    - Offensive Security Certified Professional (OSCP) vs Certified Revocation List (CRL)

- Issuance to entities
- Key escrow
- Certificate
- Tokens
- Stapling
- Pinning
- Cryptocurrency/blockchain
- Mobile device encryption considerations
- Elliptic curve cryptography P-256, P-384, P-521
- 4.5 Given a scenario, select the appropriate control to secure communications and collaboration solutions.
  - Remote access
  - Resource and services
  - Desktop and application sharing
  - Remote assistance
  - Unified collaboration tools
    - Conferencing
      - Web
      - Video
      - Audio
    - Storage and document collaboration tools
    - Unified communication
    - Instant messaging
    - Presence
    - Email
    - Telephony and Voice over Internet Protocol (VoIP) integration
    - Collaboration sites
      - Social media
      - Cloud-based

1. Your organization currently uses FTP to transfer files, and you are tasked with upgrading a file transfer solution that answers the need for both integrity and confidentiality. Which of the following is true about the current state of business?

   A. Port 20 used for transfer and port 21 used for control

   B. Port 20 used for control and port 21 used for transfer

   C. Port 20 used by the client and port 21 used by the server

   D. Port 20 used for integrity and port 21 used for confidentiality

2. You are the new CISO for a software organization revising security best practices. Which of these statements regarding best practices is the most accurate?

   A. They should be endorsed by end users.

   B. They should be extremely specific.

   C. They should by extremely general.

   D. They should be as short as possible.

3. As the senior security architect, you create a security policy and standards that instruct employees to use strong passwords. You find that employees are still using weak passwords. Revising the procedures for creating strong passwords, which of these do you LEAST likely require for employees?

   A. Change your password every 90 days.

   B. Use a combination of numbers, letters, uppercase and lowercase letters, and special characters.

   C. Use a minimum number of characters.

   D. Use a Merriam-Webster dictionary.

4. You are part of a small startup nonprofit that has grown to a development stage where a security policy is necessary. Which of these do you NOT include in your security policy?

   A. Purpose

   B. Scope

   C. Compliance

   D. Procedures

5. Employees in your organization must use a Windows 10 desktop with a multicore CPU, a minimum of 8 GB of memory, and a solid-state drive. Which of these describes these technical aspects?

   A. A policy

   B. A procedure

   C. A standard

   D. A responsibility

6. A virtual machine hosted on an ESX server in your data center contains confidential data that is no longer needed by your company. You recommend shutting down the virtual machine and deleting the VM disk (VMDK) from the host. What is the security risk?

    A. Data retention

    B. Data encryption

    C. Data protection

    D. Data remanence

7. Your organization has grown and needs to hire someone for information management. This role is responsible for security marking and labeling. Which of the following BEST describes the role's responsibility?

    A. Security marking/labeling is the process of using internal data structure from within information systems to determine criticality.

    B. Security labeling is more important than security marking and is required for all information, including marketing information released to the general public.

    C. Security marking and security labeling are the same.

    D. Security marking and labeling will reflect compliance, requirements, applicable laws, directives, policies, and standards.

8. You are tasked with deploying a system so that it operates at a single classification level. All users who access this system have the same clearance, classification, and need to know. What is this operating mode?

    A. Closed

    B. Dedicated

    C. Peer to peer

    D. Compartmentalized

9. As a security architect of a medical complex, you are concerned that attackers can steal data from highly secure systems. You are trying to prepare for a system attack that exfiltrates data through existing channels in small increments. What are you trying to prevent?

    A. Encryption

    B. Backdoors

    C. Covert channels

    D. Viruses

10. A third-party software vendor disclosed that a backdoor was left in a product by mistake. What is this called?

    A. A security patch

    B. A rootkit

    C. A virus

    D. A maintenance hook

11. What form of storage decays over time and must be refreshed constantly?

    A. RAM

    B. Hard Drive

    C. ROM

    D. BIOS

12. You are building a decentralized privilege management solution for your financial organization with user accounts that are defined on each system rather than a centralized server. Which of these BEST describes this?

    A. A workgroup

    B. RADIUS/DIAMETER

    C. Client/Server

    D. Terminal services

13. You are tasked with creating a single sign-on solution for your security organization. Which of these would you not deploy in an enterprise environment?

    A. Directory services

    B. Kerberos

    C. SAML 2.0

    D. Workgroup

14. Your growing startup wants to take advantage of single sign-on. Which of the following is NOT an advantage?

    A. Eliminating multiple user accounts and passwords.

    B. Signing on once for access to resources.

    C. Convenient and leads to fewer tech support password resets.

    D. The attacker needs only one password to compromise everything without two-factor authentication.

15. Your healthcare startup does not currently have any written security standards, so you are creating a security policy. Which of these statements should go into a security standards document?

    A. All personally identifiable health information (PHI) must be encrypted using AES to ensure customer privacy and confidentiality.

    B. First, you must select the data you want to encrypt, right-click the file, and select encryption. Then, select a password.

    C. All data must be encrypted.

    D. HIPAA compliance requires customer privacy.

16. The National Institute of Standards and Technology (NIST) recommends the physical destruction of data storage media at what stage of media life?

    A. Initial

    B. Backups

C. Final

D. Retention

17. Your organization's security policy specifies a length of time to keep data, after which the data must be destroyed to help mitigate the risk of that data being compromised. This type of policy helps reduce legal liability if the data becomes unrecoverable. What type of policy is this?

   A. Data protection

   B. Data remanence

   C. Data retention

   D. Data destruction

18. Your job as an information protection specialist is to prevent unauthorized individuals from examining or capturing intellectual property. What do you use to protect the confidentiality of this data?

   A. Cryptography

   B. Sanitization

   C. Legal documentation

   D. Zeroization

19. You are selected to manage a systems development and implementation project. Your manager suggests that you follow the phases in the SDLC. In which of these phases do you determine the controls needed to ensure that the system complies with standards?

   A. Testing

   B. Initiation

   C. Accreditation

   D. Acceptance

20. You have completed the SDLC's accreditation process for a system your organization is going to deploy globally. Management has approved the system. What phase in SDLC comes next?

   A. Documentation

   B. Acceptance

   C. Accreditation

   D. Implementation

21. You assisted your networking organization in upgrading the speed and capabilities of your wireless local area network (WLAN). Currently, everyone utilizes equipment based on 802.11g using central access points. Which of the following would enhance the speed?

   A. 802.11a

   B. 802.11b

   C. 802.11n

   D. WiMAX

22. Your CISO asks you to develop deployment solutions for internally developed software that offers the best customization as well as control over the product. Cost is not an issue. What is the BEST solution for you to choose?

   A. Hosted deployment solution with a lower up-front cost but requires maintaining the hardware the software is residing on

   B. Cloud-based deployment solutions that require a monthly fee only

   C. Elastic virtual hosting based on need

   D. An on-premise traditional deployment solution

23. You decide to use a Type 2 hypervisor to deploy commercial software to test for suitability, vulnerabilities, and functionality. Your CISO questions your decision to use a Type 2 hypervisor instead of a VMM. Which of these is not a valid explanation?

   A. A virtual machine monitor (VMM) is another name for a hypervisor. A hypervisor is software that is able to virtualize the physical components of computer hardware.

   B. A Type 1 hypervisor is installed on a bare-metal server, meaning that the hypervisor is its own OS. Type 2 hypervisors use a host OS that is compatible with commercial software.

   C. A virtual machine (VM) is an instance of a device running on a hypervisor. It is a computing virtual environment that relies on a hypervisor to communicate with the physical hardware it is installed on.

   D. A virtual machine is a term used to describe Internet-enabled streaming services or web applications that give end users the ability to activate software locally.

24. A new program that you are in charge of requires replacing legacy equipment. This equipment touches every major operational system in the company. You establish security requirements and engage with the infrastructure and networking. What is your next step?

   A. Document all the requirements, both technical and nontechnical.

   B. Organize a tabletop exercise with all the technical personnel.

   C. Communicate the security requirements to all the stakeholders.

   D. Meet with database and application consultants for migration advice.

25. You conduct a security assessment and find legacy systems with vital business processes using standard Telnet protocols. What should you do to mitigate the risk?

   A. Migrate from IPv4 to IPv6.

   B. Install PuTTY.

   C. Move the system to a secure VLAN.

   D. Unplug the system until a replacement can be ordered.

26. You are a security architect for a large enterprise bank that recently merged with a smaller local bank. This acquired bank has a legacy virtual cluster, and all these virtual machines use the same NIC to connect to the LAN. Some of the VMs are used for HR, and some are used to process mortgage applications. What is the biggest security risk?

   A. Shared NICs negatively impacting the integrity of packets

   B. Bridging of networks impacting availability

    C. Availability between VMs impacting integrity

    D. Visibility between VMs impacting confidentiality

27. Your CIO requests a meeting with you, the security manager, to discuss the SQL administrators' request for a service-oriented architecture (SOA) and an application programming interface (API). In SOA and APIs, services are provided over a network. What is your biggest concern?

    A. Users and services are centralized and available only during business hours.

    B. SOA manages all the legacy systems that are vulnerable.

    C. SOA is deployed using VMs and is exploited using VMEscape.

    D. Users and services are distributed over the Internet, which can be open to outside threats.

28. In the last five years, your manufacturing group merged twice and acquired three startups, which led to more than 75 unique customer web applications. To reduce cost and improve workflows, you are put in charge of a project to implement centralized security. You need to ensure a model with standard integration, and accurate identity information and authentication as well as repeatability. Which is the BEST solution?

    A. Implementation of web access control and relay proxies

    B. Automated provisioning of identity management

    C. Self-service single sign-on using Kerberos

    D. Building an organizational wide granular access control model in a centralized location

29. A large enterprise social media organization underwent several mergers, divestitures, and acquisitions over the past three years. Because of this, the internal networks and software have extremely complex dependencies. Better integration is necessary. Which of the following integration platforms is BEST for security- and standards-based software architecture?

    A. API

    B. Point to point

    C. SOA

    D. ESB

30. A new business was acquired by your organization. Your CISO tells you that you will oversee the project merging the two organizations. As the security manager, what do you do first?

    A. Develop an interconnection policy and perform a risk analysis.

    B. Deploy a golden image operating system to all end users' computers.

    C. Develop criteria and rate each firewall configuration.

    D. Implement NIDS on all desktops and conduct security awareness training for all new employees.

31. Your company decided to outsource certain computing jobs that need a large amount of processing power in a short duration of time. You suggest the solution of using a cloud provider that enables the company to avoid a large purchase of computing equipment. Which of the following is your biggest concern with on-demand provisioning?

A. Excessive charges if deprovisioning fails

B. Exposure of intellectual property

C. Data remanence from previous customers in the cloud

D. Data remanence of your proprietary data that could be exposed

32. You are a systems administrator and are asked to draft a policy for several mission-critical legacy application servers that will be replaced in six months. What policy do you create?

A. Data provisioning

B. Data remanence

C. Data retention

D. Data encryption

33. You are an IT manager and the software list your employees must use has grown to the point that it's mandated that you implement federated identity SSO. It needs to be an extensible markup language used to exchange provisioning requests for account creation. Which of the following is BEST for this task?

A. SAML

B. cURL

C. SOAP

D. SPML

34. You are a small company administrator who is hosting multiple virtualized client servers on a single host. You are told to add a new host to create a cluster. The new hardware and OS will be different, but the underlying technology will be compatible. Both hosts will be sharing the same storage. What goal are you trying to accomplish?

A. Increased availability

B. Increased confidentiality

C. Increased integrity

D. Increased certification

35. Your news organization is dealing with a recent defacement of your website and secure web server. The server was compromised around a three-day holiday weekend while most of the IT staff was not at work. The network diagram, in order from the outside in, consists of the Internet, firewall, IDS, SSL accelerator, web server farm, internal firewall, and internal network. You attempt a forensic analysis, but all the web server logs have been deleted, and the internal firewall logs show no activity. As the security administrator, what do you do?

A. Review the external firewall logs to find the attack.

B. Review the IDS logs to determine the source of the attack.

    C. Correlate all the logs from all the devices to find where the organization was compromised.

    D. Reconfigure the network and put the IDS between the SSL accelerator and server farm to better determine the cause of future attacks.

36. After a meeting with the board of directors, your CEO is looking for a way to boost profits. They identified a need to implement cost savings on non–core-related business activities, and the suggestion was made to move the corporate email system to the cloud. You are the compliance officer tasked with making sure security and data issues are handled properly. What BEST describes your process?

    A. End-to-end encryption, creation, and the destruction of mail accounts

    B. Vendor selection and RFP/RFQ

    C. Securing all virtual environments that handle email

    D. Data provisioning and processing, while in transit and at rest

37. New zero-day attacks are released on a regular timeline against many different technology stacks. Which of the following would be best for you, as a security manager, to implement to manage the risk from these attacks?

    A. List all inventory, applications, and updated network diagrams.

    B. Establish some type of emergency response hierarchy.

    C. Back up all router, firewall, server, and end-user configurations.

    D. Hold mandatory monthly risk assessment meetings.

38. You are a server administrator for a large enterprise using Windows, Linux, and macOS. You need to find a web service that enables HTTP and SMTP using XML-based protocols. Which technology is BEST for this way of exchanging information?

    A. HTTPS

    B. SSL

    C. SOAP

    D. SAMLv2

39. Your global software organization is required to conduct a BIA for any new company acquisition. Your organization has acquired a new software startup. Your organization and the startup both outsource the LMS and CMS for education to noncompatible third parties. What are you most concerned about?

    A. Data sovereignty

    B. Encryption

    C. Data migration

    D. Disaster recovery

40. Your hospital just merged with another hospital in another state that falls under a different legal jurisdiction. You are tasked with improving network security. Your CISO suggests data isolation by blocking communication between the two hospitals. How do you accomplish this?

   A. Implementing HIDS

   B. Building gateway firewalls

   C. Configuring ERP

   D. Creating network segmentation

41. You have been newly hired as a CISO for a governmental contractor. One of your first conversations with the CEO is to review requirements for recovery time and recovery point objectives, and enterprise resource planning (ERP). Who should you bring to the roundtable to discuss metrics surrounding your RTO/RPO?

   A. Board of directors

   B. Chief financial officer

   C. Data owners and custodians

   D. Business unit managers and directors

42. You are a security engineer for a government agency attempting to determine the control of highly classified customer information. Who should advise you on coordinating control of this sensitive data?

   A. Sales

   B. HR

   C. Board of directors

   D. Legal counsel

43. Two CISOs brought their IT leadership together to discuss the BIA and DRP for a merger between two automobile manufacturers. Their first priority is to communicate securely using encryption. What is the BEST recommendation?

   A. DNSSEC on both domains.

   B. TLS on both domains.

   C. Use SMime in select email transmissions.

   D. Push all communication to the cloud.

44. You are a security engineer for a healthcare organization. You are evaluating controls for PHI as well as financial data. Based on this table, what is the best classification?

Data	Confidential	Integrity	Availability
PHI	High	Medium	Low
Financial	Medium	High	Low
PII	High	Medium	Low
Industrial	Low	Low	High

A. High confidentiality, High integrity, Low availability

B. High confidentiality, Medium integrity, Low availability

C. Medium confidentiality, High integrity, Low availability

D. Low confidentiality, Low integrity, Low availability

45. After the latest acquisition, your security manager asked you to review the business continuity plan. Your organization is required to meet compliance and other regulatory requirements relating to confidentiality. Upper management is concerned that you may miss some of the requirements, which would make your newly blended organization fail an audit. What should you do to improve the existing business continuity plan?

A. AAR

B. BIA

C. RPO and RTO

D. Gap analysis assessment

46. You own a small training business with two classrooms. Your network consists of a firewall, an enterprise-class router, a 48-port switch, and 1 printer and 18 laptops in each classroom. The laptops are reimaged once a month with a golden patched image with up-to-date antivirus and anti-malware. User authentication is two-factor with passwords and smart cards. The network is configured to use IPv4. You also have a wireless hotspot for students to connect their personal mobile devices. What could you improve on for a more resilient technical security posture?

A. Enhanced TLS controls

B. Stronger user authentication

C. Sufficient physical controls

D. IPv6

47. You are hired by a large enterprise as a systems security consultant to evaluate and make recommendations for increasing the network security posture. It is your first meeting with the stakeholders. What is your first question?

A. What are your business needs and the corporate assets that need to be protected?

B. What hardware and software do you currently have, and what would work best for securing your network?

C. What is your budget?

D. When is your next audit, and who will be on my team to carry out this security plan?

48. After merging with a new acquisition, you come to work Monday morning to find a metamorphic worm from the newly acquired network spreading through the parent organization. The security administrator isolated the worm to spreading on TCP port 445. What do you advise the administrator to do to immediately to minimize the attack?

A. Run Wireshark to watch for traffic on TCP port 445.

B. Update antivirus software and scan the entire enterprise.

C. Check your SIEM for alerts for any asset with TCP port 445 open.

D. Deploy an ACL to all HIPS: DENY-TCP-ANY-ANY-445.

49. In an enterprise environment, which common security services would include firewalls and enterprise-grade border routers?

    A. Access control

    B. Cryptography and encryption

    C. Boundary control

    D. Authentication and automation

50. You are a security architect building out a new hardware-based VM. Which of the following would LEAST likely threaten your new virtualized environment?

    A. Patching and maintenance

    B. VM sprawl

    C. Oversight and responsibility

    D. Faster provisioning and disaster recovery

51. You are exploring the best option for your organization to move from a physical data center to virtual machines hosted on bare metal servers. Which of the following is the BEST option for that move?

    A. Type 1 hypervisor

    B. Type 2 hypervisor

    C. iPaas

    D. Iaas

52. You are exploring the best option for your organization to move from a physical data center to VMs hosted on bare-metal servers. Moving to a Type 1 hypervisor was discussed, but they were difficult to deploy. Now, it's been decided to use hosted hypervisors. Which of these is the BEST option for that move?

    A. Type 1 hypervisor

    B. Type 2 hypervisor

    C. iPaas

    D. Iaas

53. A server holding sensitive financial records is running out of room. As the information security manager, what is the BEST option?

    A. First in, first out (FIFO)

    B. Compress and archive oldest data

    C. Move the data to the cloud

    D. Add disk space in a RAID configuration

54. Your HR recruiter is having difficulties finding qualified applicants for an open IT security manager role. Your department discussed moving deployment solutions to a third party that will operate and maintain the processes. Which of the following deployment solutions is this most likely to be?

A. Cloud

B. Hosted

C. On-premise

D. Automated

55. Your company hires a third party to provide cloud-based processing that will have several different types of virtual hosts configured for different purposes, like multiple Linux Apache web server farms for different divisions. Which of the following BEST describes this service?

A. SaaS

B. PaaS

C. IaaS

D. AaaS

56. You have joined a company that licenses a third party's software and email service that is delivered to end users through a browser. What type of organization do you work for?

A. IaaS

B. SaaS

C. PaaS

D. BaaS

57. As a security architect, you decided to build a multiple virtual host with different security requirements. Several virtual hosts will be used for storage, while others will be used as databases. What should you do with these hosts?

A. Encrypt all hosts with AES.

B. Store each host on a separate physical asset.

C. Move these virtual hosts to the cloud for elasticity.

D. Verify that each server has a valid certificate.

58. Your company has a subscription to use a third party's infrastructure, programming tools, and languages to develop and build out a new cloud-based ESB application. Which acronym properly defines this type of service?

A. PaaS

B. IaaS

C. SaaS

D. MaaS

59. Your organization needs to be able to use a third party's development tools to deploy specific cloud-based applications. Platform as a service (PaaS) is the choice that has been approved to launch these cloud services. Which of the following is NOT a true statement?

   A. PaaS can use an API to develop and deploy specific cloud-based services.

   B. Cloud storage is a term used to describe the use of a third-party vendor's virtual file system as a document or repository.

   C. You can purchase the resources you need from a cloud service provider on a pay-as-you-go basis.

   D. With PaaS, you must buy and manage software licenses.

60. You work in information security for a stock trading organization. You have been tasked with reducing cost and managing employee workstations. One of the biggest concerns is how to prevent employees from copying data to any external storage. Which of the following BEST manages this situation?

   A. Move all operations to the cloud and disable VPN.

   B. Implement server virtualization and move critical applications to the server.

   C. Use VDI and disable hardware and storage mapping from a thin client.

   D. Encrypt all sensitive data at rest and in transit.

61. You are leading a project for your organization moving to a thin client with the server architecture hosted in the cloud. You are meeting with upper management, and they have asked for your advice about using thin clients. Which of the following is a security advantage?

   A. Thin clients are economical and require less security. There is no storage, and the server is protected in the cloud.

   B. Thin clients are encrypted with AES, both at rest and in transit.

   C. Attackers will have less opportunity to extract data from thin clients.

   D. Thin clients do not require external security auditing.

62. Your newly formed IT team is investigating cloud computing models. You would like to use a cloud computing model that is subscription based for common services and where the vendor oversees developing and managing as well as maintaining the pool of computer resources shared between multiple tenants across the network. Which of the following is the BEST choice for this situation?

   A. Public

   B. Private

   C. Agnostic

   D. Hybrid

63. Your organization opted into a public cloud solution for all of your business customers' testing environments. Which one of these is NOT a disadvantage?

   A. TCO can rise exponentially for large-scale use.

   B. Not the best solution for security and availability for mission-critical data.

    C. Low visibility and control of the environment and infrastructure, which may lead to compliance issues.

    D. Reduced complexity and requirements of IT experts as the vendor manages the environment.

64. Your newly formed IT team is investigating cloud computing models. You want to use a cloud computing model that is dedicated to your organization. The data center and all resources are located at the vendor's site but are isolated through a secure network and not shared with any other customer. Which of the following is the BEST choice for this situation?

    A. Public

    B. Private

    C. Agnostic

    D. Hybrid

65. Your organization opted into a private cloud solution for all your large, highly regulated technical customers. Which one of these is a disadvantage?

    A. Dedicated environment

    B. Compliance with regulations

    C. Scalable and high SLA performance

    D. Expensive solution and difficult to scale

66. Your newly formed IT team is investigating cloud computing models. You want to use a cloud computing model that is orchestrated as an integrated infrastructure environment. Apps and data can share resources based on business and technical policies. Which of the following is the BEST choice for this situation?

    A. Public

    B. Private

    C. Agnostic

    D. Hybrid

67. Your organization has opted into a hybrid cloud solution for all your strategic organizations with multiple verticals with different IT requirements. Which one of these is an advantage?

    A. Flexible, scalable, reliable, and improved security posture

    B. Strong compatibility and integration requirements

    C. Complexity as the organization evolves

    D. Can be very expensive

68. As the IT director of a nonprofit agency, you have been challenged at a local conference to provide technical cloud infrastructure that will be shared between several organizations like yours. Which is the BEST cloud partnership to form?

    A. Private cloud

    B. Community cloud

    C. Hybrid cloud

    D. Data centers

69. Your objectives and key results (OKR) being measured for this quarter include realizing the benefits of a single-tenancy cloud architecture. Which one of these results is NOT applicable to a single-tenancy cloud service?

    A. Security

    B. Reliability

    C. Ease of restoration

    D. Maintenance

70. Your objectives and key results (OKR) being measured for this quarter include realizing the benefits of a multitenancy cloud architecture. Which one of these results is NOT applicable to a multitenancy cloud service?

    A. Financial

    B. Usage

    C. Vulnerabilities

    D. Onboarding

71. As you investigate the itemized receipts from your cloud provider, you notice some VMs being spun up that either were not authorized or have been left running for extended time periods with no usage. What is this called?

    A. VM sprawl

    B. VM escape

    C. VM jacking

    D. VM migration

72. A guest OS escapes from within VM encapsulation to interact directly with the hypervisor. If the VM becomes compromised, this can give an attacker access to all the VMs as well as the host machine. What is this scenario called?

    A. DoS

    B. VM escape

    C. VM jacking

    D. VM isolation

73. One of the concerns you have for your hypervisor environment is the flooding of network traffic to leverage a host's own resources. The availability of botnets to rent on the Dark Web make it easy for attackers to carry out a campaign against specific virtual servers or applications with the goal of bringing services down. What is this type of an attack called?

    A. VM DoS

    B. VM scraping

    C. VM isolation

    D. VM migration

74. You are tasked as a security engineer with mitigating risk for your virtual machines. The first task is to identify all virtual environments and any active security measures currently in place. After you check for antivirus, IDS, and vulnerability scanning, which of these should you do next?

    A. VM isolation

    B. VM mitigation

    C. VM traffic monitoring

    D. VM sprawl

75. You are a cloud security consultant working with a large organization that is advocating applying the highest level of protection across all cloud assets. You suggest this is not what the priority should be. What would be a more strategic priority?

    A. Determining what to protect through data discovery and classification

    B. Running anti-malware software on all cloud instances

    C. Using vulnerability scanning software on mission-critical servers

    D. Implementing threat mitigation strategies

76. While running IaaS environments, you retain the responsibility for the security of all operating systems, applications, and network traffic. Which of these would not be advantageous to deploy to protect this cloud environment?

    A. Advanced anti-malware applied to the OS

    B. Application whitelisting and machine learning–based protection

    C. Memory exploit prevention for single-purpose workloads

    D. Negotiation of an SLA spelling out the details of the data the provider will share in case of an incident

77. You decided to create your own company that will be a service provider integrating security services into a corporate entity with a subscription model. This will be cost effective for companies when they investigate the total cost of ownership (TCO) of cybersecurity. What business model have you just created?

    A. DaaS

    B. PaaS

    C. SECaaS

    D. Iaas

78. You are a security analyst with an enterprise global financial organization. The company just experienced an advanced persistent threat (APT) type of attack that was traced to ransomware delivered to end users via a phishing campaign. One of your IT analysts forwarded the email to the phishing@mycompany.com address. You want to rip open the ransomware to see what it does and what asset it touches. What do you build?

    A. Cloud sandbox

    B. On-premise sandbox

    C. An SLA with a penetration tester

    D. A hypervisor

79. Your organization has increasingly turned to using cloud access security broker (CASB) vendors to address cloud service risks, enforce security policies, and comply with regulations. Which of these is not one of the pillars of CASB?

    A. Visibility

    B. Data security

    C. Threat protection

    D. Database normalization

80. One of the biggest issues your CISO has with migrating to more cloud environments is the process of acquiring and releasing resources. Technical as well as operation issues are associated with these processes. What type of procedure documentation should you create to help with this?

    A. How to authenticate and authorize

    B. How to dynamically provision and deprovision

    C. How to use SaaS, IaaS, and PaaS

    D. How to build a Type 2 hypervisor

81. Not having complete control over networks and servers is a real concern in your organization, and upper management asks you if the company's data is genuinely secure now that you have migrated to the cloud. They have asked you to be present at the next board of directors' meeting to answer questions regarding cloud security and content filtering. With all the news of the latest breaches, you know they are going to have questions. Which of these questions would NOT apply to this meeting?

    A. How is our data protected in the cloud?

    B. Who has control over our data in the cloud?

    C. Who has access to our data in the cloud?

    D. Why move to the cloud?

82. You are reading about the latest breach of a cloud web application server One key element in the breach was no vTPM was being utilized for encryption. The attack targeted a flaw in the security settings, specifically failing to auto-encrypt files, which left the entire network and every device connected to it vulnerable to attack. Configuration vulnerabilities in the cloud can include which of the following?

    A. Unpatched security flaws in server software

    B. SSL certificates and encryption settings not configured properly

    C. Enabled and accessible administrative and debugging functions

    D. All of the above

83. You are a program developer for a large retail organization. Your CISO returned from a large conference and asked you to clarify exactly what the benefit of a container is over virtual machines. Which of these is the BEST succinct answer?

    A. In a VM, hardware is virtualized to run multiple OS instances. Containers virtualize an OS to run multiple workloads on a single OS instance using a container engine.

    B. In a container, hardware is virtualized to run a single OS, where a VM can run multiple applications across multiple assets with a single OS.

C. A VM is virtualized technology, but a container is not.

D. A container is the same thing as a virtual machine, just smaller in size.

84. As a leader in your organization in DevOps, you want to convince your CISO to move toward containerization. Which of these is not an advantage to using containers over VMs?

A. Reduced and simplified security updates

B. Less code to transfer, migrate, and upload

C. Quicker spinning up applications

D. Large file size of snapshots

85. At the latest IT department meeting, a discussion on the best virtual methodology centered around using VMs versus containers. Which of these statements BEST aligns with those two models?

A. VMs are better for lightweight native performance, while containers are better for heavyweight limited performance.

B. VMs are for running applications that need all the OS has to offer, while containers are better when maximizing number of applications on minimal resources.

C. VMs share the host OS, while containers run on their own OSs.

D. Containers are fully isolated and more secure, whereas VMs use process-level isolation.

86. Containerization provides many benefits in flexibility and faster application development. Which of the following statements is false?

A. Containers share the host OS's kernel during runtime.

B. Containers do not need to fully emulate an OS to work.

C. One physical server running five containers needs only one OS.

D. Containers are pure sandboxes just like VMs are.

87. You are a security analyst reviewing corporate settings on multiple assets. You notice some settings were disabled and are allowing untrusted programs to be installed on mobile devices. What settings should be adjusted so that applications can be sandboxed and tested before deploying securely?

A. Updates

B. Digitally signed applications

C. Containerization

D. Remote wiping

88. After merging two disparate networks, a security incident led you to the discovery of an attacker gaining access to the network, overwriting files and installing backdoor software. What should you use to detect attacks like this in the future?

A. Containerization

B. Firewalls

C. VM patch management

D. FIM

89. A newly installed application has a large database and needs additional hardware. Your budget is stretched tight, and your CIO will not approve new purchases for the data center. Which cloud hosting option would BEST fit your need?

A. SaaS

B. PaaS

C. IaaS

D. SECaaS

90. Your CISO asked you to help review system configurations and hardening guides that were developed for cloud deployment. He would like you to make a list of improvements. What is the BEST source of information to help you build this list?

A. Pentesting reports

B. CVE database

C. Implementation guides

D. Security assessment reports

91. You and a colleague are discussing the differences between 2FA and MFA. They say it's the same thing, and you are explaining to them that it isn't. Which is the BEST statement that describes the difference?

A. Multifactor authentication (MFA) requires users to verify their identity by providing multiple pieces of evidence that can include something they know, something they have, or something they are. MFA can be push based such as sending an SMS to a phone to approve or decline. Two-factor authentication (2FA) is a user providing two authentication methods like a password and a fingerprint.

B. 2FA and MFA have the same process with the caveat that 2FA must be two separate types of authentication method. MFA could be two or more of the same method.

C. 2FA is safer and easier for end users than MFA.

D. Multifactor authentication (MFA) requires users to verify their identity by providing at least two pieces of evidence that can include something they know, something they have, or something they are. Two-factor authentication (2FA) is a user providing two or more authentication methods like a password and a fingerprint.

92. Your employees have various computer systems they must access during a workday. A security audit shows that many of them are reusing passwords. Your CISO is interested in a system that will allow employees to use one set of credentials to access all systems. What type of authentication is this called?

A. Single sign-on

B. 2FA

C. MFA

D. Biometrics

93. Your CISO wants to implement a solution within the organization where employees are required to authenticate once and then permitted to access the various computer systems they are authorized to access. The organization uses primarily Microsoft products. Which solution is BEST suited for this organization?

   A. Kerberos

   B. SSL

   C. OTP

   D. Kubernetes

94. Your organization uses an authentication system that enables users to authenticate once and includes a service that grants tickets for specific services. Of the following options, which technology BEST matches this description?

   A. OSPF

   B. Kerberos

   C. LDAP

   D. Biometrics

95. Your organization wants to automate the process of assigning corporate resources to employees. For example, when an HR rep enters data into the HR system for a new employee, the organization wants the HR system to reach out to various other systems like the email system to configure resources for the new employee automatically. What automated identity management propagation solution could perform this task?

   A. SPML

   B. SOAP

   C. Active Directory

   D. SSO

96. Your organization has partnerships with various other companies that require employees of each company to access information from the others. Of course, each company has an authentication process for their employees. What identity management system would allow employees of each company to log in to their respective company and also access the needed information at the others?

   A. SSO

   B. SSL

   C. Federal Identity Management

   D. Kerberos

97. You are logged into a website. While performing activities within the website, you access a third-party application. The application asks you if it can access your profile data as part of its process. What technology is this process describing?

   A. OATH

   B. OAUTH

   C. Malware

   D. Cookies

98. You are a system admin for a large organization with many deployed web services. You are looking for a protocol to implement that would allow the web services to communicate over HTTP using XML. What solution would suit your needs?

    A. SOAP

    B. SAML

    C. Kerberos

    D. LDAP

99. You visit a website that requires credentials to log in. Besides providing the option of a username and password, you are also given the option to log in using your Facebook credentials. What type of authentication scheme is used?

    A. SAML

    B. OAUTH

    C. ClosedID

    D. OpenID

100. You are managing a new project to bring the OAUTH framework into the organization. Which one of these statements is incorrect?

    A. OAUTH gives a third-party application access to resources.

    B. OAUTH is an open standard authorization framework.

    C. OAUTH is designed around four roles: owner, client, resource server, and authorization server.

    D. OAUTH shares password information with third-party applications.

101. You need to develop a security logging process for your mission-critical servers to hold users accountable for their actions on a system after they log in. What is this called?

    A. Authorization

    B. Authentication

    C. Verification

    D. Accountability

102. Your IT management team is wary of open-source tools and does not want to implement an OASIS open standard tool for authentication. Which tool will not be considered based on the scenario?

    A. OAUTH

    B. SAML

    C. SPML

    D. XACML

103. You are conducting a security survey and want to ensure that only one authenticated person at a time can enter the building at a specific point and time. What is the BEST way to authenticate, and what perimeter defense do you recommend?

 A. Badge through a turnstile

 B. Signature through a mantrap

 C. Presentation of an ID at a closed gate

 D. Bollards and physical locked door

104. Your organization needs an AAA server to support the users accessing the corporate network via a VPN. Which of the following will be used to provide AAA services?

 A. RADIUS

 B. L2TP

 C. LDAP

 D. AD

105. You determined that there is a need for a client-based technology using a sandbox to limit the amount of system resources utilized by a program. If the program attempts to exceed those resources, the browser terminates the program. Which of these technologies uses sandboxing as a security control?

 A. Java applet

 B. ActiveX

 C. SAML

 D. SOAP

106. Which of the following access control principles should you implement to create a system of checks and balances on employees with heightened privileged access?

 A. Rotation of duties

 B. Need to know

 C. Mandatory access control

 D. Separation of duties

107. Your company hired a third-party company to fulfill compliance requirements to test for weaknesses in your company's security. The contractor attempted to hack wireless networks and enter secure areas without authorization and used phishing to gain access to credentials. What BEST describes this process?

 A. Vulnerability scans

 B. Active reconnaissance

 C. Penetration test

 D. Passive reconnaissance

108. You need to find a web-based language that is used to exchange security information with single sign-on (SSO). Which of the following is the BEST language to use?

    A. SOAP

    B. Kerberos

    C. SAML

    D. API

109. You work for a software company and learned that a certain developer hard-coded secret authentication credentials into one of your applications. What is this called?

    A. Backdoor

    B. Logic bomb

    C. Maintenance window

    D. Isolation

110. Your network administrator wants to use an authentication protocol to encrypt usernames and passwords on all Cisco devices. What is the BEST option for them to use?

    A. RADIUS

    B. DIAMETER

    C. CHAP

    D. TACACS+

111. You need to review the logs in the finance department from application servers to look for any malicious activity. What BEST describes your activity?

    A. Identification

    B. Authentication

    C. Malware analysis

    D. Accountability

112. Your IT manager wants to move from a centralized access control methodology to a decentralized access control methodology. You need a router that authenticates users from a locally stored database. This requires subjects to be added individually to the local database for access, which creates a security domain, or sphere of trust. What BEST describes this type of administration?

    A. Decentralized access control requires more administrative work.

    B. Decentralized access control creates a bottleneck.

    C. Decentralized access control requires a single authorization server.

    D. Decentralized access control stores all the users in the same administrative location using RADIUS.

113. Your company hired customer service representatives from a third-party vendor working out of a remote facility. What is the BEST way to prevent unauthorized access to your systems?

    A. Two-factor authentication (2FA)

    B. Site-to-site VPN

    C. Encrypted VDI

    D. IPSec to the required systems for the vendor

114. You are a security administrator helping a network engineer troubleshoot RADIUS authentication problems. You see the following message in the logs: RADIUS message received from invalid client 192.168.1.109. What should you check first to remedy the situation?

    A. Examine the RADIUS policy

    B. Register the RADIUS server

    C. Modify the authenticated client

    D. Add the IP address of the authorized client

115. Your enterprise is dealing with an increase in malicious activity traced back to insiders. Much of the activity seems to target privileged users, but you don't believe much of this activity is from the employees on your network. What will most likely deter these attacks?

    A. Role-based training and best practices

    B. More frequent vulnerability scans

    C. Full disk encryption

    D. Tightening security policy for least privilege and separation of duties

116. Your company currently uses Kerberos authentication protocols and tickets to prove identity. You are looking for another means of authentication because Kerberos has several potential vulnerabilities, the biggest being which of the following?

    A. Single point of failure

    B. Dynamic passwords

    C. Limited read/write cycles

    D. Consensus

117. The Domain Name System (DNS) maintains an index of every domain name and corresponding IP address. Before someone visits a website on your corporate network, DNS will resolve your domain name to its IP address. Which of the following is a weakness of DNS?

    A. Spoofing

    B. Latency

    C. Authentication

    D. Inconsistency

118. Your CIO approached the CISO with the idea to configure IPSec VPNs for data authentication, integrity, and confidentiality. Which of the following reasons would help support the CIO's goals?

A. IPSec only supports site-to-site VPN configurations.

B. IPSec can only be deployed with IPv6.

C. IPSec authenticates clients against a Windows server.

D. IPSec uses secure key exchange and key management.

119. You work for a university and are monitoring your dedicated faculty wireless network. You see many mobile devices not authorized to use this network, and malicious activity has been reported. Your IT security manager suggested adding contextual authentication. Which of the following falls in that category?

A. GPS

B. IDS

C. MAC filtering

D. Bluetooth

120. You just accepted a CISO position for a small customer service business, and your first priority is to increase security and accessibility for current SaaS applications. The applications are configured to use passwords. What do you implement first?

A. Deploy password managers for all employees.

B. Deploy password managers for only the employees who use the SaaS tool.

C. Create a VPN between your organization and the SaaS provider.

D. Implement a system for time-based, one-time passwords.

121. You are a SQL database administrator managing security initiatives. Based on controlling the confidentiality of your customers' financial information, what controls BEST meet the need of your company?

A. UPS and partial disk encryption

B. IPS generator and strong authentication controls

C. Vulnerability scanning and peer review of all changes

D. CMDB and an analysis of all code modifications

122. Your credit card company identified that customers' top transaction on the web portal is resetting passwords. Many users forget their secret questions, so customers are calling to talk to tech support. You want to develop single-factor authentication to cut down on the overhead of the current solution. What solution do you suggest?

A. Push notification

B. Hardware tokens

C. Login with third-party social media accounts

D. SMS message to a customer's mobile number with an expiring OTP

123. You are a service provider responsible for ensuring that an audit for PCI-DSS occurs and that the correct documentation is completed by the relevant parties. This is part of the assessment you provide. What is this process called?

   A. Service provider request

   B. Attestation of compliance

   C. Payment requests

   D. Security standards council

124. You purchase software from an online store. On the download page next to the link to download the software, there is a string of characters that looks like SHA256: e2ad113ea0d826d8c208bd0eabd3fb4b76c7d85618d4f38b5d54d4788a5ececa. What is the string of characters after SHA256 used for?

   A. Serial number of software

   B. Product ID of software

   C. Encryption key to decrypt the software

   D. Unique identifier of the software

125. You need to provide software for your end users to download. You want the users to be able to verify that the software has not changed during the download process. How might you provide this verification?

   A. Compute a hash of the software and list it along with the software on a server for download. End users can then use the hash to verify that the software hasn't been altered.

   B. Encrypt the software and list the encrypted software along with the encryption key on a server for download. End users can then use the encryption key to verify that the software hasn't been altered.

   C. The user can attempt to install and run the program. If it installs and operates properly, it hasn't been altered.

   D. Have the user authenticate first. If the user is authenticated, the software they download must be genuine.

126. You want to send a confidential message to a colleague in such a way that only the colleague can read it. You encrypt the message and then send it. What key is used to encrypt the message?

   A. Your public key

   B. Your private key

   C. Your colleague's public key

   D. Your colleague's private key

127. You want to send a confidential message to a colleague in such a way that only the colleague can read it. You encrypt the message and then send it. What key is used to decrypt the message?

    A. Your public key

    B. Your private key

    C. Your colleague's public key

    D. Your colleague's private key

128. You want to send an email securely to a colleague in such a way that the colleague is sure it came from you. What key would you use to sign the email so that the colleague is sure it came from you?

    A. Your public key

    B. Your private key

    C. Your colleague's public key

    D. Your colleague's private key

129. You want to send an email securely to a colleague in such a way that the colleague is sure it came from you. What key would your colleague use to decrypt the email, ensuring that the message came from you?

    A. Your public key

    B. Your private key

    C. Your colleague's public key

    D. Your colleague's private key

130. Your colleague hashes a message, encrypts the associated hash with her private key, and sends it to you. What is this process called?

    A. Digital signature

    B. Nonrepudiation

    C. Digital transfer

    D. Digital privacy

131. Your colleague hashes a message, encrypts the message with your public key, encrypts the associated hash with her private key, and sends it to you. What will this process do?

    A. Provides confidentiality, integrity, and nonrepudiation

    B. Provides availability, confidentiality, and integrity

    C. Provides availability, integrity, and nonrepudiation

    D. Provides availability, confidentiality, and nonrepudiation

132. You have an application that requires data to be encrypted on legacy equipment with minimum hardware resources. Which type of cipher is BEST suited for this situation?

    A. Stream cipher

    B. Serial cipher

    C. Block cipher

    D. Parallel cipher

133. You have an application that requires data to be encrypted on legacy equipment with minimum hardware resources. Which of the following ciphers BEST suits your needs?

    A. Twofish

    B. RC4

    C. AES

    D. Blowfish

134. You have an application that needs to send large amounts of data in a secure fashion. Which of the following ciphers is BEST suited for this need?

    A. ECC

    B. RC4

    C. 3DES

    D. AES

135. You suspect that an employee is stealing company information, but you're not sure how they are removing the information from the premises. During an investigation, you find a folder with numerous pictures in it. Later, you also discover that many of these pictures were emailed to an external email account. What may you deduce from this information and want to investigate further?

    A. Someone loves photography and sharing photos via email.

    B. Information could be hidden in the photos.

    C. The recipient of the photos could be in the marketing department.

    D. You could reach out to human resources to bring this person in for a discussion and review the NDA they signed.

136. You investigate an incident of malware on a corporate computer, and you come across a steganography program on an employee's laptop. It turns out that this tool was downloaded for free onto the system and that the downloaded file is the source of the malware. What might explain this information?

    A. Company information may be extracted using the steganography tool by the employee who downloaded it as well as the developer of the program itself.

    B. Someone downloaded the steganography tool to protect data as a form of encryption.

    C. You should reverse engineer the unauthorized software to determine how it works.

    D. You only need worry about the malware. You can always trust employees.

137. You are a forensic investigator analyzing a copyrighted video file for hidden information. You only have the file. What type of analysis technique will you use?

    A. Known message

    B. Known stego

    C. Stego only

    D. Chosen

138. You found a suspicious USB in the corporate parking lot and brought the USB back to your lab for testing in a sandbox. It contains unreadable documents and audio files. You pick one that is abnormally large to analyze, looking for hidden information. What is this process referred to as?

    A. Stego-analysis

    B. Stegoanalysis

    C. Steganography

    D. Steganalysis

139. You examine a file for hidden information but do not find any. What technique might the attacker use to make it more difficult to detect the hidden information?

    A. Encryption

    B. Deception

    C. FIM

    D. Randomization

140. Your company relies on certificates to verify entities it does business with. It is important that the validity of certificates is verified as quickly as possible. What method of checking certificate validity is BEST for this situation?

    A. CRL

    B. OCSP

    C. CLR

    D. OSCP

141. Your CISO is concerned with the secure management of cryptographic keys used within the organization. She wants to use a system where the keys are broken into parts, and each part is encrypted and stored separately by contracted third parties. What is this process called?

    A. Key objectives

    B. Key revenue

    C. Key escrow

    D. Key isolation

142. You manage a CA on your global corporate network. When a certificate authority revokes a certificate, what certificate information is placed on the revocation list?

    A. Certificate's private key

    B. Certificate's public key

    C. Certificate's serial number

    D. Certificate's hash

143. You work with a certificate authority to create digital certificates for your organization. You do not want to use OCSP stapling which holds the certificate and will be the one to provide status of any revocation. What cryptographic key do you provide to the certificate authority?

    A. You don't provide keys to the certificate authority.

    B. You provide both the private and public keys.

    C. You provide the private key.

    D. You provide the public key.

144. You need a hardware solution that will provide your employees a secure way to store digital certificates and private keys in multiple domains. The solution must be mobile. Which of the following options BEST suits your need?

    A. Wild card PKI token

    B. PKI badge

    C. Token ring

    D. RAID

145. You were tasked with choosing the correct encryption for your mobile device management program. Which asymmetric encryption algorithm is BEST suited for mobile devices?

    A. AES

    B. ECC

    C. IDEA

    D. Serpent

146. You intend to use asymmetric encryption to transmit various amounts of data from one endpoint to another over the Internet. You are concerned that if the private key used for this transmission is compromised, all encrypted data will be exposed. What technology could you use that generates temporary session keys based on your asymmetric keys?

    A. Perfect Forward Secrecy

    B. Pretty Good Privacy

    C. Public Key Infrastructure

    D. PaaS

147. Your company generates documents intended for public viewing. While your company wants to make these documents public, it stills wants to prove the documents originated from the company. How can these documents be marked in such a way that information about their origin is maintained while not distorting the visual contents of the documents?

    A. Blowfish

    B. Steganographic watermarking

    C. Digital signatures

    D. PKI

148. Your end users are using mobile devices to access confidential information on the corporate network. You need to ensure the information is kept secure as it is transmitted to these mobile devices. Encryption is a requirement. Of the following answers, which one BEST describes a major concern with implementing encryption on mobile devices?

   A. They have more processing power than other computing devices.

   B. They typically have less processing power than other computing devices.

   C. Increased complexities.

   D. Obfuscation.

149. Your small company wants to utilize asymmetric encryption to send secure emails but doesn't want the expense of using a certificate authority or a pinned certificate. Which of the following options is a good alternative?

   A. PKI

   B. CA/RA

   C. GPG

   D. Kerberos

150. Your business cannot overlook the need for allowing remote access by employees. You never know when an employee will need to connect to the corporate intranet from a remote location. The first thing to do is create a comprehensive network security policy. Which one of these will not fit into that policy?

   A. Definition of the classes of users and their levels of access

   B. Identification of what devices are allowed to connect through a VPN

   C. The maximum idle time before automatic termination

   D. Whitelist ports and protocols necessary to everyday tasks

151. You must decide what to do to formulate an efficient and effective security policy that includes the network, cryptocurrency and blockchain. This technology will enable electronic transactions that are resilient even when large amounts of money are at stake. What type of an assessment should you do?

   A. Risk assessment

   B. Penetration test

   C. Compliance audit

   D. Black-box testing

152. You have a three-layer line of defense working to protect remote access to your network, which includes a firewall, antivirus software, and a VPN. What action should your network security team take after standing up this defense?

   A. Log all security transactions.

   B. Monitor alerts from these assets.

   C. Check the firewall configuration monthly and antivirus weekly.

   D. Run tests for VPN connectivity once every 24 hours.

153. You are a security architect and were asked to review the project for a new VPN. You were asked to review a solution that operates on the network layer of the OSI model and uses authentication and encryption and cryptographic keys to protect data moving between hosts. What type of VPN remote access solution is this?

   A. L2TP

   B. XAUTH

   C. IKE

   D. IPSec

154. You have decided that an IPSec VPN is not a good fit for your organization. Employees need access only to specific applications, not the entire network. What VPN option would work BEST in this situation?

   A. SSH

   B. SSL

   C. IKE

   D. RDP

155. You need a way to enable tech support from your organization to have complete remote access to your systems. It has become difficult to walk end users through a complicated set of steps, so it is best to let a well-trained technician do it for them. Which of the following are the major risks with desktop sharing and remote access?

   A. Authentication and access control

   B. Authorization and verification

   C. Validation and isolation

   D. Regulation and application

156. You need to prevent attackers from being able to access copyrighted and digitally protected data from a group of transactions, even if they are able to break the encryption for a single communication sent over the Web by devices creating a unique session key for each transaction. What is this called?

   A. Perfect Forward Secrecy

   B. Pretty Good Privacy

   C. GNU Privacy Guard

   D. IETF standards

157. Your SMB organization is exploring a tool that combines VoIP, video, chat, and email together in one messaging system. What type of tool is this called?

   A. Cloud computing

   B. Unified communications

   C. Global transformation

   D. Competitive collaboration

158. You are a network engineer for an SMB. You are evaluating the placement of your new unified communications (UC) server. Your UC server does have some built-in capabilities for attack mitigation, but you do not want to solely rely on it. Where should you place this UC server?

    A. Sequestered behind a firewall

    B. Connected directly to the Internet

    C. Between two web servers, email and messaging

    D. Connected directly to your intranet

159. An email with a document attachment from a known individual is received with a digital signature. The email client is unable to validate the signature. What should you NOT do?

    A. Contact the sender.

    B. Contact your security administrator.

    C. Open the attachment to see if the signature is valid.

    D. Determine why the signature is not valid before you open the attachment.

160. You would like to periodically update records in multiple remote locations to ensure the appropriate levels of fault tolerance and redundancy. What is this is known as?

    A. Shadowing

    B. Mirroring

    C. Archiving

    D. Fail safe

161. Users are reporting to you that some Internet websites are not accessible anymore while on VPN. Which of the following will allow you to quickly isolate the problem causing the network communication issue so that it can be reported to the responsible party?

    A. IPConfig

    B. Ping

    C. MMC

    D. Tracert

162. What is the best security practice for keeping your collaborative software updated with patches and bug fixes as well as knowing how those updates will impact the system?

    A. Patch management

    B. Vulnerability management

    C. Encryption

    D. Security policy and procedures

163. The art of having people divulge sensitive information about the organization or about themselves by masquerading as a valid identity in your collaboration platform is known as which of the following?

   A. Dumpster diving

   B. Phishing

   C. Social engineering

   D. Active reconnaissance

164. Your team is conducting a risk assessment to assign an asset value to the collaboration servers in your data center. The primary concern is how and what to replace in the case of a disaster. Which one of the following is the BEST choice?

   A. Purchase cost

   B. Depreciated cost

   C. Retail cost

   D. Replacement cost

165. You are working with upper management to classify data to be shared in your collaboration tool, which will create extra security controls limiting the likelihood of a data breach. What principle of information security are you trying to enforce?

   A. Confidentiality

   B. Integrity

   C. Accountability

   D. Availability

166. You chose a vendor for your collaboration tool and will sign an agreement that requires that a vendor not disclose confidential information learned during the scope of the proof of concept, deployment, and usage of the tool. Which document needs to be signed by both your organization and the vendor?

   A. SLA

   B. MOU

   C. NDA

   D. RFP

167. VoIP is dependent on continuous reliable packet flow. It is an issue in the face of attacks. High levels of packet loss raise questions about VoIP reliability. Which of these attacks could be called the "busy signal" of VoIP?

   A. DDoS

   B. SQLi

   C. MiTM

   D. Bluejacking

168. You evaluate several unified communication vendors. You have a need for one with their own data center facility hosting their own instance of the platform with built-in redundant power, remote backup, and secured entry as well as 24/7 staffing. Why would a UC vendor have minimal data center security?

A. Cost savings

B. Compliance requirements

C. Ease of setup and use

D. Perfect forward secrecy

169. You investigate a breach and trace it back to your unified communications tool. The malicious user attacked the UC network and spoofed a MAC address to register an employee's soft phone and made international calls through your UC network. Which one of the following options would NOT have affected this attack?

A. Vulnerabilities in the UC platform

B. Weak firewall configurations

C. Social media posts

D. Cipher lock on the server room door

170. You are a security manager looking to improve security and performance of your unified communications server. Which of the following options might help with decreasing the attack surface?

A. Adding more users

B. Adding more devices

C. Turning off unused services

D. Ease of setup

171. Your organization is analyzing the risk of using more and more diverse technology. Your task is to look at video collaboration tools because it houses your most important information, customer data, and innovative ideas in one single space. With data security in mind, what do you suggest doing to protect against privileged users compromising sensitive data?

A. Deploying flexible levels of access across the platform

B. Creating alerts when specific data file types have been uploaded

C. Putting individual projects in their own dedicated spaces with restricted access

D. Creating a strict password policy

172. The audio collaboration tool that your company uses follows a username and password login model. If an employee's credentials are compromised, it could give attackers access to financial information, intellectual property, or client information. How would you mitigate this type of risk with a collaboration tool?

A. Strict password guidelines

B. Only use HTTPS

C. Restrict usage to VPN

D. Disable SSO

173. You recently were made aware that your collaboration tool is sending daily summaries to employees, contractors, and vendors through a publicly shared email service. You suspect this might be risky. If there is a vulnerability in your email server, you're opening up even more security risks. What should you have employees do instead?

   A. Turn off the feature.

   B. Use a tool that has a "recent activities" summary that pops up when a user securely logs in.

   C. Set up an export via VPN.

   D. Perform weekly check-in phone calls to review all the summaries.

174. While doing risk analysis, you realize that you set up a presence collaboration tool using the URL mycompanyname.appname.com. What should you do to protect this collaboration tool from an attacker randomly finding this login portal?

   A. Choose a tool that enables your IT team flexibility to control security settings and to determine a URL structure that is customizable.

   B. Make sure that the entire team using the tools understands encryption.

   C. Require strict usernames and passwords.

   D. Check for compliance if you are a healthcare organization.

175. You are a healthcare provider accessing a cloud-based server where your collaboration tool resides. What is the most important question you need to ask the vendor/host of this cloud-based server?

   A. Is this server HIPAA HITECH compliant?

   B. Is this server SCADA compliant?

   C. What is your SLA if the server goes down?

   D. What is my TCO of this software?

176. You are choosing a collaboration tool to be used across the finance department. For evaluation, which of the following questions is NOT as important as the others?

   A. How established is the solution?

   B. What support is required to roll out the solution?

   C. Can we change the brand logo and color scheme?

   D. What training and best practices can you offer to avoid issues in the future?

177. Management of your hosted application environment requires end-to-end visibility and a high-end performance connection while monitoring for security issues. What should you consider for the most control and visibility?

   A. You should consider a provider with connections from your location directly into the applications cloud ecosystem.

   B. You should have a T1 line installed for this access.

   C. You should secure a VPN concentrator for this task.

   D. You should use HTTPS.

178. Your organization has a policy that passwords must be at least 12 characters long; include a combination of upper- and lowercase letters, numbers, and special characters; and be changed every 30 days. Which of the following solutions will enforce this policy organization-wide?

    A. Active Directory GPO

    B. LDAP

    C. RADIUS

    D. DIAMETER

179. Your organization was the victim of brute-force attacks where the attacker discovered usernames and continually tried to log in to the corporate network using various passwords until the account was compromised. What following option could reduce the likelihood of a brute force attack being successful?

    A. Allow only one attempt for privileged users.

    B. Configure Group Policy in Active Directory to lock out an account for 10 minutes after five unsuccessful login attempts.

    C. Create federated identities with Shibboleth and WAYF. SSO.

    D. Have stricter password requirements.

180. To enter your facility, a guest must sign in and present a picture ID. A security guard will check both for accuracy, and if both match, the guest is allowed to enter into the building as long as they are escorted by a sponsor. What has the security guard performed?

    A. Identity proofing

    B. Identity authentication

    C. Identity accounting

    D. Identity confidentiality

181. Phishing is a successful way to initiate a security breach. One of the collaboration-based attacks your company suffered last quarter was phishing using malicious URLs via an instant messaging tool. Which of the following is why this attack is so successful?

    A. Your guard was down, you were worried about deadlines, and you trusted those people.

    B. You logged into the collaborative tools with credentials.

    C. Phishing is only used for emails.

    D. Malicious files or URLs are not blocked automatically in IMs.

182. You are evaluating remote desktop software that enables help-desk personnel to remotely access a user's computer for troubleshooting purposes. For ease of use, you want the product to be browser based. While evaluating a product, you notice a padlock next to the URL in the browser. What does the padlock indicate?

    A. You are connected using HTTP.

    B. You are connected using SSH.

    C. You are connected using TLS.

    D. You are connected using TPM.

183. You want to access network equipment on the corporate LAN remotely. A colleague suggests using the program PuTTY. After downloading and running PuTTY, you find that it offers various means of remote connectivity. Which of the following options is the most secure option?

    A. Telnet

    B. SSH

    C. FTP

    D. HTTP

184. You are a network engineer and need to access network equipment on the corporate LAN remotely. The solution to provide this function must include a secure login per user that is easily managed. Tracking login activity is also important. Which of the following is the BEST solution?

    A. Common passwords should be set on each network device.

    B. A common username and password should be set on each network device.

    C. Unique usernames and passwords should be set on each network device.

    D. Use a RADIUS solution and have each network device configured to use it.

185. Your company is migrating systems from on-premise systems to a data center managed by a third party. Remote access must be available at all times. Controls on access must be auditable. Which of these controls BEST suits these needs?

    A. Access is captured in event logs.

    B. Access is limited to single sign-on.

    C. Access is configured using SSH.

    D. Access is restricted using port security.

186. You are evaluating a remote desktop solution that is browser based. While performing the evaluation, you discover that the latest version of SSL is used to encrypt data. Which statement is true about this connection?

    A. The connection is using SSL, and it is secure.

    B. The latest version of SSL is version 1.96.

    C. SSL is obsolete. TLS should be used instead.

    D. TLS is obsolete. SSL is the best solution.

187. You found that an attacker compromised a web conferencing server utilizing a known vulnerability of the software. Which option should be performed to prevent this intrusion?

    A. Install a firewall in front of the server.

    B. Keep the web conferencing software patches up to date.

C. Install AV on the web conferencing server.

D. Ensure HTTPS is always used.

188. You have a user who wants to conduct video conferences from his computer. He finds a free program that does what he wants and downloads it. The program was published for only a few months. Unfortunately, the free program includes malware and infects his system and others. What technology could have prevented this situation from occurring?

A. Redlisting

B. Blacklisting

C. Graylisting

D. Whitelisting

189. Your CISO is concerned that employees are posting confidential information on social media. Which of the following two options BEST addresses this issue?

A. Block social media sites from corporate resources.

B. Train employees on the importance of not divulging company information on social media.

C. Forbid employees from having social media accounts.

D. Create a corporate policy outlining the requirement not to divulge corporate information on social media sites and the consequences of doing so.

190. You want to implement a technology that will verify an email originated from a particular user and that the contents of the email were not altered. Of the answers provided, which technology provides such a function?

A. Digital signature

B. Symmetric encryption

C. Asymmetric encryption

D. Nonrepudiation

Chapter

5

Research, Development, and Collaboration

THE CASP+ EXAM TOPICS COVERED IN THIS CHAPTER INCLUDE:

✓ **Domain 5: Research, Development, and Collaboration**

- 5.1 Given a scenario, apply research methods to determine industry trends and their impact to the enterprise.

    - Perform ongoing research

        - Best practices

        - New technologies, security systems, and services

        - Technology evolution (e.g., RFCs, ISO)

    - Threat intelligence

        - Latest attacks

        - Knowledge of current vulnerabilities and threats

        - Zero-day mitigation controls and remediation

        - Threat model

    - Research security implications of emerging business tools

        - Evolving social media platforms

        - Integration within the business

        - Big data

        - AI/machine learning

    - Global IA industry/community

        - Computer Emergency Response Team (CERT)

        - Conventions/conferences

        - Research consultant/vendors

- Development approaches
  - DevOps
  - Security implications of agile, waterfall, and spiral software development methodologies
  - Continuous integration
  - Versioning
- Secure coding standards
- Documentation
  - Security Requirements Traceability Matrix (SRTM)
  - Requirements definition
  - System design document testing plans
- Validation and acceptance testing
  - Regression
  - User acceptance testing
  - Unit testing
  - Integration testing
  - Peer review
- Adapt solutions to address
  - Emerging threats
  - Disruptive technologies
  - Security trends
- Asset management (inventory control)
- 5.3 Explain the importance of interaction across diverse business units to achieve security goals.
  - Interpreting security requirements and goals to communicate with stakeholders from other disciplines
    - Sales stuff
    - Programmer
    - Database administrator

- Network administrator
- Management/executive management
- Financial
- Human resources
- Emergency response team
- Facilities manager
- Physical security manager
- Legal counsel
- Provide objective guidance and impartial recommendations to staff and senior management on security processes and controls.
- Establish effective collaboration within teams to implement secure solutions.
- Governance, risk, and compliance committee

1. IT security is a rapidly evolving field. As a security professional, you need to stay current of industry trends and potential impact on an enterprise. Many of these changes will lead to you adopting which of the following?

    A. Best practices

    B. Digital threats

    C. Antivirus programs

    D. NIST

2. As a system administrator, you need to show that you did what any reasonable and prudent organization would do in certain circumstances for a legal defense. What is this minimum level of security called?

    A. Due diligence

    B. Due care

    C. Standards

    D. Policies

3. Your company holds large amounts of company data in electronic databases as well as personally identifiable information (PII) of customers and employees. What do you do to ensure that implemented controls provide the right amount of protection?

    A. Best practices

    B. Forensics

    C. Due diligence

    D. Auditing

4. As CIO, you took the proper steps to implement a standard of due care by fostering an environment of due diligence. You created an ecosystem that enforces more than the minimum level of required security. What are these efforts called?

    A. Best practices

    B. Due care

    C. Baseline

    D. Modeling

5. While implementing best practices, you determine that the security fix for a specific asset costs more than the asset is worth to the organization. What must be maintained?

    A. SSH

    B. Due care

    C. CVE

    D. Fiscal responsibility

6. You look to implement best practices and have identified other departments or people who have experience with their implementation. Where else might you look for guidance on cybersecurity best practices?

    A. NIST

    B. ADA

    C. FBI

    D. GLBA

7. Your best practices are outlined in the compliance requirements of Payment Card Industry-Digital Security Standard (PCI-DSS). This standard specifies the digital framework around what type of organization?

    A. Any organization, regardless of size or number of transactions that stores any card-holder data

    B. The financial industry excluding trading companies

    C. Only publicly traded mortgage companies and banks

    D. Retail organizations that have more than 30,000 transactions a month

8. As a security analyst for a large retail organization, you research best practices for PCI compliance levels. How do you know to what level your organization must build the security framework?

    A. Transaction volume for 6 months

    B. Transaction volume for 12 months

    C. Financial total for 6 months

    D. Financial total for 12 months

9. New security technology is necessary because data thieves found another way of stealing your company's information. The inadequacy of usernames and passwords is well known. Which of these is a new and more secure form of authentication to research?

    A. Hardware authentication

    B. Rule-based access control

    C. Vulnerability management

    D. Incident detection

10. One of your administrator's username and password combinations was compromised. An attacker with those credentials can engage your network in nefarious ways. What do you use to trigger a red flag alerting you of this type of behavior?

    A. IDR

    B. UBA

    C. RBAC

    D. AM

11. One of your managers asked you to research data loss prevention techniques to protect data so that cyberattackers cannot monetize the stolen data. What DLP do you recommend?

    A. Encryption and tokenization

    B. HIPAA and PCI

    C. I&AM management

    D. NIST frameworks

12. You examine activity in a data center on the corporate network. There is nonuser behavior that is malicious and suspicious. What type of model would you use to determine your reaction?

    A. COBIT

    B. Advanced threats

    C. Machine learning

    D. GDPR

13. Your organization migrated to the cloud to host your traditional on-premises IT. Which on-premises security technique should you NOT research and adopt in the cloud?

    A. Virtual firewalls

    B. Virtual IDS and IPS

    C. Virtual security hardware

    D. Virtual physical security

14. While doing research on current best practices, you find the Internet Engineering Task Force (IETF) authored memorandums applicable to your new project. How does the IETF list these official documents?

    A. RFQ

    B. RFP

    C. RFC

    D. IAB

15. While investigating threats specific to your industry, you found information collected and analyzed by several companies with substantive expertise and access to source information. Which of these is the LEAST beneficial item to your organization after subscribing to threat intelligence information?

    A. Determining acceptable business risks

    B. Developing controls and budgets

    C. Making equipment and staffing decisions

    D. Creating a marketing plan for your product

16. You are reading threat intelligence reports focusing on the triad of actors and capability as well as tactics and techniques. You try to make informed decisions regarding this intelligence. Which of these is NOT a type of assessment you make with cyberthreat intelligence?

A. Strategic

B. Arbitrary

C. Operational

D. Tactical

17. You and your organization are performing an annual threat modeling exercise. You look for potential threats coming from physical or digital vulnerabilities. Using the most popular Microsoft IT threat-modeling methodology, you try to find threats that align to your product. What is this methodology called?

A. STRIDE

B. PASTA

C. TRIKE

D. VAST

18. You have mission-critical software running on a server in your data center with a known security flaw. The software vendor does not have a patch in place to fix the problem, and there is potential attacker exploitation. What is this called?

A. No-day vulnerability

B. Zero-day vulnerability

C. Patch vulnerability

D. Java vulnerability

19. A zero-day vulnerability was found in your organization and presents a serious security risk. To keep your computer and data safe, it is smart to be proactive. Which of these options has the lowest priority to secure endpoints?

A. Use comprehensive security software that protects against threats.

B. Install new software updates when they become available from the manufacturer or vendor.

C. Remove unnecessary software and features and update drivers.

D. Develop some security awareness processes to be followed sometime in the future.

20. Your security manager petitioned management to disallow social media account access on company-issued property. Upper management feels that giving up social media is not a reasonable option. You were asked to take steps to protect your company against common social media threats. Which one of these is a big risk to your company?

A. Unattended social media accounts

B. Strict privacy settings

C. Social media policy

D. Audits

21. You believe you successfully locked down your company's social media accounts. While doing more research, you find another malicious attack vector related to social media. Which of these could enable an attacker to gain access to your social media account through app vulnerabilities?

A. Imposter accounts

B. Third-party apps

C. Privacy settings

D. Authentication

22. You have a team of people working on social media messaging and customer service. While you may focus on threats coming from outside the organization, research has shown that employees are more likely to cause cybersecurity incidents. What is your first line of defense?

A. Limit the number of people who can post on your company's social media accounts.

B. Share the individual login information for social network accounts with only marketing personnel.

C. When someone leaves the organization, disable their social media access.

D. Create brand guidelines that explain how to talk about your company on social media.

23. Your business is using social media and created a social media policy. These guidelines outline how your employees will use social media responsibly and protect you from security threats and legal trouble. Which of the following would not be included in your social media policy?

A. Guidelines on brand and copyright

B. Rules regarding confidentiality and personal social media use and who to notify if a concern arises

C. Guidelines on password creation and rotation

D. Latest threats on social media

24. While researching how your retail organization should regulate social media use and access, you discovered that cybercriminals use social media botnets to disseminate malicious links and collect intelligence on high-profile targets. A common attack you need to watch for includes leveraging a hashtag for a specific organization and distributing malicious links that appear in your new feeds. What is this social media attack called?

A. Hashtag hijacking

B. Trend-jacking

C. Retweet storm

D. Spray and pray

25. Your pharmaceutical company uses social media for press releases. A hacktivist organization believes your pharmaceutical company makes too much money on the drugs it sells. After your company tweets a press release about a new drug treatment approved by the government, traffic on social media explodes with a negative comment. This comment is immediately retweeted by the thousands. What type of attack is this?

   A. Click farming

   B. Retweet storm

   C. Spray and pray

   D. Watering hole

26. You were asked to perform a quarterly audit on your social media accounts. Social media security threats are constantly changing. Attackers are coming up with new strategies, so a regular audit should keep you ahead of an attacker. Which of the following is most important and should be included in your regular audit?

   A. Privacy settings, access, and publishing privileges

   B. All network attack vectors and access management

   C. Social network trending of competitors

   D. All mentions of your company on the Internet

27. Your manufacturing company uses sensor data to detect production processes that malfunctioned. You are concerned that an attacker could undermine the quality of your big data analysis by fabricating data. What would this vulnerability revolve around?

   A. Fake data

   B. Fraud detection

   C. Alarming trends

   D. Wrong quality

28. You work for the power company that supplies electricity to three states. You rely heavily on the data you collect. Once your big data is collected, it undergoes parallel processing. Data is split into numerous arrays, and a mapper processes them to certain storage options. What is the biggest threat to this process?

   A. Encryption

   B. Inadequate key/value pairs

   C. Poisoning

   D. Perimeter security

29. You work in IT for a medical research facility. You need to grant different levels of access for multiple roles within your agency. End users can see no personal information even if it could theoretically be helpful for medical researchers. People can access needed dataset but view only the information they are allowed to see. What do you use to separate this data?

   A. A data warehouse

   B. RAID 1+0

   C. SAN

   D. NAS

30. A new objective for your department is to establish data provenance or historical data records. Moving forward, you must now document the data's source and all manipulations performed on it. Every data item will have detailed information about its origin and the ways it was influenced. Why is this crucial to the security of the data?

   A. Unauthorized changes in metadata can lead you to the wrong datasets.

   B. Authorized changes to the data warehouse can lead you to the wrong datasets.

   C. Traceable data sources make it difficult to find security breaches.

   D. Traceable data sources make it difficult to find fake data generation.

31. You work for a luxury car manufacturer. Your CEO wants to use machine learning and artificial intelligence to build models of customer buying patterns and to use those models to make future predictions for a competitive lead. Machine learning engines learn for themselves and constantly evolve. Optimization is hard and it is nearly impossible to trace how decisions are made. You risk ending up with a car that no one wants. What is this called?

   A. Transparency

   B. Computational power

   C. Massive datasets

   D. Model drift

32. One of your enterprise security vendors was working toward incorporating machine learning into old products. What would machine learning help with the most?

   A. Malware detection

   B. Provisioning

   C. Incident remediation

   D. Compliance

33. You are a security analyst working for a casino. You work with a security firm and have traced the origin of a ransomware attack to a connected fish tank in the casino lobby. The attack was stopped within seconds, and the threat was mitigated. What would have led to the quick discovery of the attack?

   A. Signatures

   B. Endpoint analysis

   C. Machine learning algorithms

   D. Immunity learning

34. You are the CIO of an organization with many governmental contracts. You were challenged by the board of directors to reduce staff and the need for staff to do repetitive, low-value, decision-making activities so that your staff can work strategically. What tool would you use for this?

   A. Machine learning

   B. Zero-day exploits

   C. Triaged threats

   D. Human resources

35. You are tasked with building a team that will handle computer security incidents. What has this team been called historically?

A. NIST

B. CERT

C. ADA

D. Red Cross

36. You were selected to manage a systems development project. Your supervisor asked you to follow the proper phases in the systems development life cycle. Where does the SDLC begin?

A. Functional requirements

B. System design specifications

C. Initiation

D. Implementation

37. You finished the initiation and planning stage of the system development life cycle for a project you're managing. Next, you need to evaluate how the system fits end-user needs. What stage in the SDLC is this?

A. Development

B. Implementation

C. Acceptance

D. Requirements

38. Your system completed all the system design specifications defining how information enters a system, how it flows through, and what should be produced. What part of the system development life cycle comes next?

A. Development

B. Documentation

C. Acceptance

D. Rejection

39. You documented the controls that are required for a system including how data is edited, the type of logs that will be generated, and any system revision processes. According to the SDLC, what phase comes next?

A. Certification

B. Common controls

C. Integration and test

D. Requirements definition

40. You have reports from an independent third party that have verified the systems you designed meet all the functional and security specifications documented. The next important process requires that a certified person compare the system against a set of standards, verifies that best coding practices were followed, and that there is a process where management then approves the system. What are these two processes called?

- **A.** Functionality and testing
- **B.** Certification and accreditation
- **C.** Acceptance and implementation
- **D.** Replacement and production

41. You have almost completed the SDLC for an assigned project and are ready to complete the phase that pushes the system to production. What is this phase called?

- **A.** Revisions
- **B.** Operations
- **C.** Accreditation
- **D.** Implementation

42. The SDLC phases are part of a bigger process known as the system life cycle (SLC). The SLC has two phases after the implementation phase of the SDLC that address post-installation and future changes. What are they called?

- **A.** revisions and replacement
- **B.** evaluation and versioning
- **C.** authentication and monitoring
- **D.** compliance and functionality

43. You have been selected to manage a systems development project. Your supervisor told you to follow the SDLC phases. What happens during the accreditation process?

- **A.** The system is tested and is waiting for certification.
- **B.** A system is accepted by the data owner, even if it's not certified.
- **C.** All testing is completed and certified for security requirements.
- **D.** The system is tested but not certified.

44. You have turned a system project over to operations. Which of the following are you not responsible for in the SDLC?

- **A.** Acceptance
- **B.** Licensing
- **C.** Development
- **D.** Evaluation

45. You are a software engineer and need to use a software development process that follows a strict predetermined path through a set of phases. What type of method is this called?

- **A.** Agile
- **B.** Waterfall

    C. Adaptable

    D. Verifiable

46. You are a software engineer and prefer to use a flexible framework that enables software development to evolve with teamwork and feedback. What type of software development model would this be called?

    A. Prototyping

    B. Ceremony

    C. Agile

    D. Radical

47. You are a software developer, and as part of the testing phase in the SDLC, you need to ensure that an application is handling errors correctly. What is the BEST tool for you to use in this situation?

    A. Fuzzer

    B. Compliance

    C. Access control

    D. Remediator

48. You are working on a high-risk software development project that is large, the releases are to be frequent, and the requirements are complex. The waterfall and agile models are too simple. What software development model would you opt for?

    A. Functional

    B. Cost estimation

    C. Continuous delivery

    D. Spiral

49. You want to enhance your overall compliance and protect your company more carefully. You also want to prioritize which web applications should be secured first and how they will be tested. What do you need to sit down with your IT security team and build?

    A. Web application security plan

    B. Web application–level attack list

    C. Business logic justifications

    D. Container security

50. You have an application that performs authentication, which makes checking for session management, brute forcing, and password complexity appropriate. What else might you check for?

    A. SQLi

    B. Ransomware

    C. Privilege escalation

    D. Static analysis

51. To protect your company's web applications, you first must determine any highly problematic area of the application. You have applications that enable users to use large amounts of data like blog posts. When these blog posts are done through HTML, they are at a high risk of what type of attack?

    A. NGINX

    B. Injection

    C. Arbitrary

    D. Recursive

52. You are creating a web application security plan and need to do white-box security testing on source code to find vulnerabilities earlier in the SDLC. If you can find vulnerabilities earlier in the process, they are cheaper to fix. What type of testing do you need to do?

    A. SAST

    B. CAST

    C. DAST

    D. FAST

53. You are creating a web application security plan and need to do black-box security testing on a running application. What type of testing do you need to do?

    A. SAST

    B. CAST

    C. DAST

    D. iAST

54. You completed the inventory of your existing web applications and must sort them in order of priority. Your list is quite long, and if you do not prioritize, it will be difficult to know which application to focus on first. What should NOT be a category rating?

    A. Normal

    B. Baseline

    C. Serious

    D. Critical

55. You had a discussion with the nontechnical members of your upper management team and explained why eliminating all vulnerabilities from all web applications is not possible or needed. By limiting yourself to testing the vulnerabilities that pose a threat, what will you save the company?

    A. Time and money

    B. Compliance and experience

    C. Testing and implementation

    D. Recurrence and risk

56. For security reasons, during the system development life cycle you are looking at security at the hardware level as well as software. You need a CPU that will separate memory areas so that one is used for instructions and one is used for storage. What is this called?

    A. NX

    B. CN

    C. AR

    D. C++

57. In your role as a hospital's security architect, not only do you have to worry about confidentiality attacks like attackers stealing PHI, you also must worry about availability attacks like a DoS. One of the most popular attacks you want to thwart is a buffer overflow attack. Which of the following is a technique designed to protect against buffer overflow attacks?

    A. MAC

    B. OSPF

    C. ASLR

    D. RLSA

58. Your organization is blending its development team with the operations team because the speed at which you're rolling out applications is faster than ever. Applications change with new services required in production, so you have undertaken the challenge of eliminating those silos of development and operations. What is this called?

    A. Incremental

    B. DevOps

    C. Agile

    D. Waterfall

59. You are reviewing the code for a new application that will be used for a specific function and used for only a short period of time. What is this type of code called?

    A. High-quality code

    B. Low-quality code

    C. Code analyzing

    D. Static code

60. You are using continuous integration involving different members of your team while developing a new application. You meet every day after lunch to review, which can mean multiple integrations every day. What are the security implications of using continuous integration?

    A. There are no security issues.

    B. Errors will not need to be fixed because the next integration will fix them.

    C. Encryption will be impossible because of timing.

    D. Errors need to be handled as soon as possible.

61. Your team replaced version 1.2 of software with 2.0. The newest version has a completely different interface in addition to updates. What is this called?

A. Versioning

B. Coding integration

C. Secure coding

D. Vulnerability assessment

62. You built an Excel spreadsheet for system security test activities. Included in this spreadsheet are an identification number, a description of the requirement, the source of the requirement, the objective of the test, and the verification method of this test. What is this spreadsheet called?

A. NIST

B. OSCP

C. OSPF

D. SRTM

63. You are conducting a unit test on a new piece of software. By looking at an individual program, how do you ensure that each module behaves as it should?

A. Input/output

B. BIOS

C. Processes running

D. Services running

64. You are doing a peer review of software and walking through each line of code, examining each object, method, and routine. You are inspecting code granularly to find any possible errors or areas for improvement and to see if all security concerns are met. What is the main disadvantage to doing a peer review?

A. Money

B. Damage

C. Time

D. Reproducibility

65. While performing unit testing on software requested of your department, you found that privilege escalation is possible. Privilege escalation means that an attacker can elevate their privilege on a system from a lower level to an administrator level. What two techniques do you need to test?

A. Vertical and horizontal

B. Left and right

C. North and south

D. Ring 1 and Ring 3

66. You are shopping on a popular website for computer parts. As you move from page to page, cookies are being used to maintain session state. This means the cookie is used to store needed information, such as the selections made on previous pages. Not all websites protect cookies when they are transmitted over HTTP because HTTP is stateless. If an attacker gets ahold of your cookie, what can they not do with it?

   A. Modify the cookie content

   B. Rewrite session data

   C. Inject malicious content

   D. Eat it

67. According to the Center for Internet Security, the number-one control of the top 20 controls is to know what assets you have. Having an asset and data inventory is a basic part of any security program, but it may look easier than it is. Vulnerability scanning will give you a lot of information about your assets, including IP address and operating systems, but it will not be able to give you which of the following?

   A. Hostname

   B. Business context and prioritization

   C. Age of vulnerabilities

   D. Risk scores

68. As a risk manager, you know that accurate inventories are critical for many reasons. You receive an alert of multiple failed logins on a root account on a server. How do you decide the criticality of responding to the alert?

   A. Use the inventory to find what service this server provides and what data is stored on it.

   B. Use the inventory to find the physical location and unplug the machine from the network.

   C. Use the inventory to find the environment the asset services and send an email to operations.

   D. Log into the machine and watch tasks that are running while deploying antivirus software.

69. You identified an SSL cipher weakness on a human resources web server named MS16_HR. You know that this weakness throws you out of compliance for a specific human resources web application. You have been written up during an audit for allowing SSLv2 on another web application used by human resources. Why would an inventory help with these risks?

   A. These three findings are related to the same risk.

   B. These three findings are not related to the same risk.

   C. A software inventory would not help with this risk.

   D. DHCP would be more helpful in this scenario.

70. The second CIS control of the top 20 controls is knowing software inventory. A feature of Nmap is the ability to remotely detect operating systems. By default, Nmap will attempt to identify which of the following using the nmap-os-db file?

   A. Hostname and IP address

   B. OS vendor, generation, and device type

   C. FQDN and open ports

   D. OS patch level and DNS

71. As a CIO, you are concerned with the lack of skilled cybersecurity professionals and the difficulty of keeping good talent. According to sources, in 2019 there were 1.3 million cyber positions available worldwide and climbing. To change this trend, what must our industry do?

   A. Provide formal education and development programs.

   B. Perform more trending analysis.

   C. Use more artificial intelligence (AI).

   D. Deploy more IaaS, SaaS, and PaaS.

72. You deployed more than half of your enterprise into the cloud, but you still have concerns about data loss, unauthorized access, and encryption. What continues to be the vulnerability in cloud infrastructure that leads to the most breaches?

   A. Misconfiguration

   B. SIEM

   C. SaaS

   D. Machine learning

73. You are a network defender and are finding it difficult to keep up with the volume of network attacks. What can you leverage to help with early detection and response to these threats, especially new ones?

   A. Machine learning

   B. SIEM

   C. DevSecOps

   D. Security as Code

74. The rise of the Internet of Things (IoT) has presented challenges for your organization's security team while they are trying to secure your corporate network. Attacks on IoT have been steadily trending upward as attackers enlist devices to launch attacks. What is the BEST method to combat this threat?

   A. Adding network intrusion devices

   B. Performing inventory management

   C. Adding more security tools

   D. Reducing the attack surface

75. The Internet was developed with voluntary cooperation and collaboration. Collaborative security is based on responsibility, confidence, protection, evolution, and consensus. The purpose of collaborative security does NOT include which of the following?

A. Ensuring continued success of economic and social innovation

B. Encouraging participants to share responsibility

C. Making sure security solutions are compatible with human rights

D. Providing involuntary top-down corporate organization that thinks locally and acts globally

76. You work for a security software company. For any sales customer conversation to be productive, customers must understand what you're saying, see the value in what is offered, and build trust. How do you convey value and persuade a customer to purchase your software?

A. Marketing

B. Sales enablement

C. Product training

D. All of the above

77. As a security engineer, you are comfortable with the security aspect of information technology. However, real security requires being able to communicate with stakeholders. You read security reports, and any findings that are related to risk are given to department heads for review. This collaboration technique is which of the following?

A. Independent review

B. Structured review

C. Strategic alignment

D. Security controls

78. As a security engineer, you are comfortable with the security aspect of information technology. However, real security mandates requirements and goals being communicated to stakeholders. You read security reports, and the findings related to risk are reviewed during a meeting with all appropriate people in attendance. Which of the following describes this approach?

A. Independent review

B. Structured review

C. Strategic alignment

D. Security controls

79. You are a security engineer and will be holding a meeting to discuss risk analysis processes. Individuals at this meeting will review your prepared material and write down their responses for you, as the team leader, to review. What is this collaboration method called?

A. Independent review

B. Structured review

C. Unmodified Delphi

D. Modified Delphi

80. What are the three components of implementing information security programs?

    A. People, processes, policies

    B. Assets, authentication, authorization

    C. Backups, broadband, BCPs

    D. Servers, SaaS, supply chains

81. As a technical project manager, you are collaborating with programmers working quickly to develop code. Some common problems that programmers face are debugging their code, keeping up with technology, and which of the following?

    A. Understanding the user

    B. Being very well paid

    C. Keeping up with high demands

    D. Being curious

82. You are working as the "Sec" part of a DevSecOps team. Developers are working quickly to get out code, while security is working to keep the network safe. "Ops" is comprised of network engineers who are tasked with keeping services and software up and running and available. What might cause difficulties between you and the network engineers?

    A. Objectives

    B. Committees

    C. Training

    D. Debugging

83. You work as a database administrator for a large enterprise. You are tasked with making sure only authorized users have access to the data. This requires the implementation of a rigorous security infrastructure for both production and test databases. What is this control called?

    A. Background checks

    B. Job rotation

    C. Mandatory vacation

    D. Least privilege

84. You have interviewed several candidates for a position that is open in your security department. Human resources will need to conduct a background check before offering a position to your final candidate. Why is a background check necessary?

    A. Helps provide the right person for the right job

    B. Is a single point of failure

    C. Reinforces a separation of duties

    D. Improves performance

85. You have an accountant on staff who refuses to take a vacation. Your CISO has asked you to start collecting data, emails, and messages on your unified collaborative software. After two weeks, this accountant is forced to take a vacation. Why would a mandatory vacation be required?

    A. To uncover misuse

    B. Job rotation

    C. Separation of duties

    D. Confidentiality

86. You work in the training department of a software company and have only one full-time trainer. What can you do to prevent a single point of failure if that trainer should become ill and unable to teach?

    A. Job rotation

    B. Dual control

    C. NDA

    D. Mandatory vacation

87. You have policies and procedures in place for the finance department. One of the policies and procedures requires one person to input account payables and another to do account receivables. You have another control in place where one person writes the check and another signs the check. Another control in place states that if an expenditure is over $5,000, it requires two signatures. What is this control called?

    A. Dual control

    B. Job rotation

    C. Nondisclosure agreement

    D. Nonrepudiation

88. You hired a new person to be on your security team, and HR is helping them fill out all the proper paperwork. Before they can be privy to any classified information, they must sign a document that helps prevent any disclosure of sensitive information. What is this document called?

    A. MTTR

    B. MOU

    C. NDA

    D. RFQ

89. You identified people who should be on your IT security steering committee. These are individuals who are from various levels of management and who you meet with to discuss security issues. Another name for these people could be which of the following?

    A. Employees

    B. Consultants

    C. Stakeholders

    D. Users

90. You have been tasked with a goal of keeping something from happening. What type of control would you want to put in place?

  A. Detective

  B. Preventative

  C. Corrective

  D. Recovery

91. You want to gather your team together to evaluate potential corrective and recovery controls for your company. You want to encourage them to contribute and evaluate, taking an active role in the discussion. The three-tiered approach consists of brainstorming ideas for solutions, evaluating the best possible solutions, and which of the following?

  A. Decide

  B. Commit

  C. Administer

  D. Recover

92. Forming a response team and assigning responsibilities is a critical step in emergency response planning. If your team is not familiar with their assigned role, important actions could be missed when a security incident occurs. Overall, a cyber emergency response team should analyze incident data, discuss observations, manage communications, remediate, and close the incident with what response?

  A. Understanding lessons learned

  B. Negotiating a contract

  C. Building an SOC

  D. Performing risk analysis

93. You need a strategy for managing your organization's overall governance, risk management, and compliance regulations. What is the structured approach to aligning IT with business objectives?

  A. GRC

  B. ITIL

  C. PMI

  D. CRMA

94. Establishing effective communication to obtain collaboration requires the support of senior management. How can upper management support be made apparent?

  A. Not providing resources for implementation

  B. Delaying approval for monitoring and policies

  C. Decreasing budget

  D. Voicing support and approval for strategies

95. The facilities manager should be part of the physical security controls team because they are responsible for the care and maintenance of the building. Physical controls protect against theft and loss. Examples of physical controls do NOT include which of the following?

   A. Mantraps

   B. Locks

   C. CCTV

   D. Password policies

96. Your organization has a remote workforce and often works with multiple global offices, partners, and contractors. You are a security engineer and have been asked to collaborate on security goals. All communications must be encrypted and remain on site. All users must use the same programs, and those programs must be patched regularly. Which solution do you recommend?

   A. Deploy an SSL reverse proxy and have end users use full disk encryption with the TPM chip.

   B. Install an SSL VPN to your data center and have users connect with a virtual workstation image.

   C. Create a portal using web-based software. Your company hosts the database.

   D. Use a terminal server and use remote management tools to standardize workstations.

97. You are implementing a new program to handle e-business transactions. The project has multiple stakeholders. The audit division controls the database, the physical team controls the data center, and the development team is responsible for the front end of the web application. As technical project manager, you are responsible for which of the following?

   A. Ensuring the process is secure from start to finish

   B. Ensuring that the customer experience is seamless

   C. Ensuring all audit processing is compliant

   D. Building a security control library

98. Your organization opened new offices on a different continent. This expansion requires internal security as well as compliance. Existing policy states that all employee activity could be monitored. What would be the reason that policy could change?

   A. Teams in other countries fall under different legal or regulatory requirements.

   B. The time it takes to export data to the data warehouse.

   C. Cybersecurity shortage of qualified analysts.

   D. Social networking initiatives.

99. A hospital database is hosting PHI data with high volatility. Data changes constantly and is used by doctors, nurses, and surgeons, as well as the finance department for billing. The database is located in a secure network where there is limited access. What is the most likely threat?

    A. Internal fraud

    B. Malware

    C. Compliance

    D. Inappropriate admin access

100. You work for a small bank that implemented least privilege but is still concerned about compliance, fraud, and identity theft. Which of the following BEST addresses the risk team's concerns?

    A. Awareness training

    B. Job rotation

    C. Mandatory vacations

    D. Background checks

101. You work for a health provider as an information security officer. Upper management, including medical staff, requested using the internal email systems on their personal smartphones. Which of the following concerns you the most?

    A. Radiation from smartphones affecting patients

    B. Compliance

    C. Email server could crash

    D. Smartphones as rogue access points

102. Your company has been fined for a security breach that resulted in the loss of sensitive customer information. As part of improving security, you recommended hiring a third-party training company to provide security awareness classroom training. What should the primary focus of the training be?

    A. Data handling policies

    B. Possible vulnerabilities and threats

    C. Data classification

    D. Explanation of how customer data is created, used, shared, and managed

103. Which of the following is a use case for configuration management software?

    A. Incident remediation

    B. Continuance

    C. Asset management

    D. Collaboration

104. Disciplinary actions for noncompliance should be included in security policy. These actions should be strong enough to deter violating policy, including suspension, termination, or legal prosecution. Who has to endorse the security policy?

    A. Senior management

    B. Human resources

    C. All employees

    D. Contractors

105. Which of these should not be covered in your security policy?

    A. Details and procedures

    B. Exceptions to policy

    C. Password policy

    D. Access control of client data

106. If you wanted to require employees to follow certain steps to avoid malware, you would create a procedure. If you wanted to require employees to use specific software to avoid malware, which of the following would you create?

    A. Policy

    B. Standard

    C. Baseline

    D. Scope

107. In a comprehensive security program, which of the following documents is considered to be discretionary?

    A. Policies

    B. Procedures

    C. Guidelines

    D. Baselines

Chapter

6

Practice Test 1

1. You are setting up a new virtual machine. What type of virtualization should you use to coordinate instructions directly to the CPU?

   A. Type B.

   B. Type 1.

   C. Type 2.

   D. No VM directly sends instructions to the CPU.

2. You just purchased a web application and want to assess for any vulnerabilities. What would be the BEST option going forward?

   A. Black-box test

   B. White-hat test

   C. Vulnerability assessment

   D. Patch management

3. Bob and Alice work in Finance. What control should you put in place that requires two employees to work together to complete a single action to prevent fraud?

   A. Job rotation

   B. Single point of failure

   C. Education

   D. Dual control

4. The security triad does NOT include which of the following?

   A. Verification

   B. Availability

   C. Confidentiality

   D. Integrity

5. You received some weird messages and links in your instant messaging application. What is this called?

   A. Spamming

   B. Phishing

   C. Pass-the-hash

   D. Spimming

6. You are working with authentication and authorization and need a process that separates this into three separate processes. What do you choose?

   A. RADIUS

   B. DIAMETER

   C. TACACS+

   D. TACAX

7. You are tasked with implementing security measures and with presenting to the board of directors what symmetric encryption you will offer your organization. Your presentation will discuss which of the following?

A. Accounting

B. Authentication

C. Nonrepudiation

D. Integrity

8. You are interviewing for a lucrative job with a new software company. You will have access to all the source code. What should this company do before they make you an offer?

A. Perform a background check

B. Have you sign an NDA

C. Complete your healthcare enrollment

D. Obtain a blank check for your direct deposit

9. In cryptography, the process of taking clear text and turning it into something unreadable by a human being is called _____.

A. confidentiality

B. encryption

C. work factor

D. TCP/UDP

10. You are a security architect and will be deploying encryption in your enterprise environment. Which encryption algorithm is the only one appropriate for streaming but has been found to be vulnerable?

A. DES

B. AES

C. Blowfish

D. RC4

11. You are examining the OSI model. Layer 2 broadcast traffic stays in a local area network known as a broadcast domain. Every device in a broadcast domain recognizes a specific MAC address and passes the traffic to other devices in the broadcast domain. What MAC address is recognized?

A. 127.0.0.1

B. 8.8.8.8

C. 00 00 00 00 00 00

D. FF FF FF FF FF FF

12. You have completed a port scan of an email server and identified that TCP port 4444 is being actively used. What application might be using that specific port?

    A. Metasploit

    B. Back Orifice

    C. CobaltBlue

    D. Armitage

13. You have been hired by a startup to organize and document the IT assets so that planning, management, and expansion can be budgeted and streamlined. What is this practice called?

    A. NIST

    B. HIPAA

    C. Enterprise architecture

    D. Vulnerability assessment

14. As a security architect, you have implemented controls that will restrict Internet access for any end user on a secure siloed system. What is this control called?

    A. Least privilege

    B. Need to know

    C. Accounting

    D. Job rotation

15. You have implemented address space layout randomization (ASLR) in your enterprise. What type of attack is ASLR meant to protect an organization from?

    A. SQLi

    B. Social engineering

    C. DDoS

    D. Buffer overflow

16. You have deployed a centralized desktop solution that uses servers to serve up an operating system to a host system. What is this technology called?

    A. VDI

    B. VM

    C. Unix

    D. AS450

17. You are a security administrator. You are examining a packet capture file (PCAP) from Wireshark. You see traffic addressed to 119.0.23.5. What class address is this?

    A. Class A

    B. Class B

    C. Class C

    D. Classless

18. You are using Nmap to do a port scan on your network and find port 53 open. What protocol would you suggest is being used?

    A. DHCP

    B. DNS

    C. IMAP

    D. HTTPS

19. You are a security engineer, and your legal department and human resources department have reached out to you because of employee fraud. They have asked you to prove the authenticity of an email an employee sent to the bank requesting an unauthorized wire transfer. What would you recommend for nonrepudiation?

    A. IPv4

    B. Physical signature

    C. Certificate

    D. Digital signature

20. You have created a plan to roll out cloud computing. Which of the following is NOT an advantage?

    A. Scalability

    B. Increased cost

    C. Accessibility

    D. Decreased cost

21. You have used a tool that returned the value of a data center server operating system as Microsoft Windows Server 2016. What is this called?

    A. Footprinting

    B. Handprinting

    C. OS fingerprinting

    D. Protocol scanning

22. Bob and Alice handle sensitive information for your healthcare organization. The company has swapped their individual roles for the next three months. What security tenet does this meet?

    A. Least privilege

    B. Dual control

    C. Job rotation

    D. Background check

23. Which of the following storage techniques should you deploy if you want the option to selectively provide availability to some hosts and to restrict availability to others by using a masking process?

    A. NAS

    B. SAN

C. iSCSI

D. LUN

24. You are troubleshooting email services and the lack of retention of emails on hosts. You discover port 143 is open. What service is probably running?

   A. POP3

   B. IMAP

   C. SMNP

   D. HTTP

25. Your CIO is reviewing a contract with a new software vendor. He has asked for a clause to be added for software escrow. Why would this be necessary?

   A. Vendor bankruptcy

   B. Off-site backup

   C. Payment over time

   D. Performance measurements

26. You have scanned your network and found port 123 open. What service makes use of this port?

   A. SNMP

   B. SQL

   C. NTP

   D. SSL

27. You have done a quarterly audit and found an expired certificate being used to log into a host. What should have happened to that certificate when it expired?

   A. Added to the CRL

   B. Added to the OCSP

   C. Renewed with new expiration date

   D. Deactivated and added to the ACL

28. You are editing an ACL. What device are you most probably configuring?

   A. A switch

   B. A modem

   C. A router

   D. A hub

29. You are investigating an attack that has used fake caller ID and VoIP. What is this type of attack called?

   A. SQLi

   B. Phishing

   C. Spimming

   D. Vishing

30. Alice is an administrator who works in the finance department. She has clicked a link in an email that has executed unwanted actions in a web application she is using. What type of attack is this?

A. XXS

B. CSRF

C. SQLi

D. Buffer overflow

31. You have been asked to interview a candidate for your department. You have a list of questions to ask and have time to ask some of your own. Which of the following would be a violation to ask a candidate about?

A. Education

B. References

C. Certifications

D. Religion

32. You have to terminate an employee. When should you also terminate their network access?

A. End of day

B. End of week

C. Beginning of shift

D. At time of termination

33. While architecting a new storage array, you have been told to make use of SMB or NFS. What type of storage should you implement?

A. SSD

B. Tape drive

C. SAN

D. NAS

34. While building out a new VoIP architecture, what also should be added to add redundancy?

A. Power

B. Budget

C. Legal

D. ISP

35. What document in your organization is the highest tiered, providing an overall view of security?

A. Procedures

B. Policies

C. Baselines

D. Standards

36. What is used to maintain session state when your employees are surfing from one web page to another?

    A. Cookie

    B. URL

    C. Syn/Ack

    D. Session

37. You have been tasked with building out a pentesting team and to use a tool called Kali. What is Kali?

    A. A port

    B. A protocol

    C. An operating system

    D. A browser

38. Your end users are having difficulty signing into the network. Your investigation of the situation leads you to believe it is what type of attack?

    A. Port scanning

    B. DDoS

    C. Pass-the-hash

    D. Trojan

39. You are a Windows administrator. Which of these is difficult for Kerberos to offer on a Windows ecosystem?

    A. Faster connection

    B. Manual authentication

    C. Interoperability

    D. Handling a large number of security groups

40. You are reviewing your annual budget and are looking for places to cut back. You want to find a way to get one certificate to cover all domains and subdomains for your organization. What type of certificate do you need?

    A. Validated certificate

    B. Assured certificate

    C. Physical certificate

    D. Wildcard certificate

41. You work for a software company and are building an SLA template. The SLA is what the IT organization as a whole is promising to the customer. Which of the following documents can be used to support the SLA?

    A. PLA

    B. OLA

    C. NDA

    D. DBA

42. You would like to add storage to a mission-critical server in the data center. This storage needs to appear to the operating system as a local disk that can be formatted and used locally. What storage technology is the BEST option in this situation?

   A. NAS

   B. DAS

   C. SAN

   D. USB

43. Your company is experiencing degraded VoIP call quality. What is this called?

   A. Jitter

   B. Stutter

   C. Spikes

   D. Latency

44. You are building out your security department and need a document to define the minimum level of security. What document do you need?

   A. Policy

   B. Standard

   C. Baseline

   D. Guideline

45. Your company is migrating web applications from IPv4 to IPv6. IPv6 uses addresses of what length in bits?

   A. 8

   B. 16

   C. 64

   D. 128

46. For security reasons, you are moving from LDAP to LDAPS for your standards-based specification for interacting with directory data. LDAPS provides for security by using which of the following?

   A. SSL

   B. SSH

   C. PGP

   D. AES

47. You are using RC6, which is a symmetric encryption algorithm. Which of the following is NOT an advantage of using symmetric encryption?

   A. Faster

   B. Key exchange is easier

   C. Confidentiality

   D. Single key

48. Your company has a new CIO. She has a favorite vulnerability management tool and a relationship with that software company. You are migrating to the new software. What document would require the most changes?

   A. Policies

   B. Guidelines

   C. Baselines

   D. Procedures

49. To optimize the network, you have begun VLAN tagging by putting a VLAN ID into a header to identify which network it is in. With this system, individual domains can be created with the help of this VLAN tagging system. The standard that supports this is which of the following?

   A. 802.11a

   B. 802.1q

   C. 802.13b

   D. WiMax

50. You need a tool that will allow you to build a connection between two software packages, extending the functionality of both. What is this called?

   A. API

   B. RFP

   C. IBM

   D. AES

51. You need to upgrade your current tunneling protocol because it does not provide authentication or confidentiality. What would be a good replacement for L2F?

   A. PPTP

   B. LDAP

   C. L2TP

   D. ISP

52. You are a security architect who has written more than half of your company's security policy. Who ultimately is responsible for the content in your company's security policy?

   A. Security department

   B. Senior management

   C. CIO

   D. Employees

53. Your CIO has asked you to identify control types and control functions for risk mitigation. What type of control type and function would a honeypot be?

   A. Detective/technical

   B. Preventative/physical

C. Corrective/administrative

D. Recovery/technical

54. You want to build fault tolerance into your hardware systems. Which of the following is a way of preventing a disruption arising from a single point of hardware failure?

   A. Database with customer information backed up in a data warehouse

   B. Duplicate alternative power sources

   C. Using an identical server with all operations running in parallel

   D. A duplicate database

55. You have written the following conditional statements: IF the user is logged in, AND the user has the correct permissions, THEN show the user the configuration page. What is this an example of?

   A. Race conditions

   B. Amorphous thinking

   C. Logical connectives

   D. Formal logic

56. You are looking for a replacement for POP3. Which of the following protocols offer advantages over POP3 for mobile users?

   A. HTTPS

   B. NTP

   C. IMAP

   D. SMTP

57. DNSSEC provides authority and data integrity. DNSSEC will not protect against which of the following?

   A. Spoofing

   B. Kiting/tasting

   C. Verification

   D. Masquerade

58. You need an encryption algorithm that offers easier key exchange and key management than symmetric offers. Which of the following is your BEST option?

   A. Asymmetric

   B. Quantum

   C. Hashing

   D. Scytale

59. You have built an access control list for a router that is subject to PCI DSS. The ACL you have built contains four commands that deny HTTP, POP3, FTP, and Telnet. No traffic is coming through the router. What is the most likely reason?

    A. Traffic is dropped because of the "deny TCP any HTTP" statement.

    B. Traffic is dropped because of the "deny TCP any FTP" statement.

    C. Traffic is accepted but not forwarded to the proper location.

    D. There are no permit statements in the ACL.

60. Which of the following protocols could be used for exchanging information while implementing a variety of web services in your organization?

    A. SOAP

    B. HTTP

    C. SNMP

    D. ASP

61. In forensics, what is the process that dictates how to control, protect, and secure evidence, should it ever need to be admitted to a court of law?

    A. Containment

    B. Cryptoanalysis

    C. Encryption

    D. Chain of custody

62. You are working on a business continuity and incident response plan. What is the control type of this corrective control function?

    A. Functional

    B. Technical

    C. Authoritative

    D. Administrative

63. You have been asked to make a change to software code. What type of testing do you complete to make sure program inputs and outputs are correct?

    A. White-box

    B. Black hat

    C. Code review

    D. Regression

64. You have been tasked with delivering security awareness training to all employees at least once a year due to FISMA requirements. What type of control is security awareness training considered?

    A. Preventative

    B. Protective

    C. Administrative

    D. Corrective

65. During a routine Wireshark capture on your network, you see a great deal of traffic over port 80. What protocol is typically running over port 80?

A. HTTPS

B. HTTP

C. HTML

D. NTTP

66. You are examining DNS records in your DNS management panel. You need to assign a value to a record of a domain and a TTL. What record would you alter?

A. TTL record

B. A record

C. B record

D. NS record

67. You are performing risk analysis on authentication systems in your enterprise. You are using a one-way encryption hashing algorithm. Which of the following is a hashing algorithm?

A. AES

B. Skipjack-128

C. Blowfish

D. SHA-512

68. You are evaluating the security policy of a large enterprise. There are many elements and points of enforcement, including email and remote access systems. XML is the natural choice as the basis for the common security policy language. What language standard should be implemented with XML for a fine-grained, attribute-based access control?

A. OASIS

B. SAMLv2

C. SOAP

D. XACML

69. You are using a process where the product or system being evaluated is called the "target of evaluation" and rated on evaluation levels of E0 through E6. What is this process called?

A. TCSEC

B. Z notation

C. ITSEC

D. Common Criteria

70. You are building a network intrusion detection system (NIDS). What can a NIDS do with encrypted network traffic?

A. Look for viruses

B. Examine contents of email

    C. Bypass VPN

    D. Nothing

71. You have built an extended ACL, which will allow you to be very specific about what you allow into your environment. The extended ACL that you have written can process all EXCEPT which of the following?

    A. ICMP

    B. TCP

    C. DES

    D. UDP

72. You have been handling an incident and have finally arrived at the final step of the incident response process. What is the final step?

    A. Recovery

    B. Announcement

    C. Public relations

    D. Lessons learned

73. You are configuring SNMP on a Windows server. You have found that you are currently running SNMPv2c. Why would you want to upgrade to SNMPv3?

    A. Cryptographic security system

    B. Party-based security system

    C. Easier to set up

    D. Supports UDP

74. Using Microsoft Network Monitor, you have captured traffic on TCP port 23. Your security policy states that port 23 is not to be used. What client-server protocol is probably running over this port?

    A. SNMP

    B. Telnet

    C. PuTTY

    D. FTP

75. TCP is connection oriented, while UDP is connectionless. Which of these is NOT a valid header in a UDP packet?

    A. Source port

    B. Destination port

    C. Length

    D. Sequence number

76. You are having difficulties reaching tech support for a specific web application that has crashed. You have to find the agreement between your company and the provider. What is the document that requires a provider to maintain a certain level of support?

A. NDA

B. SLA

C. MOU

D. MTTR

77. Which of the following would be considered a detective and administrative control?

A. Fences and gates

B. IDS and honeypots

C. IPS and antivirus

D. Audit logs

78. Which of the following would be an early form of encryption also known as a transposition cipher?

A. ROT13

B. Scytale

C. Steganography

D. Anagrams

79. You are working toward implementing the Bell–LaPadula model in your enterprise. What is the Bell–LaPadula model based on?

A. Confidentiality

B. Integrity

C. Availability

D. Authentication

80. Most of your staff works remotely. What is the most secure remote access protocol for mobile users on corporate devices?

A. PPTP

B. PPP

C. RAS

D. L2TP

81. Your stakeholders are concerned about data privacy. Geolocation data could be found in which type of file?

A. PDF

B. MP4

C. XLS

D. JPG

82. You have finished conducting an audit to verify the protection mechanisms you have placed on information systems. What is this type of audit called?

    A. Information security audit

    B. Operational audit

    C. Forensic audit

    D. Procedure audit

83. You have seen the IT department disposing of software, hardware, and documents in the regular dumpster. Which of these do you recommend to upper management?

    A. Hire a third party to take care of the disposal of all equipment.

    B. Remove the dumpster.

    C. Create a policy for data destruction.

    D. Shred all documents.

84. You have been instructed to remove all data from a hard drive with the caveat that you want to reuse the drive. Which of the following would be the BEST option?

    A. Put the hard drive in the microwave for two minutes

    B. Empty the recycle bin

    C. Degauss the drive

    D. Perform a seven-pass bit-level drive wipe

85. You are calculating the SLE for a backup drive that crashed in a mission-critical server. The drive and content are valued at $15,000. The exposure factor is 20 percent. What is the SLE?

    A. $300

    B. $3,000

    C. $75,000

    D. $12,000

86. You want to form a legal partnership with another organization. Which of these is the BEST description of a partnership?

    A. A business that legally has no separate existence from the owner

    B. A business where the owners are not personally liable for the company's debts

    C. A form of business operation that declares the business is a separate legal entity from the board of directors

    D. A legal form of business between two or more individuals who share management and profits

87. The manufacturer of a motherboard advertises the presence of a TPM chip. What is TPM used for?

    A. Speed

    B. Encryption

   C. Hyperthreading

   D. Authentication

88. You are reviewing a contract your organization has made with a governmental agency. Some of the contract is not available to you because it is classified. What is the lowest level of the governmental model of information classification?

   A. Confidential

   B. Secret

   C. Sensitive

   D. Top Secret

89. Your company is conducting new web business with companies with home offices in the EU. Under the rules of GDPR, visitors to the website may exercise their EU data rights that include which of the following?

   A. Not be informed of a breach

   B. To have their presence on a site erased

   C. To not be taxed on purchases

   D. Receive a healthy discount

90. As you are building a business continuity plan, you are investigating cybersecurity threats for your manufacturing organization. Cyber threats to your business would not include
_____ .

   A. ransomware

   B. DDos

   C. intellectual property theft

   D. resource management

91. You have received an RFQ response from a software company, which makes a tool that will allow you to record all changes in a single change management tool. This tool will track scheduling change, implementing change, the cost of change, and reporting. What type of software is this called?

   A. Vulnerability management

   B. Change control

   C. Security information and event management

   D. Automation

Chapter 7

Practice Test 2

1. According to your security policy, you should have step-by-step guides for both vulnerability management and patch management. Where will you find those guides?

    A. Procedures

    B. Baselines

    C. Guidelines

    D. Audits

2. You are in a team meeting and would like to solicit ideas and feedback from the team. You would like this process to be anonymous and build consensus. What is the BEST methodology to accomplish this?

    A. Virtualization

    B. Code review

    C. Modified Delphi

    D. Quantitative analysis

3. Your company is looking at ways to improve processes as well as cut costs in the call center. What would be the most likely solution?

    A. Hire more employees.

    B. Acquire another company to do the work.

    C. Outsource the work.

    D. Form a partnership.

4. You have upgraded SSL to TLS on a web application. What type of encryption is TLS?

    A. Hybrid

    B. Hashing

    C. Steganography

    D. Asymmetric

5. You have both mycompany.com and www.mycompany.com pointing to the same application hosted by the same server. What type of DNS record is this found in?

    A. Authentication

    B. SOA

    C. CNAME

    D. AWS

6. You are a software project manager evaluating whether certain criteria have been met before deployment can start. What is this stage?

    A. Testing

    B. Design

    C. Implementation

    D. Analysis

7. You travel a great deal for work. What tool would you use to find a hidden infrared camera in your hotel room?

    A. Fuzzer

    B. Metal detector

    C. Tethering

    D. Smartphone

8. You work for a large marketing agency and often handle accounts for competing companies. What security model would you implement to prevent employees working on one account from seeing what is happening on another competing account?

    A. Clark–Wilson

    B. Biba

    C. Bell–LaPadula

    D. Brewer and Nash

9. You work for a global construction company and have found cloud computing meets 90 percent of your IT needs. Which of these is of least importance when considering cloud computing?

    A. Data classification

    B. Encryption methodology

    C. Incident response and disaster recovery

    D. Physical location of data center

10. You are conducting a risk analysis for your company, specifically looking at quantitative data. Which of these would NOT be considered quantitative?

    A. Volume

    B. Temperature

    C. Pressure

    D. Reputation

11. Your organization is undergoing an external penetration test. You see the following data passed in a web page field: `password' OR 1=1;--`. What is this attack?

    A. CSRF

    B. XSS

    C. SQLi

    D. Buffer overflow

12. You are monitoring your IT environment to detect techniques like credential dumping. Credential dumping is extracting usernames and passwords from a computer to then pass those credentials to other machines on a network. Where are the credentials stored on a Windows machine?

    A. In the SAM

    B. In PSEXEC

    C. In Documents and Settings

    D. In WUTemp

13. You have investigated a breach into your network. You found lower-level credentials used to access files and functions reserved for higher-privilege credentials. What is this called?

    A. Phishing

    B. Dumpster diving

    C. Privilege escalation

    D. Pass-the-hash

14. You have joined an ERM team and completed a risk assessment for your organization. After evaluating all cyber risk, you have found an area that needs to be mitigated by risk transfer mechanisms. Which of these would be an example of risk transfer?

    A. Patching

    B. Pentesting

    C. Insurance

    D. Simulations

15. You want to calculate the ALE of the email server in your data center. The email server is valued at $10,000. The exposure factor is 10 percent, and the server has failed twice in the past two years. What is the ALE?

    A. Not enough information

    B. $1,000

    C. $100

    D. $2,000

16. You are helping develop a security policy that focuses on social engineering. You are working on a section that helps employees avoid malware downloads via phishing. What would NOT be beneficial in this policy?

    A. Do not use public WiFi.

    B. Anti-malware and anti-phishing software.

    C. Digital certificates.

    D. Do not share personal information in email.

17. You are working for the federal government as a vulnerability management supervisor. You are attempting to enable automated measurement and policy compliance because of FISMA. What protocol are you most likely to use?

    A. HTTPS

    B. SCAP

    C. STATE

    D. HIPAA

18. As a security architect, you have created a blended Windows and Linux environment. What is the technology you want to use that will virtualize an instance on top of either operating system's kernel?

A. Hypervisor 1

B. Hypervisor 2

C. Containerization

D. Automation

19. Who in your organization is responsible for setting goals and directing risk analysis?

A. Board of directors

B. CIO

C. Senior management

D. Human resources

20. Your training manager is copying MP4 security awareness videos to mobile devices from their laptop. What is this called?

A. Uploading

B. Downloading

C. Blueloading

D. Sideloading

21. You are explaining cryptography to upper management, specifically hashing and data storage. Which of these is NOT a hash algorithm?

A. DES

B. SHA-1

C. MD5

D. SHA-3

22. You have been given a USB with hardware drivers from a co-worker. How can you ensure that the drivers have not been tampered with?

A. Hashes on the Internet

B. Hashes on the developer's website

C. Scan with a vulnerability scanner

D. Scan with asymmetric algorithms

23. You are investigating a method for transaction-level authentication using shared secrets and hashing for DNS. You want to authenticate dynamic updates and responses. What protocol do you use?

A. OSPF

B. TSIG

C. ICMP

D. IGMP

24. You have connected your laptop to the Internet by using your smartphone. What is this called?

   A. Vishing

   B. Tethering

   C. Scanning

   D. Hopping

25. You need a formal state transition system for your computer security policy that aligns with integrity controls. You want to group by data and subject. Which security model do you choose?

   A. Bell–LaPadula

   B. Brewer and Nash

   C. Chinese Wall

   D. Biba

26. You have taken your workstation into the hardware lab to get reimaged with the newest operating system. While there, you notice some new machines on the workbench with the USB port filled with glue. What type of security approach is this?

   A. Redundant

   B. Reciprocal

   C. Vector oriented

   D. Protective oriented

27. You work for a publicly traded company. While evaluating your organization's information classification, some information can be given the lowest-level classification. The lowest level of public-sector information classification is which of the following?

   A. Secret

   B. FOUO

   C. Public

   D. Unclassified

28. Your CIO has included the use of HSM in security baseline documentation. What is HSM used for?

   A. Managing keys for authentication

   B. Managing CRLs

   C. Managing data in transit

   D. Managing TPM

29. You have calculated the single loss expectancy of a mission-critical asset by multiplying the asset value by the exposure factor. What else should your team review for qualitative costs?

   A. Cost of repair

   B. Value of lost data

C. Lost productivity

D. Public relations

30. You feel comfortable with the security mechanisms your department has put in place for data at rest. You are more concerned about data in transit. Which of these do NOT concern you?

   A. Insecure protocols

   B. Key mismanagement

   C. Man-in-the-middle attacks

   D. Bad sector on a hard drive

31. Your company has set up a new e-commerce website. It is agreed that risks exist, but the benefit of the added cash flow outweighs the risk. What is this called?

   A. Risk acceptance

   B. Risk reduction

   C. Risk transference

   D. Risk rejection

32. Identifying all potential threats is a huge responsibility. Threats can be categorized into all of the following EXCEPT which one?

   A. Human error

   B. Equipment malfunction

   C. Malicious software

   D. Financial loss

33. You work for a large hospital complex as a security program manager. As business partners, your supplier asked you to exchange documents using EDI. What does this mean to your hospital?

   A. Using purchase orders

   B. Postal mail, fax, and email

   C. Order management systems

   D. Using an electronic format

34. Your department is inundated with requests for PII. What type of controls should you put in place to protect this information?

   A. Encryption, strong passwords, MFA, and backups.

   B. Keep old media with personal data indefinitely.

   C. Do not automate updates; it can break workflows.

   D. Use public WiFi, not a corporate wireless network.

35. The users on your network should have only the access needed to do their jobs. What is this security control called?

   A. Single point of failure

   B. Least privilege

   C. Separate of duties

   D. Mandatory vacations

36. You need an IDS but have no security budget. What IDS tool listed is open source?

   A. Nexpose

   B. Nessus

   C. Snort

   D. PuTTY

37. You are using Nmap to complete a scan of your network. You want Nmap to perform all three steps of a TCP session. Which of the following command should be executed?

   A. -sL

   B. -sn

   C. -sU

   D. -sT

38. Which method of encryption is going to make use of a single shared key?

   A. SHA

   B. ECC

   C. DES

   D. AES

39. One of your salespeople has been asked to travel overseas on business and wants to make sure the corporate Windows laptop will be secure if it is stolen or lost. What do you tell the salesperson?

   A. Make sure they change their password before they leave.

   B. The laptop has a TPM chip and BitLocker enabled.

   C. Always use VPN.

   D. Install WS-Security and enable RDP.

40. You are looking for an antivirus detection tool that uses a rule or weight-based system to determine how much danger a program function could be. What type of antivirus do you need?

   A. Behavioral

   B. Signature based

   C. Heuristic

   D. Automated

41. What is it called when you have two different files that are hashed with the same encryption algorithm and it produces the same hash output?

A. XOR

B. Collision

C. Array

D. Variables

42. You need to capture network traffic and have downloaded Wireshark. What format does Wireshark use to save packet data?

A. .pcap

B. .exe

C. .wsdata

D. .fers

43. On Thursday, you had several employees complaining that their wireless signal had deteriorated in the last few days. On Monday, you installed a new WAP. What tool would you use to conduct a wireless site survey?

A. Wireshark

B. Nmap

C. John the Ripper

D. InSSIDer

44. Windows supports remote access protocols through the GUI. Remote access allows you to connect to a remote host in a different location over a network or over the Internet. What tool is native in Windows that provides this access?

A. Teamviewer

B. Remote Desktop Connection

C. Terminal Desktop Server

D. Wireshark

45. You need to configure a Windows 10 client for a remote access VPN using IPSec/L2TP. Why is a VPN so important for remote employees?

A. VPN traffic is accessible.

B. VPN traffic is encrypted.

C. VPN allows you remote access.

D. VPN is an option if you are on your home network.

46. You have an end user who has called the help desk because they visited a website that instructed them to reset their DNS. What is the command you use at the Windows command line to accomplish this?

A. netstat

B. tracert

C. `ipconfig /renew`

D. `ipconfig /flushdns`

47. You are testing Group Policy and firewall settings on an end user's workstation. You want to see whether there are certain active TCP connections. What command-line tool do you use?

A. `netstat`

B. `netsh`

C. `ping`

D. `ipconfig`

48. You are troubleshooting a Cisco IOS. What command will show the router's current configuration?

A. `show ?`

B. `show interface`

C. `show running-config`

D. `show ip route`

49. You want to replace an access point's removable antenna with a better one based on the needs gathered by a wireless site survey. You want to be able to focus more energy in one direction and less in another. What type of antenna should you purchase?

A. Directional

B. Omnidirectional

C. Parabolic dish

D. Radio

50. With 80 percent of your enterprise in a hybrid cloud model, which of the following is NOT a key enabling technology for the cloud?

A. Fast WAN

B. High-performance hardware

C. Inexpensive servers

D. Complete control over process

51. You need to run a sysinternals utility on a Windows machine that will allow you to monitor file systems, the Registry, processes, threads, and DLL activity in real time. What tool do you use?

A. Paint

B. Procmon

C. Autorun

D. Procexp

52. An Excel file on your Windows desktop is named Confidential. You want to hash this file using PowerShell and SHA1. What is the command that you run?

A. `Get-FileHash '.\Confidential.ppt' -Algorithm SHA1`

B. `Get-FileHash '.\Confidential.xls' -Algorithm SHA1`

C. `Get-FileHash '.\Confidential.doc' -Algorithm SHA1`

D. `Get-FileHash '.\Confidential.xls' -Algorithm MD5`

53. To prepare for appropriate preventative measures, you have downloaded a tool that will allow you to check weak credentials on your network. Which of the tools listed will perform a simple dictionary attack on NTLM passwords?

A. L0phtcrack

B. Wireshark

C. Maltego

D. Social-Engineer Toolkit

54. You are a privileged user launching Nmap. You use the default `nmap` scan: `#nmap target.` What is the default option?

A. `-sS`

B. `-A`

C. `-O`

D. `-SYN`

55. Your penetration tester is using Kali Linux and has listed John the Ripper as a tool he will use in an upcoming black-box test. What is John the Ripper used for?

A. Packet capture

B. Wireless site survey

C. Password cracking

D. Compliance

56. You have started a new position as a security analyst for a small startup and found they are using Telnet. You want to use a more secure tool for data exchange. Which of the following will BEST suit your needs?

A. PuTTY

B. Metasploit

C. Wireshark

D. Nmap

57. You have several employees who have created IT help-desk tickets regarding fake SMS text messages. What form of attack is this?

A. Phishing

B. Smishing

C. Pharming

D. Phreaking

58. You are investigating a new tool that helps identify, analyze, and report on threats in real time based mostly on logs. What is the BEST solution?

A. SIEM

B. Antivirus

C. XSS

D. Port scanner

59. You have written very tactical documentation that is explicit in the steps and processes required to meet regulations or compliance. It is a mandatory action or rule designed to support and conform to a policy. What is this document called?

A. A guideline

B. A procedure

C. A standard

D. A policy

60. What kind of attack can happen when a program or process tries to store more data in a space than it was originally designed to hold?

A. SQLi

B. XSRF

C. Buffer overflow

D. SIEM

61. You have an employee who has downloaded a health app on their iPhone. The app is tracking physical location and accessing photos and videos, as well as browser activity. What is this called?

A. Worm

B. Trojan

C. Virus

D. Ransomware

62. What protocol runs over port 25 and will be used to send mail to other mail servers?

A. SMTP

B. POP3

C. IMAP

D. S/MIME

63. One of your employees has turned in their two-week notice. When you schedule their exit interview, what document should you review?

A. SLA

B. NDA

C. MOU

D. I-9

64. You are a security analyst. You have been approached by the HR director who is suspicious of a specific employee. There is suspicious documented behavior, but the HR director would like you to conduct a full digital investigation. What should this process start with?

A. The suspected employee takes a mandatory vacation.

B. The authorities are called to investigate.

C. A meeting is set up with the employee and their supervisor.

D. A complete backup is taken of the employee's hard drive.

65. An end user has called you to question a macro they are running in Excel. The macro runs, and their sent folder mail program fills up with email. What is most likely happening?

A. Macro virus

B. Micro virus

C. Trojan

D. Spyware

66. You are being interviewed for a system administrator's role. You are asked what the benefits are of using Group Policy. You list all but which of the following?

A. Applying security

B. Controlling a user's environment and settings

C. Not needing the host on the domain

D. Modifying the registry

67. You have evaluated different types of access controls. Which of these are easiest to bypass?

A. Fingerprint

B. Password

C. Iris scan

D. CAC card

68. You want to ensure that a terminated employee returns all the equipment and data that belongs to your company. What defense do you deploy?

A. Asset maintenance

B. Asset tracking

C. Destruction and disposal

D. Offsite backups

69. What is the purpose of creating information in images by changing the least significant bit in each byte?

   A. Copyright protection

   B. Certificates

   C. Manual signature

   D. Message digest

70. Which of the following can be used to encrypt disk drives, email messages, and files?

   A. L2TP

   B. PGP

   C. LDAP

   D. S/MIME

71. You need to use a protocol that is utilized to synchronize the time on your network devices, phones, and workstations so that your SIEM processes log files consistently. What protocol should be used in this situation?

   A. VoIP

   B. NMP

   C. NTP

   D. TFTP

72. You want to create an IT disaster recovery solution for your organization, and your budget is small. The MTD for your company is five days. Any downtime more than five days will harm the company. Which of the following is your BEST option?

   A. Hot site

   B. Warm site

   C. Cold site

   D. Reciprocal site

73. You only want hosts from the mycompany.net domain to access your company's intranet. Your firewall is configured with the implicit deny rule. What should you add first to your ACL?

   A. Deny all

   B. Allow all

   C. Deny mycompany.net

   D. Allow mycompany.net

74. You have several hard drives in a server that need to be wiped. Which of the following is the BEST data sanitation method that will prevent data remanence on solid-state drives if you want to use the drive again?

   A. Quick format

   B. Full format

    C. Degaussing

    D. Hardware-specific erasing

75. You want to configure a tool that will gather information about intruders and the attack methods they are using. It needs to have valuable information and be specifically designed to attract malicious activities. What type of tool would you build?

    A. Botnet

    B. Zombie master

    C. Honeypot

    D. Honeynet

76. The OKRs for the security team are to set up more in-depth defense layers in the organization. Which of these is considered proactive rather than reactive?

    A. Running Nessus/Nexpose

    B. Using attribution

    C. Adhering to compliance and regulations

    D. Implementing quality of service

77. Which of the following BEST describes the hardware layering model that uses system calls to communicate with the CPU?

    A. OSI

    B. Ring

    C. Lattice

    D. Biba

78. You want to monitor all traffic passing through a switch. Which of the following would be the BEST option to accomplish that task?

    A. IDS device

    B. DMZ network

    C. SPAN ports

    D. OSI model

79. You have event logging turned on so that you can build a chronological list of steps to provide documentary evidence of the sequence of activities that affect a specific operation or event. What is this called?

    A. Audit trail

    B. Vulnerability scanning

    C. Patch management

    D. Compliance and reporting

80. You work for a healthcare provider and would like your department to come up with alternatives for storing medical imaging files long term. Which of the following options would be the most likely to raise concerns?

    A. SSD on-site

    B. HDD off-site

    C. Data centers

    D. Offshoring

81. For a mission-critical server running vital web applications, you have built a RAID level, providing striping for speed and mirrors for redundancy. Which of these have you most likely created?

    A. RAID 0

    B. RAID 5

    C. RAID 6

    D. RAID 10

82. What technique would you want to implement to map hardware memory addresses to applications?

    A. Paging

    B. Swapping

    C. Virtual memory

    D. Indexing

83. You have been analyzing the backup schedule for a SQL database. Your CIO has said the company has an RPO of 48 hours. What is the minimum backup schedule for the SQL database?

    A. 24 hours

    B. 6 hours

    C. 48 hours

    D. 12 hours

84. You work as a DBA for a major credit card company. You want to create a rule that searches a large volume of data for credit card accounts that show transactions in multiple locations during a small time period. What is this called?

    A. Machine learning

    B. Artificial intelligence

    C. Data mining

    D. Data warehousing

85. You are monitoring security configuration changes over time. Which of these management tasks is most likely to involve taking a snapshot of a security configuration to compare to future configuration?

    A. Change management

    B. Baselining

C. Guidelines

D. Software updates

86. An employee has lost his private key. This key provides access to a database holding confidential health information. Without this key, this employee cannot perform his everyday tasks. As the security administrator, what do you do first?

A. Revoke the key

B. Reissue a key

C. Recover the key

D. Replace the key

87. Your CISO has tasked you with mitigating zero-day exploits. Which of these is the BEST way to protect your organization from zero-day issues?

A. Update and patch on a cycle.

B. Use vulnerability assessments.

C. Do not use software that has a zero-day vulnerability.

D. Harden a system for only the required functions.

88. You have been appointed the new data custodian. What will your new role entail?

A. Data protection

B. Data classification

C. Data backups

D. Data entry

89. You have received an RFQ for 100 new laptops for your company. You need to decide if you should purchase the additional warranty. The additional warranty will cost $5,500. You estimate that four laptops each quarter will fail, costing $1,000 each. What is the SLE?

A. $500

B. $1,000

C. $250

D. $4,000

90. You have architected your network to hide the source of a network connection. What device have you used?

A. Proxy firewall

B. Border router

C. Layer 3 switch

D. Bastion host

Appendix

Answers to Review Questions

Chapter 1: Risk Management

1. A.

A vulnerability is a weakness in system design, procedure, or code. It can be exploited for a threat to destroy, damage, or compromise an asset. A threat is the circumstance or likelihood of a vulnerability being exploited. The likelihood of the threat is the probability of occurrence or the odds that the event will actually occur.

2. A.

The BEST definition of a risk in IT is a vulnerability in your ecosystem and the high probability of compromise with a known active threat actor.

3. B.

A breach of physical security can be instigated by a trusted insider or an untested outsider. Intruders, vandals, and thieves remove sensitive information, destroy data, or physically damage or remove hardware.

4. C.

Virtual Machine Escape is an exploit where the attackers can run code on a VM that enables an OS to interface directly with the hypervisor. This type of exploit of a vulnerability can be a huge risk. The attacker could then have access to the host operating system and all other VMs running on that host.

5. D.

The procedures already exist; they just aren't being followed. Mandatory training is deemed essential for your organization to ensure its meeting policies, standards, guidelines, and procedures are being followed.

6. A.

The only answer that works is threat reports and a trend analysis. ISA, MSA, and RFI are business documents that come after management has approved the budget line item.

7. D.

If a manager can fire an employee, they must understand the repercussions and risks of a hostile termination, and the former employee's accounts need to be disabled. If the employee has access to sensitive accounts, those passwords must be changed immediately.

8. A.

The best strategy for patch management is to test all updates in a safe environment before deploying them to production.

9. C.

The contractual shifting of risk from one party to another is an example of transferring risk. Purchasing an insurance policy is an example of risk transference.

10. A.

The most important security controls of any device that will be mobile are the ability to wipe that device should it become lost or stolen, as well as the ability to control access to that same device. Encryption provides a layer of physical and digital security. The track record of the vendor in correcting security flaws plays an important part in the risk assessment.

11. D.

The vital new healthcare system being exploited might ruin the company. The healthcare industry is a prime target of cyberattacks and faces hostile cybersecurity issues that have financial and reputational impacts for hospitals, pharma, and other healthcare institutions.

12. A.

The first phase of any attack will be active and passive reconnaissance. Using social media capriciously will open your organization to knowledge that can be used against you. Some malicious actors will use job descriptions found on the Internet to determine what technology your organization is using to craft a social engineering attack.

13. C.

The act of encrypting nonvolatile memory will make the biggest impact and increase the work factor of anyone who attempts to break into the phone. A PIN would not be a strong enough deterrent, not when this phone has apps that connect to the corporate intranet. A complex password is better than a PIN.

14. A.

The best way to ensure that email is kept secure is to verify that all logins to the system are encrypted and that the cloud provider has signed both a nondisclosure agreement (NDA) and a service-level agreement (SLA) with your organization.

15. B.

The act of input validation is the proper testing of any input supplied by a user or application. It prevents invalid data from entering the database or information system.

16. D.

Organizations have evolved, and people are doing more work remotely and while traveling. The need for constant access and connection is real in a fast-moving organization. Security policies must evolve to enable usability, risk evaluations must be done, and all mobile devices must be encrypted.

17. A.

The business impact analysis (BIA) is a systematic process to determine the potential effects of failure to processes and systems that are critical to business operations, whether the interruption is a natural disaster, an accident, or an upgrade.

18. D.

The need for usability and productivity sometimes gets prioritized over security. Some problems with many organizations are the silos of people, the processes, and a lack of communication. This is an instance where risk management and strategies must communicate with those users and decision-makers and influence their behaviors. Not many outside of IT will know what the SDLC is, and it's our job to teach them.

19. A.

The strategy of risk mitigation enables an organization to prepare and lessen the effects of threats facing them. Risk mitigation requires you to take steps to reduce the negative effects of threats and disasters and to ensure business continuity.

20. A.

The ALE is the ARO × SLE. The SLE is EF × AV. In this question, you have two equations to solve. The SLE is 10% × $1,000, which is $100. The ALE is 2 × $100.

21. D.

The principle of least privilege is an important concept in IT security. It is the practice of limiting access rights for users to the bare minimum permission they need to get their job done. You may see this abbreviated as POLP.

22. A.

An incident is an event that could lead to loss of, or disruption to, an organization's operation, services, or functions. Incident management is a term describing the activities of an organization to identify, correct, and analyze to prevent a future occurrence.

23. D.

The role of a digital forensic analyst or a digital forensics examiner is to protect computer systems, recover files, document and analyze data, and provide reports and feedback or testify in court. This role also assists in the creation of documentation for best practices.

24. D.

The ISA is a contract between a telecommunication organization for the purpose of connecting networks and exchanging traffic. It is found detailed in NIST SP 800-47. This document regulates the security-relevant aspects of two entities operating under distinct authorities.

25. A.

IT outsourcing is a phrase used to describe the practice of seeking resources or subcontracting outside of an organizational structure for all or part of the IT function. Most large organizations outsource a portion of any given IT function.

26. C.

Networks can be built with a multitude of hardware and software. When you are attempting to join two disparate networks, many problems can occur with connectivity, latency, and vulnerabilities due to the two separate entities becoming one. Before making any technical changes, both networks should be examined and documented, and a risk analysis should be performed.

27. D.

The role-based access control is an approach to restricting system access to authorized users that supports the separation of duties and facilitates the administration of security for administrators and users.

28. A.

A line-by-line code review and simulation uncovers vulnerabilities and enables behavior to be watched in a safe location with minimized risk.

29. C.

A great many people view USBs as passive storage when, in fact, they are one of the best vehicles for transferring malware. Many penetration testers use a USB type of attack, knowing that end users do not understand the repercussions.

30. A.

The biggest issue with any type of BYOD is the loss of data (data exfiltration), and the best fix is to be able to remotely wipe the device should it become lost or stolen.

31. D.

The biggest threat to merging two disparate organizations is the security of both networks becoming one. With different physical assets, tactical standards, and operational procedures combining with a productivity objective, the danger of overlooking the security risks and vulnerabilities in the merged network is high.

32. B.

The best option for the CISO is to investigate whether the outside firm has a service-level agreement (SLA) with the subcontractor, which will protect the organization legally. If the contract does not exist, the CISO must insist that one be created, or he or she should exit the contract as soon as possible.

33. A.

All organizations have vulnerabilities. As the saying goes, the only completely secure asset is the one encased in concrete and buried 6 feet under. If you have no budget and minimal vulnerabilities that are protected under compensating controls, then accepting risk is the only option.

34. B.

The biggest security risk to adopting service-oriented architecture (SOA) is a lack of understanding, and because understanding is lacking, you have a lack of governance. It can also increase solution costs. You need all the applications to work together to save money and to not be in isolation from each other. SOA should be deployed where everyone, including customers, suppliers, and employees, is enabled as a partner in the system.

35. A.

With the evolution of adding wireless access (802.1x) to any network, you have increased capability due to its ease of use and movement. You also have an increased risk due to your data traveling over the airwaves, a higher total cost of ownership due to more security, an increased head count, and more assets being purchased and maintained on the network.

36. D.

Web-based meeting software for collaboration has become increasingly important to organizations. You cannot disallow it completely; otherwise, you lose competitiveness. Our job is to perform quantitative and qualitative software analysis and to choose the best, cheapest, and most secure software and configure it properly.

37. A.

The process of data classification is extremely important to making processes repeatable. Once you have a document classified as Secret or Classified, you know exactly how to treat it according to the CIA triad. Each organization is unique, so you must develop the right security controls based on risk analysis and decide which security controls to implement.

38. D.

The third-party organization should be contractually obligated to perform security activities noted in the business documents between the parties. Evidence of those contracts should be negotiated, investigated, and confirmed prior to beginning the project.

39. D.

The process of scraping data is also called data extraction. It is the process of importing data from a local file or a website, then extracting the data that is usually not human-readable but can be parsed to extract output intended to be human-readable.

40. C.

This is hardware. You can put an operating system on almost any hardware out there. When old equipment has maintenance issues, it is sometimes difficult to find the parts and perform regular updates to those assets.

41. D.

Gap analysis involves comparing the actual performance with desired or potential performance. If your organization does not properly use the resources available, it might be performing below its potential.

42. D.

White-box testing validates inner program logic and security functionality.

43. A.

The vulnerability time is the time from when the vulnerability is discovered and the vulnerability is patched. The vulnerability window is when an IT asset is most vulnerable. This window has become increasingly important because it is currently much larger than it was in the past. The cycle of creating malware based on known vulnerabilities keeps getting shorter and shorter.

44. B.

The standard security practice of mandatory vacations prevents fraud. While an employee is on vacation with no access to the system, software, or network, you have ample opportunity to perform an audit. You should have a separation of duties set in place where one person writes the check and another signs the check.

45. D.

Security awareness training is vital to any customer-facing organization because 80–85 percent of most compromises today begin with some form of social engineering. Unfortunately, it's usually the first thing cut from the IT budget.

46. A.

The first step of integrating businesses/partnerships is to develop an interconnection agreement and then perform a qualitative and quantitative risk assessment. You must set your goals and measure where you are from a security vantage point.

47. A.

The first stage of any interaction with a third party is an RFI. After you receive the information, you can then ask for a quote (RFQ) so that you know approximately how much the service/asset will cost. After you've decided on a vendor, you can formally ask them for a request for proposal (RFP), which should supply a firm cost, an SLA, and other requirements.

48. D.

Terminal servers enable businesses to centrally manage host applications, enabling access to company resources from anywhere and any device. Applications are installed once and regularly updated.

49. A.

Training and policy enforcement are key ways to prevent social engineering attacks. Many end users are not aware of the risks involved. Training raises awareness and should provide clear instructions for dealing with and reporting suspicious activity, including to whom to forward the suspected email.

50. C.

The best way to control dumpster diving is to control what leaves the facility by way of disposal and what form that takes. Larger enterprise organizations will hire third-party organizations for their shredding, while some organizations will create policy based on what type of document has been manufactured. Either way, this must be included in your policies and procedures, communicated to staff, and periodically audited.

51. A.

Using qualitative methods of assessing means you gather information that cannot be readily translated into numbers. Often, feelings or actions can affect a situation and do not require technical expertise.

52. D.

Due diligence is verifying that those responsible are doing the right thing. Due care is acting responsibly. It is creating policies, procedures, and guidelines to protect information or assets in a way that is reasonable.

53. A.

The five steps in risk assessment are as follows: (1) Identify hazards or anything that can do harm to the health and safety of assets, including people. (2) Decide what the vulnerabilities are and who/what could be harmed. (3) Assess the threat landscape and take action after you have recorded the impact of that exposure to the organization. (4) Make a record of the findings. (5) Review the risk assessment.

54. D.

Risk analysis involves looking at how objectives might change due to the impact of an event or incident. Once a risk is identified, it is analyzed both qualitatively and quantitatively so that the proper steps can be taken to mitigate them. These steps are documented in procedure controls and will be implemented as soon as an incident occurs.

55. C.

The BIA that your team is working on is a process that enables you to identify critical functions within your business and to predict what the end results of a disruption will be. It enables you to gather information needed to develop recovery options and to limit the potential loss.

56. A.

A hurricane is a natural disaster that should be accounted for in a business impact analysis (BIA) document. A BIA should provide a plan for resuming operations after a disaster and identify which events could impact the organization's operations.

57. C.

Threat and risk assessments are the best way to identify the risks this company is facing. Pentesting will come after the controls are in place.

58. A.

Link encryption is a way to secure your data by encrypting the information at the data link layer as it's transmitted between two points.

59. C.

The most important aspect of vulnerability management processes is to understand assessing what risks exist to your organization and who/what threatens to use your vulnerabilities against you. Risk = Threat × Vulnerability.

60. C.

The replacement cost is the actual cost to replace an asset and to restore to its previous state. It is not the cash value of the asset. The difference between replacement cost and cash value is the deduction taken for depreciation. Both are based on the cost today to replace the damaged asset.

61. B.

If Alice encrypts her database, she is using an algorithm to transform readable data into unreadable data. Without knowing the key or algorithm used, you cannot reverse engineer the data. The purpose of this is to protect date from theft, malicious intent, or misuse.

62. B.

When the cost of controls is more than the benefits gained by implementing a response, then the best course of action is risk acceptance for a certain period, and then the risk is reevaluated.

63. C.

The threat in this scenario is the hacker/hacktivist or nation-state hacker who wants to use this third-party vendor as a gateway into your organization. Vetting a third-party organization is mission critical if that vendor is going to be working with any type of sensitive data or project.

64. B.

If your recovery point objective is nine hours and the last available copy of backup is at midnight, you have until 9 A.M. to get that network backup server up and running again before it exceeds the RPO.

65. A.

The recovery time objective (RTO) is the duration of time that can pass before a disruption begins to affect the flow of normal business operations. It can include the time for trying to fix the problem even if it doesn't work, the actual recovery itself, testing the fix, and communicating to others.

66. B.

The data owner has administrative control over the data and is accountable for who has access. A data custodian has technical control of that data.

67. B.

A data custodian has technical control of data. The role is focused on data at rest and data in transit, not what the data is.

68. B.

When the decision is made to outsource any IT function, process, or system, there is a risk to operations and process flows, confidentiality, continuity, and compliance. You cannot use the excuse, "It wasn't me." Regulators and compliance auditors will still hold your organization accountable for performing the correct level of due diligence to confirm that a third-party service has the right people, processes, and technology in place to support your business needs.

69. D.

In digital or cyber forensics, no matter what action has been taken and what the implied burden of proof is, you must treat the incident as if a crime has been committed. If the process is broken, the risk of challenging or diminishing the value of the evidence could make it inadmissible and reduce its value to the company. The IRT should have well-documented policies and procedures in place and have chain-of-custody rules.

70. C.

The first step to managing/deleting old data is to decide how long it must be kept. Data retention is not just about sensitive data. It is also about the different types of records and how those records get securely and permanently deleted.

71. B.

General Data Protection Regulation (GDPR) is a regulation in EU law on data protection and privacy for all citizens of the European Union and the European Economic Area. Adopted in April 2016, GDPR introduced requirements for data processors, controllers, and custodians ensuring they gain explicit consent from individuals whose data is being used for specific purposes. In addition, it granted the right to individuals to request detailed information and request that their data be deleted.

72. C.

An interconnection security agreement (ISA) specifically identifies the technical requirements for secure connections and ensures that the data is encrypted properly. A BPA is a business partnership agreement, and an MOU is a memorandum of understanding between two parties that need to work together. An NDA is a nondisclosure agreement or confidentiality agreement (CA) that is signed by two parties and outlines confidential material, knowledge, or information that the parties need to share with each other.

73. A.

Mobile devices represent the weakest security link. Every mobile device represents a potential vector of compromise by hackers. Even with passcodes, facial recognition, thumbprint scanners, and remote wipe capabilities, BYOD remains a vulnerability for many organizations.

74. A.

A master service agreement (MSA) provides a strong foundation for future business. It typically specifies payment terms, warranties, geographic location, and intellectual property ownership.

75. B.

Training is the first line of defense against security risks. You cannot protect what you don't know exists. You will need training for compliance with regulatory requirements as well as organizational objectives. Awareness is achieved through cultural attitudes combined with training.

76. D.

Disgruntled employees can hide activity so that employers do not know how bad the damage is. Funds, trade secrets, intellectual property, and even access to your entire IT infrastructure can all be put in jeopardy by an unhappy employee.

77. D.

The CIA triad principle is a security model that stands for confidentiality, integrity, and availability. All three should be guaranteed in any type of secure environment. Confidentiality is the ability to hide information. Integrity ensures that the information is accurate. Availability ensures that the information is readily accessible, and authenticity is needed for proof of origin. Cryptography and encryption are used to ensure data remains secure during transit, remains unchanged, and can be used to prove who sent it. Availability is the only one not affected by encryption.

78. D.

A keylogger, by its very nature, is meant to steal the keystrokes that the victim makes on the keyboard. Using this information, the attacker can replay websites/usernames/passwords typed in by the victim.

79. D.

Working with storage-attached networks, multipathing is a technique that enables you to build different paths to transfer data between the asset and the storage device. For example, you can have two HBAs feeding one ESXi host. If one route fails, the data can be routed through another, providing availability.

80. D.

The question said nothing about speed. Speed is good. Actually, speed is great, but still, the question targets availability. To focus on availability, create and enforce security policies appropriately, create a standard image and configuration for hardening, and have a backup.

81. C.

Virtualization creates an abstract computing platform. Many servers can be replaced by one larger physical server to decrease the need for hardware. Many hosts enable the execution of complete operating systems, and access can be restricted for security depending on the hardware access policy created by the host. In this scenario, the most secure option with a focus on confidentiality would be to assign virtual hosts to the client and physically partition storage. If confidentiality is in the question, look for encryption in the answer.

82. A.

A computer cluster is a set of connected computers that work together so they can be viewed as a single system. They are created to improve performance and availability while being cost effective.

83. A.

Visibility into the data through the traffic on these virtual machines can impact confidentiality as well as compliance issues, such as PCI for financial data and HIPAA for patient data.

84. B.

The data might not be in the same format and unable to be restored to a different application.

85. D.

Any type of transition to new software or hardware should be projectized so that processes roll out smoothly. Plans for decommissioning the existing OS, implementing testing, and verifying compliance with applicable regulations are the best life cycle. In addition, with any type of change or upgrade, be sure to have a rollback process just in case the project fails.

86. C.

HBA is a host bus adapter. It is a hardware device, like a circuit board, that provides connectivity between a server and storage-attached network used to improve performance. LUN storage is important to the configuration. An LUN is a unique identifier given to separate devices so they can be accessed in a storage disk array.

87. A.

Mean time between failures = Total uptime/number of breakdowns

Mean time to repair = Total downtime/number of breakdowns

Availability of device = MTBF/MTBF + MTTR

88. A.

The best answer is data quality procedures, verification and validation, adherence to agreed-upon data management, and an ongoing data audit to monitor the use and the integrity of existing data.

89. D.

The goal of the Bell–LaPadula confidentiality model is to keep secret data secret and share secret data when it is allowed to be shared.

90. C.

The Biba model is a state transition system for computer security. Data is grouped into ordered levels of integrity. The model was created so that subjects cannot corrupt the data. Invocation properties mean that a process from below cannot request a higher access. It can only work with the same or lower levels. (Think of it as the inverse of Bell–LaPadula, which deals with security and people.)

91. C.

The golden rule of forensics is never touch, change, or alter anything until it is documented, identified, measured, and photographed. An image is a complete image of all the contents of a storage device. A bit stream copy of an image copies all areas of a storage device. When documenting for an incident, you need to list the software/hardware used, its source and destination name, the start/end timestamp, and hashed values.

92. A.

RAID is for redundancy; the data's level of sensitivity is classified based on importance, which is correlated to security measures and who has access; and load balancers determine which server in a pool is available and route requests to that server.

93. B.

Digital signatures are a standard element of most cryptographic standards and are used to verify that a message was sent by a known sender and not altered in transmission. Encryption converts information or data into code to prevent unauthorized access. Hashes are one-way algorithms that take a variable value and create a fixed output value, which can prove that something is the same as something else without actually revealing the original value.

94. C.

Implementing controls for confidentiality ensures that data remains private. Steganography can hide messages in pictures, music, or videos. Access control lists (ACLs) are tables that tell who has permission to see an object or directory, and vulnerability management refers to finding weaknesses in software to deal with any associated confidentiality risks.

95. A.

A DoS or DDoS attack occurs when legitimate users are unable to use devices or network resources. It affects availability.

96. A.

Redundancy = availability. There are several different types of RAID. The most popular ones are RAID 0 (striping) for speed, RAID 1 (mirroring) for redundancy, and RAID 5 (parity) for error correction. You can combine RAID 0 and 1, or RAID 1 and 0, in different ways to accomplish speed and redundancy.

97. D.

A hot site is fully functional the moment disaster strikes and is ready to go at a moment's notice. A cold site has infrastructure only, perhaps four walls and HVAC. A warm site is between the two—a building with HVAC, running water, and power, and after a backup, these assets are ready to be networked and have the business up and running in a reasonable amount of time. A mobile site is an alternative site, such as an RV, that can travel in case of an emergency.

98. D.

Because time is important, as a project manager, you need to estimate how long the merge will take and then look at ROI—how much to sustain and how much to change. Involve the stakeholders in the decision-making process.

99. D.

Think strategy! You need to test for resilience and reliability of the rebuilt site before you restore any mission-critical function. The financial department and communication would be restored only after you know the foundation is good.

100. D.

The initiation of work is not dependent on time. Health and human life are the primary concerns, and you should not put that type of risk on your employees. You may return only when it has been deemed safe to do so.

101. A.

Establishing a process for off-site backups is most important. If you don't have access to your company's data, the rest of these options, while important, mean nothing.

102. D.

A BIA is when you examine elements that are business processes, while risk analysis looks at the assets themselves.

103. C.

Gap analysis is the comparison of performance, actual versus potential. It helps to identify areas for improvement and empowers an organization to quickly diagnose a problem.

104. A.

Quantitative analysis is based on numbers and calculations, whereas qualitative research is based on written descriptions. Both should be part of a BIA. If they are not included, you may not have a true picture on which to base your decisions.

105. D.

A BIA does not recommend recovery methods and responses, which take place after you have finished the BIA. It includes potential financial losses, identifies critical support areas, and defines all business units.

106. B.

With an RTO (recovery time objective) of 36 hours after an interruption, you can use a warm site to provide recovery within the stated time period and with the most reasonable cost. A cold site would take much longer to build, and a hot site would offer instant recovery but is extremely expensive to maintain with all the administration and security costs.

107. A.

Senior management will initiate the BCP in the case of a disaster or emergency. The recovery team is responsible for performing the actual steps in the BCP. Security personnel may have a role in the BCP, but they will be informed by management or the recovery team.

108. B.

A BCP and DRP are never complete. They are updated and improved over time. Management oversees a single fully integrated plan, which needs approval and testing, and may consist of multiple subplans.

109. A.

Backups provide protection for availability. It will protect your company from data loss as well as data corruption. If the primary copy is damaged, it can be replaced when there is another copy of a file.

110. C.

A structured walk-through is a paper-only test where a group discusses the plan but takes no actions in the real world. You may also hear it called a round-table exercise or a dry run. Simulation, parallel, and full interruption tests are all real-world tests.

111. C.

The absolute way to know whether a DRP test works is to perform a full interrupt test. You must get senior management's approval. Only through complete real-world implementation will you know if the plan is truly verified. The problem with a real-world full interrupt test is that it can be very costly and interrupt normal business operations if the test fails. Operations are shut down at the primary site and shifted into recovery mode.

112. A.

The best thing to do in this scenario is to hold awareness sessions for everyone. Perhaps employees need reminding of what is appropriate. New awareness programs and training should reduce this activity. Reducing permissions should happen only after retraining and auditing have no impact other than to inform you about the level of transgression. Termination should happen only after repeated attempts to train staff have occurred.

113. D.

Social engineering is malicious activity where data is disclosed by accident. It is typically performed by an attacker outside of the organization. The goal is to get the victim to disclose confidential or sensitive information. Espionage, fraud, and embezzlement are all malicious, where the attacker is internal and commits these crimes on purpose.

114. B.

User training and policy enforcement are critical to preventing social engineering attacks. Technical countermeasures can prevent automated attacks. Social engineering attacks human nature.

115. C.

Flashcards and USBs pose a security threat because they can store data, period. The size of the drive does not matter. They are small, cheap, and easy to use, and they can be connected to a system with very little possibility of detection. They can also be infected with malware so that when they are inserted, the malware spreads, creating problems for an organization.

116. C.

An IDS is used to protect against intrusion from an outside untrusted network into an internal trusted network. It can be deployed to watch for traffic that successfully circumvented the firewall, as well as for activity originating from inside the trusted network.

117. D.

The most common disadvantage to using a signature-based IDS is false positives, which can happen when the IDS identifies legitimate traffic as an attack. IDS signatures are updated by the IDS vendor in response to vulnerabilities in the wild. If you have a poorly written signature, it can produce both false positives and false negatives. False negatives occur when the signature fails to correctly identify malicious activity.

118. B.

Disconnecting the intruder is the best response if confidentiality is the importance. Allowing any more time to the intruder might enable them to pivot deeper into the network. Delaying, auditing, or monitoring the intruder is the correct response if you are going to prosecute the intruder.

119. A.

The first step after an intrusion is to document. Creating backups of logs will ensure that investigators have information about the problem. If you are unable to discover the attacker's identity, it might show other important details. After you secure the audit trail, the other answers are options.

120. A.

Account lockout is not password management. Account lockout is access management.

121. C.

Code escrow is a storage facility hosted by a trusted third party that will ensure you have access to the code even if they go out of business.

122. D.

Termination is not easy for the employer or the employee. When an employee is fired, often they are taken by HR into an exit interview, reminded of their NDA, and escorted from the premises. You must disable their network access and accounts and change the passwords to any device to which they might have had access. For example, if this employee had access to the vulnerability management program that you scan with credentials, that employee may have access to every single device on your network. These other options give that employee the ability to disrupt or cause damage to your network.

123. D.

With written job descriptions, all responsibilities should be clearly defined.

124. D.

The next best step, if you don't want to lose this employee and their contributions to the company, is to limit what they can do. Reduce the risky behavior by removing their ability to perform the associated actions. For example, if you don't want administrators clicking links in emails, you can remove URLs in emails while signed into an administrator's account.

125. A.

Security-related patches and upgrades should be applied as quickly as possible after testing on a system in a sandbox or not in production. Waiting until after you have a problem is not advantageous, and neither is having other organizations test the patch first. No two networks are identically built.

126. D.

Least privilege is assigning permissions so that users can access only those resources required to do their job. Job rotation, need to know, and separation of duties are also important to security. Job rotation avoids single points of failure, need to know promotes confidentiality, and separation of duties gives clear and direct roles to employees.

127. D.

Creating an audit trail is vital. Security policy often specifies which data should be collected, how it should be stored, and how long it will be kept. An audit trail is often used to find unauthorized activity on a network.

128. B.

Black-hat hackers have extensive knowledge about breaking into systems, which is usually for financial gain. White-hat hackers use their powers for good. Also known as ethical hackers, they use the same methods as the bad guys but get permission first. Gray-hat hackers are a combination of both. They may look for vulnerabilities in your environment but request a small fee to tell you what to fix. Yes, there are blue-hat hackers. A blue-hat hacker is someone who typically tests systems before they launch, looking for bugs.

129. B.

If you only have a single primary firewall, you have a single point of failure (SPoF), which could be catastrophic to an HA network. If all traffic must pass through a single point and it fails, no communication can happen. Clustered servers, high-speed redundant links, and switched networks all support HA by providing performance and reliability.

130. B.

The best security design methodology is to work on identifying mission-critical assets and protecting assets out, then working outwardly from there. Outside in is the opposite of assets out.

131. B.

A standard is a kind of security policy that defines how to remain in compliance with best practices and industry standards. Procedures are the step-by-step instructions on how to implement those best practices. Guidelines are used to create the procedures. Policies are at the highest level and describe the mission and goals. Policies are usually nonspecific and goal-oriented.

132. A.

You want to protect your endpoints from malware, viruses, and spyware. A host-based firewall will prevent malicious traffic, where the IDS will only report there is an intrusion. All TFA is MFA, but not all MFA is TFA. Multifactor authentication grants a user access after presenting several separate pieces of evidence that belong to different categories (including something you are, something you know, or something you have). TFA is two pieces of evidence.

133. A.

An annualized rate of occurrence (ARO) is the average number of times that something specific is likely to be realized in a year. The annualized loss expectancy is calculated by multiplying the ARO by the single loss expectancy (SLE), which is the estimated per-year loss. Simply put, ALE = ARO × SLE.

134. C.

The focus of ALE calculations is to prioritize countermeasures. A countermeasure is an action taken to counteract a danger or threat. The asset-risk pair with the largest ALE should be dealt with first.

135. A.

The valid equation in this list is ALE = ARO × EF × AV. Another valid ALE formula is ARO × SLE. The SLE is EF × AV.

136. A.

The primary purpose of change control is to prevent unmanaged change. All changes need to be managed and approved. Unmanaged change can introduce reduction in security.

137. A.

A rollback is a change-control process that makes it possible to roll back any change that has a negative effect.

138. A.

If the administrator received approval, perhaps the technical catastrophe could have been avoided with a more senior administrator's wisdom. Gaining approval is the first step in managing a needed change. Once approved, testing can be performed. Implementation, deployment, and documentation should follow after testing.

139. C.

The primary purpose of data classification is to define necessary security protection. Data classification is based on the object's value rather than the opposite—being used to assign value. Data classification doesn't control user access. User classification or clearance controls user access.

140. D.

When users are made aware that their activities can be audited, it is a preventative control. It may help them take more thoughtful actions. Auditing is a detective control when logs are reviewed.

141. D.

Senior management is always responsible for security within an organization. They are responsible for following the recommendations of the auditor.

142. A.

Accreditation is the action of officially recognizing a particular security status is qualified to perform a certain function. If a vulnerability is found during accreditation, the vulnerability must be fixed and the process started over from the beginning.

143. B.

Due care is acting responsible. Due diligence is verifying those actions are sufficient. When an organization shows due care, it means they took every reasonable precaution to protect their assets and environment. If a breach occurs, the organization is not held negligent for losses but can still be held liable.

144. A.

An AAR is a review process that ensures learning and improved performance. It analyzes what happened, why it happened, and how it can be done better.

145. A.

Bluetooth is a PAN that enables you to connect and even share data with assets that are in a close physical range. Risks include bluejacking, which is sending a text message to other Bluetooth users. Bluebugging is using someone else's phone to place calls or send texts without them knowing.

146. A.

When providing choices to users, a meeting should be held to weigh the convenience of a security process against the level of security that is required to protect the asset. Ideas can vary from person to person. You should meet with all stakeholders to both educate them and learn from them what system would be best in this scenario.

147. D.

A list of root passwords is not a requirement. A vulnerability assessment is the testing of systems and access controls for weaknesses.

148. D.

With the amount of information online today, data mining is a threat that involves taking large amounts of that information for aggregation. An attacker can use this technique to find patterns on how you conduct business and find critical times when systems are most vulnerable.

149. B.

ARO × SLE = ALE, or 12 × $1,500 = $18,000. If the computers are not protected, the company can lose $18,000 a year. You recommend mitigating the risk by purchasing the antivirus tool.

150. C.

To quantitatively evaluate risk, you must assess threat, vulnerability, and impact. The equation is Risk = Threat × Vulnerability × Impact. In our scenario, the answer is 4 × 2 × 6 = 48.

151. B.

Security domains are groupings where subjects and objects have the same security requirements. It is kept separate from other networks.

152. B.

Electronic vaulting will enable you to transmit bulk data to an off-site data backup storage facility. You can choose to back up weekly, hourly, or daily. If a server fails, you can restore data quickly, but because the information is sent over the Internet, it should be encrypted.

153. B.

The MTTR is calculated by using the total maintenance time as the numerator and the total number of repairs as the denominator. The 3 hours divided by the two times it went down gives you an MTTR of 1.5.

154. A.

Code escrow protects you from the threat of a vendor going out of business. Source code escrow is the deposit of source code of software with a third party.

155. C.

Every KPI has a measure, a target that matches your measure, and a time period, as well as a clearly defined data source so you know how each is being measured and tracked. Examples of KPI would be growth in revenue, percentage of market share, or time to market.

156. A.

KRI identification measures how risky an activity is. To identify a KRI, you need to identify existing metrics, assess gaps, establish a control environment, and track changes in the risk profile.

157. A.

Most technical project managers know how important it is to capture lessons learned. The documentation reflects both the good and bad experiences of a project. It also provides future project teams with information that can make them more effective and efficient.

Chapter 2: Enterprise Security Architecture

1. D.

Protocol decoding IDP tools can reassemble packets and look at higher-layer activity like protocols that operate at the application layer.

2. B.

A network-based intrusion detection system (NIDS) is a system used to detect intrusions traversing the network and alert on those intrusions. The alerts can come in various forms, including email and text messages.

3. A.

A host-based intrusion prevention system (HIPS) is a system used to detect intrusions on a host system like a server and stop those intrusions from compromising a system. An HIPS can also alert personnel of the intrusion detected.

4. B.

A unified threat management (UTM) system is a single device that provides multiple security functions including antivirus protection, antispyware, a firewall, and an IDP. A concern with using a UTM is that it could become a single point of failure.

5. D.

Inline network encryptors (INEs) are used in pairs and provide a means of encrypting data between two networks.

6. A.

Network access control (NAC) is a technology that enables IT staff to manage what devices can connect to a network. There are various means of authenticating a device via NAC, including using the device's MAC address and loading NAC software on the device.

7. D.

A security information and event management (SIEM) system is used to collect logs from various devices on a network and to analyze those logs, looking for security issues. Because a SIEM can review logs from various devices, it gets a holistic view of actions taking place over the network, as opposed to a single appliance analyzing only the traffic flowing through it.

8. A.

The content addressable memory (CAM) table is the table on a switch used to store MAC addresses. The CAM table maps MAC addresses to physical switch ports and is used in the forwarding of Ethernet frames from one port to another.

9. A.

Switches examine the destination MAC address of a frame entering a switch port and compare it to the MAC address and port number assignments in the CAM table. If a match is found, the frame is forwarded out of the assigned port. If a match is not found, the frame is forwarded out of all ports except the port it came in on.

10. D.

Switches use Media Access Control (MAC) addresses to forward frames. A MAC address is 48 bits in length and consists of two parts: the organizationally unique identifier (OUI) that uniquely identifies the manufacturer of the network interface card (NIC) the MAC is assigned to and the device ID or vendor-assigned number created by the NIC manufacturer.

11. C.

The predominant routable protocol used today is IP. Open Shortest Path First (OSPF) and Routing Information Protocol (RIP) are examples of routing protocols. Frames and segments are not routable or routing protocols.

12. A.

A packet filter firewall will inspect packets traversing the network and allow for the control of traffic based on source and destination IP, source and destination port, and the protocol utilized for communication.

13. B.

A demilitarized zone (DMZ) is a type of screened subnet. It is considered the public-facing part of a network because the public (i.e., customers) can reach it.

14. D.

A Web Application Firewall (WAF) is used to inspect OSI Layer 7 data for malicious activity. HTTP/HTTPS/SOAP are all web application protocols that operate at OSI Layer 7. Screened host firewalls and packet filter firewalls don't inspect OSI Layer 7 data. A DMZ is a type of screened subnet that permits external users access to a part of a private network.

15. A.

A proxy can be thought of as a middleman, where all traffic flows from a host through the proxy and out to the rest of the network or the Internet. Because the traffic flows through the proxy, the proxy can inspect the data for malicious activities. It can also help conserve bandwidth by caching data that has been requested and serving it to other users when needed.

16. D.

If a DDoS attack is launched against a server, the server may not be able to withstand the attack if the server resources are not adequate. However, if a DDoS is launched against a server that is part of a server farm with load-balancing technology implemented in it, the attack can be distributed across multiple servers, lessening the impact of the attack on any one server.

17. D.

A hardware security module (HSM) is a hardware device designed specifically to manage cryptographic keys. By performing this process in hardware as opposed to software, the process is faster. Encrypted File System (EFS) and TrueCrypt are software-based encryption technologies. Peripheral Component Interconnect (PCI) is a method of providing expansion slots in a computer.

18. C.

A microSD HSM provides hardware security module functionality on a microSD card. The microSD HSM is lightweight and mobile. An Encrypted File System (EFS) is a system used on devices for encryption purposes, not key management. A Trusted Platform Module (TPM) is a chip that is installed on a computer's motherboard for key management purposes. NTFS is a Microsoft file system.

19. B.

A buffer overflow occurs when a program writes more data to a buffer than is expected. An attacker can take advantage of this situation by injecting their own malicious code or variables into the buffer. Because these commands don't check buffer size, they make a program susceptible to buffer overflow attacks.

20. D.

A passive vulnerability scanner can intercept network traffic and analyze its content for malicious activity while not interfering with the host computer. A system scanner and application scanner are both active vulnerability scanners that do interact with a host computer and, because they do so, could cause a host computer to crash.

21. A.

Database activity monitors (DAMs) monitor databases and analyze the type of activity occurring on them. A DAM is like a SIEM, except that the DAM is concerned specifically with databases, where a SIEM is concerned with various networked devices.

22. B.

A full mesh network configuration provides for maximum redundancy in a network with all the network devices, in this case, in the core connected to each other. If one device fails, network traffic can always find another path to its destination.

23. A.

The 802.1x standard from IEEE provides for port-based network access control (NAC). It provides a means of authenticating devices that attempt to connect to the network. Based on authentication, the Ethernet port can be placed in the appropriate VLAN for that device. If a device does not authenticate, the port could be placed into a quarantined VLAN or configured for Internet access only.

24. A.

A VPN using SSL/TLS via a web browser is likely the best solution because it provides secure communication with the corporate office and ease of use since it utilizes a web browser interface.

25. C.

A VPN using IPSec in tunnel mode could be established via a border router or VPN appliance that has both LAN and Internet access. This solution is transparent to end users and does not require additional software on the host computers. Data is not secure while traversing each office's LAN. VPN via IPSec in transport mode is typically used to encrypt data from one computer to another and requires software installation on the host computers. VPN via SSL/TLS using a web browser is better suited for remote users. IPv4, unlike IPv6, does not include IPSec and is inherently unsecure.

26. D.

Secure Shell (SSH) encrypts the data being sent to and from the router, ensuring that if an attacker captures the traffic, the attacker cannot read it. The other protocols send traffic in clear text that can be read if captured.

27. D.

VLAN hopping is an attack where the attacker changes the VLAN tag of a frame so that the attacker's frame is able to access a different VLAN. To launch this attack, an attacker must establish a trunk link between the target switch port and the attacker's system. If the switch port is configured either as a static trunk port or has Dynamic Trunking Protocol (DTP) enabled on the port, a trunk link can be established. To prevent this, ensure that the Ethernet ports are configured as access ports only. DPT is a misspelling of DTP.

28. C.

A false positive alert is an alert generated but is not associated with a true attack. Having tumbleweeds hit your fence and trigger an alert is an example of a false positive alert. A true positive is an alert triggered from an attack. A true negative is no alert triggered because no attack occurred. A false negative is an attack happening with no alert triggered.

29. B.

Data loss prevention systems, also called data loss protection systems, are designed to examine data as it moves off the host system looking for unauthorized transfers. Examples of unauthorized transfers are moving data to a cloud provider, via USB, via email, etc. Network-based IDS and IPS look for malicious network-based activities. A firewall is used to filter content flowing through the unit.

30. A.

In these options, Remote Desktop Protocol (RDP) is the only protocol. It is a protocol that can be used to access a Windows system remotely via a network connection and can provide the user with a graphical interface of the desktop. Virtual Network Computing (VNC) uses the Remote Frame Buffer (RFB) protocol to enable a desktop to be viewed and controlled over a network connection. Virtual Desktop Infrastructure (VDI) is a remote desktop-hosting environment where a desktop image is hosted on a virtual machine and accessed remotely over a network. Data loss prevention is the process of detecting and preventing data exfiltration from the data owner's system.

31. B.

Virtual Network Computing (VNC) uses the Remote Frame Buffer (RFB) protocol to enable a host desktop to be viewed and controlled over a network connection. Because it is a program that runs within the operating system, it is not possible to use VNC to access the BIOS of the host as it boots up nor is it available if the OS experiences a critical failure and crashes, showing the blue screen of death.

32. A.

The first rule in a firewall list to match the packet is processed, and no further processing through the rules occurs. Therefore, rules 3, 4, and 5, as well as the implicit deny at the end of the list, are not evaluated as the packet matched rule 2 and was permitted through the firewall.

33. D.

Deep packet inspection is the process of inspecting the payload of a packet for malicious content. Other packet inspection techniques only check the header information for signs of malicious activity.

34. D.

The command enables frames with a source MAC address of 00:0E:08:34:7C:9B to pass. If a frame is received on the port with a MAC address other than 00:0E:08:34:7C:9B, the port is shut down. Shutdown is the default violation action.

35. B.

The proper way to bring a switch port out of the error-disabled state is to go to the interface and issue the shutdown and then no shutdown commands.

36. B.

To recognize a distributed denial-of-service (DDoS) attack, you must understand the normal traffic patterns of an organization. If you can't tell what your normal traffic pattern looks like, you can't identify what the attack traffic pattern looks like.

37. B.

A virtual desktop infrastructure (VDI) hosts desktop images on a server within a virtual machine and is accessed over the network via a desktop client. A virtual private network (VPN) is a way of establishing a secure link between two devices. Virtual Network Computing (VNC) is a graphical desktop-sharing system. Remote Desktop Protocol is a Microsoft proprietary protocol used to provide a graphical desktop-sharing system.

38. C.

A reverse proxy performs the function mentioned in the question. Because traffic intended for the servers goes through the reverse proxy, it can provide filtering of malicious traffic destined for the servers. A proxy sits in front of clients, receiving their requests and forwarding them on to the destination. Replies associated with these requests are also forwarded through the proxy to the clients. A basic firewall filters traffic based on packet header information. A network-based intrusion detection system (NIDS) examines traffic, looking for malicious content.

39. A.

A remotely triggered black hole is a technique where a triggering device (i.e., router) can recognize DDoS traffic and send out a routing update to other network routers, thus setting up a black hole to drop traffic. Transport security involves securing data as it traverses a network. Trunking security involves securing trunk links used to propagate VLAN traffic. Port security is concerned with a mechanism to secure ports on an Ethernet switch.

40. C.

By subdividing the network, you create an additional routing layer for messages. This additional layer can increase security or allow each subnet to be assigned to individual network administrators. Ease of troubleshooting and bandwidth utilization are other benefits as well as customizing rules between subnetworks.

41. D.

Software-defined networking (SDN) divides the function of a network device like a router or switch into planes. The control plane consists of the programmable (i.e., controlled) function of the network device. This function is separated from the network device and placed on a controller. The data plane consists of the core function of the networking device. In the case of a router, the data plane is concerned with the forwarding of data. The data plane remains on the router. The control plane communicates with the data plane to perform the overall function of the router.

42. B.

Unfortunately, most SCADA systems have little, if any, securing mechanisms in place. Therefore, two ways to secure these systems is, first, to ensure that the systems have up-to-date firmware loaded. Second, implement defense in depth whereby multiple security devices are placed in front of the SCADA systems so that they can filter out malicious content. Most SCADA systems don't support the installation of software on the systems like HIDS and antivirus products.

43. A.

Shodan is a website that crawls the Internet looking for publicly accessible IoT devices. Open Web Application Security Project is an organization concerned primarily with the security of web applications. VirusTotal is a website where you can upload files and have them checked for viruses from various antivirus vendors. Maltego is a program, not a website, that performs data mining.

44. A.

The Mirai botnet known for a massive DDoS attack in 2016 was comprised primarily of Internet of Things (IoT) devices.

45. D.

The majority of IoT devices are not developed with security in mind. Many of these devices send data over the network in clear text, use hard-coded passwords that are easily found, and have firmware that is not updated to address known vulnerabilities.

46. B.

Network access control (NAC) not only can authenticate network devices but can ensure the enforcement of corporate policies governing these devices. If a system is not in compliance with the corporate policy, the device can be quarantined until such time when the policy failures are remediated.

47. C.

The software installed on devices that will connect to the network using NAC is called an agent.

48. B.

When NAC is used but an agent is not installed on the devices, it is referred to as an agentless configuration. When using agentless NAC, the policy enforcement component is integrated into an authentication system like Windows Active Directory. The enforcement of policies is performed when the device logs on or off the network.

49. C.

Of all the answers available, only the IP address range 172.32.0.0/16 is a valid range of source IP addresses for traffic entering from the Internet. The other IP addresses are special addresses that cannot be routed over the Internet. Responses from this traffic cannot be returned to its sender and must be dropped at the border router. Because the sender can't be reached, it is a sign of malicious activity. The majority of IP traffic filtering should be performed by a firewall, but limited filtering can be performed by a router as long as the filtering doesn't adversely affect the routing function of the router.

50. A.

When changing or adding firewall rules, all rules should be tested with matching traffic. It is possible that the rule is not configured properly or that there is a contradicting rule higher up the firewall rule list that could negate the new rule. Only by testing all the rules on the firewall can the validity of the rules be verified.

51. B.

Standard versions of Linux use a discretionary access control (DAC) system that enables the creator of files to control the permissions of those files. Security-Enhanced Linux (SELinux) is a version of Linux that uses mandatory access control (MAC) where a security policy dictates the permissions associated with a file.

52. B.

SEAndroid, later renamed SEforAndroid, was an NSA project that promoted the use of SELinux in Android devices.

53. C.

A virus is malicious code capable of destroying data and corrupting systems. It generally needs help moving from one system to another. Antivirus products are designed to recognize and remove viruses from a system. Anti-malware products are able to detect various types of malware, including viruses. Anti-malware is not the correct answer as the question states that the products must detect and remove programs designed to collect information on the infected system covertly. Anti-adware products detect and remove programs designed to display advertisements on an infected user's screen.

54. B.

Anti-malware products can detect various types of malware, including viruses, Trojans, ransomware, spyware, adware, and similar malicious programs/code. Antivirus products are designed to recognize and remove viruses. Antispyware products detect and remove programs designed to covertly collect information on the infected system. Anti-adware products detect and remove programs designed to display advertisements on an infected user's screen.

55. C.

Antispyware products detect and remove programs specifically designed to covertly collect information on the infected system. Anti-malware products detect various types of malware, including viruses, Trojans, ransomware, spyware, adware, and similar malicious programs/code. Antivirus products recognize and remove viruses. Anti-adware products detect and remove programs designed to display advertisements on an infected user's screen.

56. B.

Spam filters inspect and filter malicious emails before they reach the end user. A basic firewall doesn't examine emails for malicious content. A web application firewall (WAF) examines web traffic for malicious activity. A proxy acts as a middleman between endpoints.

57. D.

A patch management system can automate the process of installing patches on systems. By automating this process, it is more likely that all systems will be patched, and none will be mistakenly missed. A security assessment identifies the current security posture of an organization. Vulnerability management is the continual process of identifying, evaluating, treating, and reporting on security vulnerabilities. A vulnerability scanner scans a network, looking for and reporting on known vulnerabilities.

58. C.

A host-based intrusion prevention system (HIPS) is a system used to detect and stop intrusions on a host and stop the activity.

59. A.

A host-based intrusion detection system (HIDS) is a system used to detect intrusions on a system and to alert on those intrusions. The alerts can come in various forms, including email and text messages.

60. A.

Data loss prevention (DLP) is a technology that monitors the system, the user, and data events on an endpoint, looking for and blocking suspicious activity.

61. C.

Whitelisting is the technique of allowing only approved programs to be downloaded to an end user's computer. If the program is not on the whitelist, either it is blocked or it sends an alert to IT, notifying them of the action.

62. D.

Blacklisting is the process of blocking known malicious things such as known malicious websites. The problem with blacklisting is that new malicious sites pop up constantly, and thus, blacklisting won't include all malicious sites.

63. B.

Because Windows Active Directory is available within your corporate environment, using Group Policy to install the antivirus product on all systems is the most efficient method for installation.

64. A.

By default, Ethernet ports on a router are shut down. To bring the port up, the `no shut-down` command must be entered after the last command listed in the question.

65. B.

The commands in option B would enable a network engineer to remotely log in to the router using the password "secret."

66. D.

When this command is entered, only SSH connections are allowed. Additional commands are required to configure SSH use on a router, but the answer is required under the `line vty 0 4` command to enable its use.

67. B.

Option B denies inbound traffic to the router from a computer with an IP address 192.168.1.25. Option A permits all inbound traffic. Options C and D deny all inbound traffic. Note, option C is an empty ACL applied to an interface that denies all traffic.

68. A.

There is an implicit deny at the end of an access control list, so if no statement matches the packet being examined, and the packet is dropped.

69. A.

It is an extended ACL that denies ICMP traffic inbound from the Internet and permits all other traffic.

70. C.

This type of configuration provides out-of-band management of the router should the primary management method fail.

71. D.

Of the options provided, option D is the most appropriate. Managing USB usage via a Group Policy prevents some users from having USB access while enabling others access.

72. C.

Wireless Equivalent Protection (WEP) is obsolete and should not be used. WPA2 or newer should be used.

73. C.

Sending the logs to a syslog server allows log retention in the event the device fails, reboots, or is compromised by an attacker and the attacker is able to turn logging off.

74. A.

Configuring NTP on all devices synchronizes the date/time on the devices, thereby synchronizing the timestamps on all logs.

75. D.

If the logs are evidence, then as evidence they can't be altered. If the timestamps are from years before the crime occurred, they may not be allowed in court.

76. D.

Whether Wi-Fi is turned on or turned off on a device typically doesn't affect Bluetooth functionality.

77. A.

All Wi-Fi standards fall under the 802.11 umbrella standard.

78. B.

Maintaining the latest firmware on an IoT device eliminates known vulnerabilities on the device. Many IoT devices can't support antivirus products or IDS systems.

79. C.

By configuring a BIOS password, an attacker with physical access to the computer could not reconfigure the boot sequence to boot to a removable drive.

80. B.

An Encrypting File System (EFS) is a Microsoft file encryption technology that enables a user to encrypt individual files.

81. D.

BitLocker is a Microsoft file encryption technology that enables a user to encrypt an entire disk and/or partitions.

82. A.

GNU Privacy Guard (GPG) is a free software package that can run on Linux and supports the encryption of data and communication using both symmetric and asymmetric encryption.

83. D.

An Encrypting File System (EFS) is a component of the New Technology File System (NTFS). Other file systems do not support EFS.

84. B.

A Trusted Platform Module (TPM) is a chipset that can be included on a computer's motherboard to store encryption keys.

85. D.

Attestation is the process of validating something is true. In this case, you hire a third-party organization to verify that the hardware components are secure.

86. A.

Secure Boot is a security mechanism included in a Unified Extensible Firmware Interface (UEFI) that ensures an OS boot loader is certified before loading it. Certification is verified using signed certificates.

87. C.

Measured Launch is a boot loader protection mechanism and relies on UEFI's Secure Boot and TPM to ensure that an OS is allowed to load and specify which parts are allowed to execute.

88. C.

Integrity Measurement Architecture (IMA) maintains a runtime list of file hashes that are compared with the files executed on a system. The file hashes are stored in a TPM where they can't be altered by malware. The comparison of hashes indicates if a file has been altered or not. If the file has been altered, it's a sign that malware may be active on a system.

89. A.

The command bash /r is not a valid bash command. All of the other commands listed place bash in restricted mode.

90. A.

A patch management system provides an automated process of retrieving, testing, and installing patches on systems.

91. C.

Secure Boot is a security feature available in UEFI. It only allows OS boot loaders certified by the software vendor.

92. D.

A Trusted Platform Module (TPM) is used to store cryptographic keys. The TPM can be embedded on a motherboard or added via a PCI card.

93. A.

Keeping your near field communication–capable device up to date and off when not in use are two recommendations that should be mentioned.

94. C.

Infrared Data Association is an infrared communication technology using infrared signals. Because infrared signals work line of sight, they are considered very secure given that sniffing traffic is difficult.

95. A.

Configuration baselining is the process of configuring a base configuration for a system that includes basic capabilities and, in this case, a basic level of security. From this baseline (also known as a *gold image*), additional features can be added.

96. C.

A standard operating environment (SOE) is a standardized base configuration of systems that normally consists of a basic operating system and software application installation. The SOE is installed on the computers, and additional features are added.

97. C.

The primary concern with Bluetooth for business considerations is that Bluetooth uses a weak encryption cipher, E0. E0 uses a 128-bit key, but cryptanalysis has shown that the E0 cipher is only as strong as a 38-bit key.

98. D.

Bluetooth is best described as a PAN. A PAN is used to create a network to connect and share data with devices that are close together. A network of a PC, a phone, a printer, and wireless headphones would be a PAN.

99. C.

Asking a user to surrender evidence is an option if the user is unaware of the breach. If the phone owner is involved directly with the activity, then confiscation is the better option. With data breaches, the chain of custody is important, and you do not want the user destroying evidence, either by accident or on purpose.

100. D.

Data at rest is stored on a device. A VPN contains moving data, which means data in transit. VPNs provide secure communications over an insecure network like the Internet. A variety of encryption protocols can be used to protect data as it moves across a VPN.

101. C.

A WPA2 is more advanced than the original WPA implementation and contains authentication, encryption (AES), and integrity (CCMP).

102. A.

Are Alexa's speech capabilities and recordings HIPAA- or PCI-compliant? If Google, Siri, or Alexa are listening to confidential business or patient discussions, the results could be horrible for the hospital.

103. A.

With the invasion of IoT, employees and customers find these devices valuable, but they can introduce risk. Updating the corporate security policy for IoT and conducting a security awareness campaign are effective mitigation tools. After performing the proper technical risk analysis, compensating controls, segmentation, and stringent network access controls can be put into place.

104. D.

When using containers, host them in a container-focused OS and reduce the initial attack surface by disabling unnecessary services. Add monitoring tools for additional visibility and then develop a strong set of security controls to preserve the integrity of the systems.

105. B.

Installing an IPS will monitor traffic moving to and from the Internet to stop attacks. Monitoring internal traffic is critical to your defense because attackers can get a foothold in a container environment and expand their reach.

106. A.

Kubernetes provides a framework to run resilient distributed systems. It takes care of scaling systems, failovers, and load balancing, and it can even be configured to kill containers that fail a health check.

107. B.

When you securely lock down and monitor the container registry, you ensure there are no rogue container environments operating insecurely that touch your systems or their sensitive data. Locking down and monitoring the container registry also ensures that only containers meeting the team's development processes and security policies are being added.

108. A.

You can ensure that your containers are free from malware and vulnerabilities and are not exposing secrets by running a container image scanner. This scanner looks at the environment and searches for custom indicators of compromise (IoC), enabling you to mitigate any risk before additional development takes place or deploying to a live ecosystem.

109. C.

Runtime self-protection controls are internal to the application. These controls should be used to manage vulnerabilities in very specific lines of code. Simple mistakes result in vulnerabilities.

110. A.

Mobile device configuration profiles are XML files, defining all settings and restrictions that should belong on your mobile devices.

111. D.

A unique device identifier (UDID) is used to identify a device for the purpose of app installation and registration. Most modern UDIDs consist of 8 characters, a hyphen, and 16 more characters, for example, 00000040-0084239fab923b3e. The first 8 characters indicate the chip manufacturer, and the last 16 characters are hexadecimal.

112. B.

App wrapping enables mobile application management admins to set up specific policies. Examples include whether user authentication is required for a specific application and whether data associated with that application is stored on the device or in the cloud.

113. A.

Mobile Device Management (MDM) is responsible for managing the hardware and cellular connection of the device. Mobile Application Management (MAM) is more granularly controlling the apps, storage, and restrictions on the device itself.

114. B.

When a device is enrolled to a Mobile Device Management (MDM) server, that server is enabled to set device-level policies and push security commands to that asset like a remote wipe or lock. It can query the device to see what is installed on that device or install needed/updated applications.

115. B.

Typically, app wrapping is performed through the use of a software development kit that enables a developer to administer management policies. This includes controlling who can download a mobile app and whether data accessed by that app can be copied and pasted.

116. B.

VNC enables you to remotely access a computer and use the desktop over the Internet. Windows does have Remote Desktop, but it is available only on certain Windows editions. Some use TeamViewer, but only VNC will enable you to install and manage your own servers and is available for all operating systems.

117. A.

Screen mirroring requires two devices: one sending and one receiving. The sending device uses a screen-mirroring protocol like Apple AirPlay on an iPhone, Google Cast on Chromebook, or Miracast on Windows devices.

118. A.

With manual OTA updates, an end user is notified when there is an available update and can decide to accept or refuse the download. This allows the end user to decide an appropriate time to install the update. An automatic OTA is done from the back end, and the update is pushed to the device.

119. D.

The Simple Certificate Enrollment Protocol (SCEP) is a standard protocol used for certificates. It is mostly used for certificate-based authentication where access to Wi-Fi, VPN, and email is deployed using certificates. Advantages include no intervention by users and secure encrypted network communication.

120. A.

There are two ways to enroll in SCEP: an SCEP server CA automatically issues the certificate, or an SCEP is requested, set to PENDING, and the CA admin then manually approves or denies the certificate.

121. A.

There is no one-size-fits-all solution, and each mobile device strategy has its own pros and cons. With bring your own device (BYOD), no wireless carrier needs to be engaged, and fast deployment is available and has a lower cost because the employee owns the device.

122. B.

A mobile strategy that works well for some organizations is choose your own device (CYOD), where there are a few select models from which to choose (for example, an organization may ask if you want a Mac laptop or a PC tablet when starting a job).

123. C.

When you are in a situation where security and data protection are of the utmost importance, company-owned, personally enabled (COPE) is the best mobile device strategy to use. COPE has strict specific procurement standards and the highest hardware costs of the three options.

124. B.

A virtual private network (VPN) enables employees to access sensitive data and systems on mobile devices while away from the secure corporate network. A VPN's traditional role is to enable employees to authenticate from anywhere in the world and seamlessly access the company's network.

125. A.

On Microsoft servers, the most secure authentication is Extensible Authentication Protocol-Transport Layer Security (EAP-TLS), which can utilize smart cards. It requires public key infrastructure (PKI).

126. D.

In a full tunnel, all network traffic is forced to go through the VPN. Depending on how it's configured, you may only have access to the internal network while the VPN is active.

127. C.

Sideloading is a term that applies to transferring a file from one local device to the other using either a USB, a lightning cable, or Bluetooth. The process involves establishing a connection between two devices and moving files to the right location.

128. A.

Android requires that all apps are digitally signed with a certificate before they can be installed. This certificate proves authorship and that the app came from you and not a suspicious entity.

129. D.

USB On-The-Go is a standardized specification that enables a device to read data from a USB device. The device becomes a USB host. You will need an OTG cable or connector.

130. A.

The benefits of tethering include getting Internet access to upload and download files and check your account balances securely through your PAN. The downsides are that there is a possible cost with your carrier, the mobile connection will be slow, and the battery on your phone or tablet can die quickly.

131. C.

Your fingerprint is a biometric. It is something you have, not something you know.

132. D.

A PIN is something you create and memorize. The others are something you physically have.

133. D.

A major challenge is the process by which the data is captured and mapped to an identity. If the process is flawed and the data is inaccurate, a partial capture of data can lead to a system failure.

134. A.

A major concern for enterprise organizations is the cost of biometric authentication. The cost of getting systems up and running, configured, and in compliance, as well as storing and maintaining the data, can outweigh the benefit of using biometrics on a larger scale.

135. C.

Only give apps permissions they must have, and delete any app that asks for more than is necessary. For example, there is no need for your flashlight app to record your voice and have access to all your pictures/video.

136. B.

This type of hacking is classic network spoofing. Placing a rogue access point near a legitimate business that has a lot of human traffic is a perfect place for an attacker to require users to create an "account" complete with a username/password to use their free services.

137. A.

This attack could also be called whaling because a specific high-ranking employee was targeted. Email monitoring is critical. Never click on email links, especially on a mobile device where the screen can be tiny compared to a desktop computer. Always enter URLs manually.

138. C.

The responsibility of secure development is on the developer and the organization to enforce encryption standards.

139. A.

New tokens must be generated with each access attempt. Improper session handling occurs when apps accidentally share session tokens with malicious attackers, enabling them to impersonate legitimate users.

140. C.

Some people have the perception that jailbreaking is used only to do nefarious things or piracy. Jailbreaking enables you to do things like change the default browser and mail client. It also enables you to use software of which the manufacturer does not approve. Not only should your company have an inventory of mobile devices, but a security policy and a scanning process should be required as well. Some companies have an annual "eyes on inventory," where mobile devices are scanned physically by IT once a year.

141. C.

Rooting is the process of gaining root access on a mobile device. This is usually done on an Android, while jailbreaking is usually performed on iPhones. Rooting gets around security architecture and can cause damage if users make a mistake. Manufacturers generally do not want end users having root access.

142. A.

Many Android phones come with a locked bootloader. A locked bootloader won't boot anything but the approved version of a specific Android ROM. Unlocking the bootloader enables you to install a custom ROM, which is an alternate version of the Android operating systems.

143. D.

If you try to insert a SIM card from a competing carrier into a phone that was locked to another carrier, a message will appear saying the phone is locked. While some carriers will unlock a phone when the contract is up, others may refuse to unlock them.

144. A.

A push notification is a way for apps to send you a message without opening the application where the notification is "pushed" to the application. The most common way identify push notifications is to look for a red circle with a number inside it on the app. The number represents how many updates/messages are waiting for the device's owner.

145. B.

A service provider could be compromised, causing important or sensitive information to be leaked. For this type of scenario, using end-to end-encryption reduces the exposure of the attack.

146. A.

Many experts say that mobile payment methodologies offered by major providers are more secure than physical cards or cash. Mobile wallets use powerful encryption to mask credit card numbers, first when you enter them and again when you pay.

147. D.

Near field communication (NFC) can be used to induce electric currents inside passive components. The passive devices do not need a power source, but rather receive power from the electromagnetic field produced by an NFC component when in range. Samsung, Android, and Apple Pay use NFC. Bluetooth works better for connecting devices for file transfers or sharing connections to speakers.

148. C.

Security is increased and risk is reduced when using tokens. The mapping from the original data to the token should be irreversible in the absence of the system that created it.

149. C.

When an original equipment manufacturer (OEM) creates a new phone, the manufacturer can take the open source operating system and customize it for their specific device. There are many, many manufacturers, so the operating system becomes more fractured over time.

150. D.

Some social networking sites are very precise when featuring locations associated with a post. This can be dangerous should the information fall into the wrong hands, putting the poster in danger.

151. A.

When a cyberattack occurs on a mobile device that is now a primary threat vector, an enterprise organization must move quickly. If data has been leaked, all affected users must be notified, because an average data breach can cost millions of dollars. It is a good idea to explore having an insurance policy.

152. B.

One of the most important ways for an organization to limit mobile device risk and threats is to enforce a strict remote lock and data wipe policy. It is another layer of protection.

153. A.

When purchasing hardware, you do not have control of the hardware's design and process. Therefore, you must purchase hardware from vetted and responsible vendors. Researchers in December 2018 discovered a UEFI rootkit called Lojack used globally by APT groups. Lojack took advantage of firmware vendors and enabled the remote flashing of firmware.

154. D.

When you have a HIDS/HIPS on an individual asset, you are monitoring and analyzing the internal workings of that system as well as network behavior. Based on how the system is configured, a HIDS/HIPS may discover what that program is accessing and if anyone or anything has altered the security policy on that machine.

155. D.

You should give the end user a list of software that is vetted and approved by IT. If comparable software is not found on that list, then the end user can request the software be tested.

156. A.

SD3 is Microsoft's defense-in-depth strategy. SD3 stands for secure by design, secure by default, and secure in deployment. Design means designers use secure coding best practices. Default means that end users install applications without changing the defaults, and deployment means it can be securely maintained with patching and auditing.

157. A.

Secure by design means combining security into your application as early in the process as possible. It involves considering security in the design state and adding security features into every aspect possible.

158. A.

Users do not often change default settings after installation. Some do not even change default passwords. Security settings should be set by default. If a feature is specifically wanted by a user, they can enable it in the future.

159. B.

An application can be maintained securely after deployment with patch management and auditing. It should also involve a process for monitoring events at regular intervals or after any failure.

160. C.

Insecure direct object references enable an attacker to bypass authorization and directly access a resource that they should not have access to, such as database records, files, or other application pages.

161. B.

Forced browsing is a technique used by attackers while searching for content that is not linked together on a web server. This is oftentimes considered to be a type of brute-force attack. An attacker may type in a URL, such as www.sybex.com/1, and then change to www.sybex.com/2 to see what else they might find.

162. D.

A double encoding attack is used to bypass a web application's directory traversal security check. HTTP accepts both decimal and hexadecimal values. The new doubled value bypasses input validation and sanitization.

163. A.

A cross-site request forgery (XSRF) is an attack that takes advantage of a software vulnerability and redirects static content from a trusted site. An example might be stealing online banking credentials and account information from a user who logs in to a legitimate banking site. CAPTCHA forms require solving some type of puzzle to validate that the user is human, revalidating the authenticity of the user.

164. A.

XSS is an attack that can be mitigated by using input validation and sanitization. Like an XSRF attack, an XSS attack attempts to steal information from a user. If a web application is not able to properly sanitize input from a user, the attacker can use form input to inject malicious code.

165. D.

When a web user accesses a decoy website or clicks a button to download a file or win a prize, they were tricked into clicking a hidden button that may result in payment of some sort on another site. It is not a CSRF, which depends on forging the entire request without the user's knowledge or input.

166. A.

Browsers and websites use HTTP to communicate, and a web session is a series of requests and responses created by an individual user. HTTP is stateless, which means each response and request are independent of each other. A web administrator uses session management to track visits to a website and movement inside the site when the user logged in.

167. B.

Developers and administrators forget or ignore how much information is shared in a server banner or a hostname. If your server is running Apache and you return the server header in your response, the attacker can use that information to find vulnerabilities for your web server version.

168. A.

When developing any application, you must assume that all users are bad actors. Developers forget to properly handle error messages, which can be leveraged for the information they contain.

169. A.

When the browser loads that page, the victim's browser makes the request using the legitimate cookie from the initial login.

170. C.

This log is SQL injection. The SQL is valid and will return all rows from the UserID table because OR 1=1 is a true statement. Developers should validate all end-user input to prevent injection attacks.

171. D.

Attackers seek domain or administrator privileges. Some tools like Metasploit harvest credentials, verify they are still active, and escalate a user account into an administrator account, bypassing all user account controls (UACs). One of the easiest ways to mitigate this is to change passwords often and to enforce strong password policies including complexity and uniqueness.

172. D.

Insecure storage of keys, certificates, and passwords is a common encryption mistake. Encryption is fairly easy to implement, but developers may overestimate the level of protection gained and not perform due diligence over other parts of the web application.

173. B.

Dumb fuzzers can provide completely random input to software with no intelligence to test for bugs. Sometimes, a program will perform certain processes only if there is specific input like a protocol definition or a rule for a file format. That allows for valid input, which is a smart fuzzer.

174. A.

Buffer overflows occur when software code has too much input, and the programmer failed to include any data input validation checks. Extra data in a buffer overflow is pushed into the execution stack and is processed, enabling the attacker to perform any system operation.

175. D.

Buffer overflow attacks are possible because programmers do not check the length and format of input data before processing. Web servers are notorious for being unprotected against buffer overflow vulnerabilities.

176. D.

Depending on your security policy and compliance, the use of cookies could be a violation of privacy. Cookies can be used to record data, web-surfing habits, etc. Secure environments and organizations concerned about privacy should restrict the use of cookies. Cookies could possibly aid an attacker in spoofing a user's identity or contain connection and session management information.

177. A.

When a computer functions normally, RAM gets used dynamically, and resources are allocated as needed. When software no longer needs the RAM, it is reallocated to the next program when necessary. In certain situations, RAM gets allocated but not freed up when no longer needed.

178. C.

In computing environments, race conditions in software or on a network can occur if two tasks are performed at the same time or if two users attempt to access a specific channel at the same instant. Attackers take advantage of the confusion of race condition vulnerabilities by gaining access to the data or unauthorized access to a network.

179. A.

Software can check the state of a resource, but the state can change between the time of check (ToC) and the time of use (ToU). This change can cause the software to crash or be a security risk if an attacker can influence the state of the resource between check and use. The most basic fix is to not to perform a check. It limits the false sense of security given by the ToC.

180. C.

Large retailers are experimenting with location-sensing technologies by tracking a customer's location through their phone's GPS capability. Some organizations use this tool as a heat map and compare stores and department layouts, which can optimize the shopping experience for customers.

181. D.

While seemingly harmless, every photo shared has a vast amount of information that is attached to it, including location with an accuracy of within 15 feet. While you are sharing posts on social media, you are also at risk from the criminal element because that photo you shared can divulge where you physically are.

182. D.

Not only do you have the business issue of lost data by attacks or by accident, you also must consider whether the vendor can verify that your data was securely deleted on demand and that remnants of the data are not still in the cloud for others to see.

183. C.

Options A, B, and D are what cloud providers *should* be doing.

184. D.

OAUTH does not share passwords with a third-party application. With OAUTH, the role of the owner is to ask the application to perform a function, and the application then tells the server the owner wants to delegate access with a token and secret key. The owner authorizes the token, and the application asks the resource server to exchange the token for an access token and a secret key.

185. A.

Prevention obfuscation makes it difficult for a computer to decompile code to reverse engineer or copy the code. An example includes renaming metadata to gibberish. Data obfuscation is aimed at obscuring data and data structures. Control flow obfuscation uses false conditional statements to confuse decompilers while keeping code intact.

186. A.

When you implement garbage collection, a process cleans up and controls what is left in memory. Garbage collection can ensure that credentials are erased from memory when they are no longer needed.

187. C.

The security offered by SSL and TLS can help prevent man-in-the-middle (MitM) attacks. These protocols are used to encrypt segments of TCP/IP traffic. A MitM attack happens when an attacker gains access to traffic sent between two devices. If the data is unencrypted, the attacker can view all the traffic. SSL and TLS are used by HTTPS over port 443.

188. A.

Network analysis is most likely going to begin with a review of web server logs. Network analysis can be done on live traffic or on logs that were recorded in a logging file. An analyst who suspects that a web server has been attacked should acquire and then analyze the logs to determine if, when, and how an attacker might have gained access.

189. A.

Object reuse is the process by which you use authentication credentials that an application or process may have in memory to authenticate a user or application.

190. D.

Encapsulation is a characteristic of object-oriented programming (OOP). OOP uses objects and instances of classes. Data that is defined for a specific class relates only to that specific class. The end result is that an object cannot accidentally read data from other objects.

191. C.

Pseudonymization uses aliases or other fake identifiers to represent data that should be protected.

192. A.

HTML5 is a solution that defines the behaviors of web page content. HTML5 encourages more interoperable implementations.

193. A.

Microsoft ActiveX controls are dangerous and should be installed only when needed, removed when no longer necessary, and downloaded only from a trusted source. ActiveX controls are insecure by design.

194. C.

Asynchronous JavaScript and XML (Ajax) is a pattern where web pages use web services using JavaScript and XML. It is used to create fast dynamic web pages, enabling parts of a web page to update, rather than reloading the entire page.

195. A.

There are two web service formats: SOAP and REST. Simple Object Access Protocol (SOAP) is used for interchanging data in a distributed environment. Representational State Transfer (REST) is an architectural style for hypermedia (think hyperlinked) systems. Of the two, SOAP has extensions for specific security concerns, while REST focuses on how to deliver and consume.

196. A.

When managing a graphical user interface with text fields and radio buttons that can trigger other text or input fields, one input state can influence another input state.

197. B.

Setting API access and a secret key pair is the most commonly used option. Key pairs provide access to the API and give each individual a secret token. If the access and secret key pairs do not match, you will not have access. Large enterprise organizations and applications use this methodology for the validation of users.

198. A.

Transport Layer Security (TLS) is a way of encrypting the data that users send across the Web while interacting with your web applications. It is critical for pages where the end user is inputting data, logging in, purchasing something, and checking out to be secured with TLS, and is indicated by the inclusion of HTTPS in the URL.

199. C.

JavaScript vulnerabilities are common in web applications. Insecure JavaScript and bad coding can cost time and money. Several tools, like ZAP and Grabber, can help examine those web applications, scanning a site for vulnerabilities.

200. D.

Patching, hardening, and firewalls are all mitigation techniques used to prevent server-side attacks. Identity management is about access control.

201. A.

When traffic increases by double digits over a short amount of time, you are usually under attack. Wireshark is the leading network traffic analyzer and captures packets to analyze. The UDP port being attacked is port 123, which is the network time protocol. End devices should be talking to an internal NTP server or reaching out to a configured NTP server. You know this is a client-side attack because it is taking place on your machine. Server-side means the action is taking place on the web server.

202. A.

You must target specific areas to identify the maximum number of high-severity vulnerabilities within the time you have to deploy the new assets.

203. B.

As soon as an organization learns of a firmware vulnerability, the company should evaluate if they are vulnerable and if a fix exists. Patch as soon as the patch is available by the vendor. If a patch is unavailable, compensating controls should be put into place if the assets affected are mission-critical assets. As more attackers learn about vulnerable firmware, the risk of exploit rises exponentially. This vulnerability exfiltrates data over ports 16992–16995 by default.

Chapter 3: Enterprise Security Operations

1. D.

A code review, also called a *peer review*, is a way that one or many people systematically check a program by reviewing its source code for mistakes.

2. A.

An organization can easily control their vulnerability management life cycle to scan specific assets during specific times. A tabletop exercise is a dry run through policies and procedures that anticipates the readiness of an organization to respond to an incident or event. Sandboxing is a process used to execute suspicious code without risking harm to a device or network, which can add another layer of protection against possible malware. Social engineering is a deceptive act used to manipulate a user into sharing information that can be used for nefarious purposes.

3. C.

A sandbox enables developers to download, install, and manipulate software in a quarantined location to test before putting it into production. Sandboxes are incredibly important to patch management and upgrading software.

4. A.

A memory dump (i.e., crash dump) is the process of taking all information in RAM and writing it to a storage drive. A memory dump is most often caused by a registry's corrupt files. It can also be caused accidentally by overclocking or overheating. Most of the time, this shows up as the blue screen of death (BSOD).

5. C.

Runtime debugging is useful to examine the state of a program during runtime. Setting breakpoints and executing small pieces of code at a time helps find why a theoretically correct piece of code does not execute the way you expect.

6. C.

A black-box penetration tester knows nothing about the environment they are testing, perhaps just a name and address. The first thing a pentester does is perform reconnaissance, trying to find out as much about the organization as possible.

7. B.

Passive reconnaissance is gaining information about a company through completely open source intelligence without actively engaging any systems or people.

8. A.

Active reconnaissance requires interaction. As the "attacker," you may start to appear in logs because you interact with systems.

9. A.

When dealing with malware, reversing binaries is important. Oftentimes, you won't have the source, so reverse engineering is how you find the location of the payload. This may also be called *binary reverse engineering*. On a side note, this code snippet is a slightly modified version of a popular bitcoin-stealing malware found on a software download site.

10. D.

An HTTP interceptor is used to inspect requests before they are handed to a server and responses before they are handed over to the application. HTTP interceptors are used for error handling and authentication for requests and responses.

11. A.

Many tools can be used to fingerprint assets. These tools gather information for you to test known vulnerabilities and exploitation. Netcat, Nmap, Telnet, or crawling cookies are all tools or techniques used to gather information about an application to further your security testing.

12. B.

Having a fuzzer, fuzzing utility, or fuzz testing is a type of testing where techniques are used to discover coding errors and loopholes in software, networks, or operating systems by inserting invalid random data called *fuzz*. The software, network, or operating system is monitored for crashes or exceptions.

13. D.

According to Gartner, social engineering is the single greatest security risk faced in cybersecurity. Social engineering is the art of manipulating, influencing, or deceiving to gain information or control of a system, process, or finances.

14. A.

Pretexting takes real knowledge of a victim and uses that to attempt to get even more information. This type of scenario will engage and increase the chance the victim will fall for the pretext.

15. A.

Spear phishing is a term used to identify the process of attempting to acquire sensitive information by masquerading as a trustworthy organization to one specific individual. If the email was sent in bulk, then it's called plain phishing. Emails claiming to be from common banks, retail sites, or social media are commonly used to lure the victim.

16. D.

Diversion is a social engineering campaign that targets vendor delivery or transport companies. The objective of this type of attack is to make the delivery of goods to another location rather than the original location.

17. D.

One technique used by attackers takes advantage of websites that people regularly visit and trust. The attacker gathers information about group of people visiting specific websites and tests those websites for vulnerabilities. Over time, the odds of that target group visiting that site and getting infected increases and then the attacker has access.

18. D.

It is no coincidence this is called baiting. What do you do to a "phish" hook? Baiting means that you dangle something interesting in front of your victim like a movie file or something labeled "confidential." Once the malicious file is downloaded and installed, the victim is infected, enabling the attacker to pivot and own the network.

19. A.

Tailgating is used by social engineers to gain access to a building or some secure area. A tailgater waits for an authorized user to open a door and time it so they can enter right behind the user.

20. C.

Quid pro quo is Latin for "something for something." In this case, someone from "IT support" calls you to say they have something for you if you do something for them. This is a good way to get malware/ransomware installed on a machine.

21. B.

Pivoting is a methodology that pentesters (and attackers) use to compromise deeper into a network. After the initial compromise, the attacker can use that system on a network to attack other systems to avoid network detection, firewall rules, or IDS. In Metasploit, you have the ability to create proxy pivots and VPN pivots to expand the attack.

22. D.

With a hard time limit set on an external exploitation, after a system is compromised, you could use the compromised system to move laterally through the network. With the internal access, you can attempt to exfiltrate the data you have been able to acquire and exploit other machines in the environment.

23. C.

Using open source intelligence sources and threat databases, you can generate your own IDS rules, leveraging the knowledge of third-party sources.

24. A.

A vast amount of open-source intelligence (OSINT) helps organizations stay safer. Using indicators of compromise (IOCs) to aid information security processes helps detect data breaches and malware/ransomware infection. With this information, you can sweep your network to identify matches, sandbox anything suspicious, and contact the authorities.

25. D.

Passive recon is when you use tools like social media to find out all you can about an organization and who works for them. Social engineering can be used to find email addresses, the types of jobs being offered, and the tools being used in that environment.

26. B.

Job boards and social media are where most attackers start passive reconnaissance. With the information gained from job boards, they know what type of products you're using and the level of expertise needed to attack your network. HR should make IT job advertisements as vague as possible to find the right person for the role.

27. A.

Whois is a protocol used to query databases that store registered users of a domain name or IP address.

28. A.

A routing table is a data set used to determine where packets are directed on a network. Routing table poisoning occurs when unwanted or malicious changes are made in the table.

29. B.

In a split DNS infrastructure, you create two zones for one domain. One of these zones is to be used by the internal network, and the external network is used by users on the Internet. This is done to hide internal information from outsiders.

30. A.

DNSSEC strengthens authentication using digital signatures based on public/private key cryptography. With DNSSEC, you have data origin authentication as well as data integrity.

31. B.

Authentication traffic is the most commonly captured and reused network traffic used in a replay attack. If an attacker is able to replay the stream of authentication packets correctly, they gain access to the same systems as the original user.

32. A.

A DoS attack is a single-source computer system initiating the attack. A DDoS is a much more orchestrated attack, enlisting the help of hundreds (if not thousands) of other source computers to completely overload the system.

33. B.

Shodan is a search engine that helps you locate devices connected to the Internet, their location, and how they are used. It is free and helps with digital footprinting. Shodan also offers a public API that enables other tools to access all Shodan's data.

34. B.

WiGLE is a search engine that maps 802.11 wireless networks. This site is searchable and has vast amounts of statistics for network admins and compliance auditors. It is also freely available to attackers.

35. C.

The primary purpose of penetration testing is to test the effectiveness of your security policies, procedures, and guidelines. It is important to obtain the proper approval before beginning a penetration test.

36. B.

A black-box penetration test occurs when the penetration tester has no knowledge of the organization.

37. A.

The black-box penetration test done by a small firm that has signed an NDA gives you a true external perspective of the environment that the CTO requires.

38. D.

In this type of situation, the best protection is to hire an expert, external red team to do a black-box test of the program/product/code.

39. A.

The Common Vulnerability Scoring System (CVSS) is a generic mathematical algorithm that scores a vulnerability based on the CIA triad, as well as attack vector, authentication, and complexity. The concern is how these vulnerabilities affect your specific environment, and for that you need a black-box test so that vulnerabilities can be prioritized based on local impact.

40. A.

A white-box test requires the expertise of testers. These tests demand competences in programming and full knowledge of the code tested. Because of that knowledge and length of code, these tests can take a long time.

41. A.

A gray-box test is an intermediary-level test. Because testers have knowledge of the system, they give input to the systems, check if the result is what was expected, and then check what the result is. This test combines the white-box and black-box test.

42. A.

A tabletop exercise is similar to a dry run. It enables you to talk through all aspects of policies and procedures without executing the business continuity plan. All stakeholders should be at this tabletop exercise so that multiple points of view of processes are examined.

43. D.

Many different products allow for configuration baseline scans. Each configuration item is evaluated on a schedule or could be evaluated with agents.

44. C.

The ISO/IEC 27001 is a framework for internal auditing, involving a complete examination of 14 different domains, including security policy, access control, compliance, and asset management.

45. C.

COBIT defines requirements for governance, management, and control of IT processes. Components of COBIT include process descriptions, objectives, maturity, and guidelines. ISO 27001 is the framework for security. ITIL is for enabling IT services and life cycles.

46. A.

An external audit must have an independent certified authority and be performed against a recognized auditable standard. This is why an external audit can hold so much value for a company.

47. A.

A red team can perform all the necessary steps that true attackers would use against you. By assuming that role, they indicate what your company is vulnerable to.

48. A.

The Committee on National Security Systems (CNSS) defines a white team as a group that is responsible for refereeing an engagement of red team attackers versus the blue team, the actual defenders of information systems.

49. D.

A white-hat hacker has a passion for helping, while the black-hat hacker is usually after financial gain. Red team and blue team members have similar skill sets—the red team being the aggressor and the blue being the defender. A white-box engagement means you know the company processes and landscape intimately, while the black-box engagement is approaching the target from the outside.

50. A.

An Address Resolution Protocol (ARP) scan is performed to learn MAC addresses. You run an ARP request to query the MAC address of a device with a known IP address. When the ARP reply is received, you populate the ARP table, which maps the IP to a MAC.

51. D.

Bollards are strong heavy posts placed in front of physical structures to prevent accidents or unauthorized vehicles crashing into a secure facility.

52. A.

Using a vulnerability scanner like Nexpose or Nessus is a good example of an organization proactively finding vulnerabilities in systems on their network. If vulnerabilities are found, they can be patched or the services disabled, hardening the system to make it resistant to future attacks.

53. B.

Boundary testing is a specific form of testing where values that are known to be out of acceptable ranges are placed into the form to see how the application handles the errors.

54. D.

An anomaly detection–based IDS is best at detecting the newest security threats. An anomaly detection device finds the oddities in network traffic behavior by taking a baseline first of what normal patterns look like. Once you have a baseline, it will compare current traffic to detect abnormal traffic.

55. D.

A SIEM monitors servers on your network, ideally providing a real-time analysis of security incidents and events. A SIEM (pronounced "SIM") can be used on hardware or software by examining and correlating logs the servers produce. A SIEM can be used to monitor alerts from an IDS and to perform trend analysis. If an anomaly is detected, rules are then written to inform security administrators.

56. A.

A honeypot is a tool used to gather information about intruders and their methodologies. This valuable threat intelligence analyzes the tools used in an attack and then uses the information to protect legitimate assets.

57. B.

Killdisk is a tool that enables you to overwrite hard drives numerous times. Hard drives contain sectors, and groups of sectors are called *clusters*. When data is written to a sector, the OS can allocate the entire cluster to that data. Deleting data by using the OS does not remove the data from clusters. It removes the filename from the file allocation table and makes the space available for writing again. The data is still there, even when you delete the contents of the recycle bin.

58. D.

You should check the DNS because the FTP server is mapped to an IP address. The DNS server is used to resolve host names or fully qualified domain names (FQDN) to an IP.

59. A.

Network access control (NAC) is a solution to support visibility and access management on a network using policy enforcement on devices and users. Organizations have to deal with mobile devices and the risks that they bring to an organization. It is important to increase visibility into those assets and strengthen the security of your network infrastructure.

60. D.

The Security Content Automation Protocol (SCAP) is an open standard used to find security flaws and configuration issues related to security and compliance. SCAP specifications standardize naming conventions and formats used by vulnerability management and policy compliance. The SCAP checklist standardizes computer security configurations, and the SP 800-53 controls framework.

61. D.

Most assets on a network produce logs to different degrees and in different formats. Log analysis is extremely important for compliance. A Security Incident/Event Management (SIEM) tool collects data from various assets, servers, domain controllers, hosts, and more. The SIEM will normalize that data, which is analyzed to discover and detect threats.

62. B.

Organizations have petabytes of data, and it is impossible for a human team to do any sort of threat hunting manually. A security incident/event management (SIEM) tool organizes that data and can use external threat intelligence for pattern matching or to find data anomalies.

63. B.

Network Mapper (Nmap) is the most popular network discovery and port scanner. It is free and open source and is used by many system administrators and network engineers for auditing local and remote networks. Port scanning sends a request to connect to a target computer on each port sequentially and records which ports respond.

64. B.

A port scan with malicious intent must go undetected. An experienced attacker would conduct the port scan in strobe or stealth mode, limiting the ports to small targets and slowing down the scan over a longer time period to reduce the chance that you, the IT administrator, get an alert.

65. A.

You must ensure that you have approval from appropriate stakeholders before taking on this task. If you do not, you could find yourself violating terms of service and, even worse, the law.

66. B.

The best known vulnerability management tools on the market today are Nessus by Tenable, Nexpose by Rapid7, and Qualys Vulnerability Management. A vulnerability scanner compares details about the target attack surface to a database of vulnerabilities, which are known securities issues with services, operating systems, and ports.

67. B.

A vulnerability scan should be used as an intruder would, without trusted credentials on a network. This type of scan can show vulnerabilities that can be accessed without logging into the network.

68. A.

In an authenticated scan, the vulnerability manager logs in as a network user, and the scan shows vulnerabilities that are accessible to trusted insiders or an attacker who has gained access to the network and taken over a trusted user's account.

69. C.

All an attacker needs is just one vulnerability to gain access to your network. At a minimum, even with quarterly compliance requirements, if you are patching weekly, then you must scan for vulnerabilities weekly. The only way to know if the patch or compensating controls you set in place have worked is to follow the vulnerability life cycle and scan after patching.

70. A.

An application scanner can help ensure that software applications are free from the flaws and weaknesses that attackers often use to exploit and exfiltrate data. Backdoors, malicious code, and threats are flaws present in both commercial and open-source software.

71. B.

Static analysis security testing (SAST) tools can scan binaries in software to find errors, vulnerabilities, and flaws in web, movie, and desktop applications. SAST is often called *white-box testing.* Dynamic analysis (DAST) tools are used for black-box testing, employing injection techniques like SQLi and CSS. Interactive analysis (IAST) is a combination of both SAST and DAST, applying analysis to all code, runtime controls, and data flow. Vendor application security testing (VAST) is a third-party risk assessment.

72. B.

Option B is the only answer that is a legitimate process. Scan the client-facing web portal to identify any ports that are exposed and services running on those ports, then determine if they are vulnerable.

73. B.

An HTTP or HTTPS interceptor like BurpSuite by Portswigger is one of the best tools out there to do web application assessments. It allows you to read and manipulate web traffic. Additionally, you can scan a target machine; interrupt the flow of traffic; and manipulate, modify, and forward information.

74. C.

Acunetix WVS (web vulnerability scanner) is used specifically for web vulnerabilities. It includes a login sequence recorder allowing you to access password-protected areas of a website, as well as scan any WordPress site for more than 1,200 vulnerabilities.

75. C.

Metasploit is an open-source collection of exploit tools that can be customized with your own tools. It is one of the most popular tools, backed by hundreds of thousands of users. As a pentester, this tool enables you to pinpoint vulnerabilities as well as integrate with Nexpose, one of the best vulnerability management tools.

76. A.

Rapid7 owns both Metasploit and Nexpose. Using these tools together enables you to find vulnerabilities and actively attempt to exploit those vulnerabilities to prioritize what needs to be fixed first.

77. A.

Network Mapper (Nmap) is a port-scanning tool. It is a free and open-source tool that enables network discovery and security auditing. It uses IP packets to determine which hosts are available, what services are running, the operating system, and more.

78. B.

Wireshark is a well-known packet capture tool that can help a pentester examine traffic on a network. It can help find vulnerabilities as well as firewall rule sets. It analyzes live packets and saves them in a `.pcap` file.

79. A.

Hashcat is the fastest cracking tool with a GPU engine. You can do straight and brute-forcing cracking, as well as reverse masking and dictionary attacks.

80. C.

Maltego is an open-source platform that can be used as a forensics platform to show the complexity in your infrastructure. With Maltego, you can find individuals, email structure, websites, domains, IP addresses, DNS, and even documents and passwords. It has a GUI interface that can be customized.

81. A.

The Social Engineer Toolkit (SET) by David Kennedy's TrustedSec is a framework for simulating attacks such as credential harvesting, phishing, and PowerShell attacks. You've seen the SMS spoofing attack on the television show *Mr. Robot*. It is Python-based and will automate these attacks, create malicious web pages, and more.

82. C.

Netsparker is a popular web application scanner that supports JavaScript and Ajax-based apps. It can find flaws like SQLi and local file inclusion and even suggest remediation actions. With Netsparker, you do not have to verify the vulnerability. If Netsparker cannot verify the flaw, it alerts you.

83. A.

The U.S. NSA recently outsourced Ghidra, a reverse engineering tool used to forensically analyze malware.

84. B.

Netcat is a utility that is features port scanning and listening and can transfer files. It can even be used strategically as a backdoor.

85. A.

The command `ipconfig /all` displays more detailed information than `ipconfig` alone. The command `ipconfig /release` forces an asset to give up its lease by sending the DHCP server a notification. You can also use `ipconfig /renew` to request a new one.

86. B.

After running `md5 "C:printer_driver.dll"`, the program returns a series of characters that you check against the checksum on the file's original download page.

87. A.

Data visualization quickly transfers information from machine analytics to the human brain efficiently and meaningfully. With visualization tools like DOMO or Google Analytics, you see the clarity of the message that the data holds.

88. A.

In a security information event management (SIEM) tool, you get near real-time alerts and analysis of what is happening on network hardware, servers, and applications. It does this by capturing logs from all those devices, aggregating the data, correlating it, looking for commonalities, and linking events together that are out of the normal range. Qradar, Arcsight, and Splunk are leading SIEM vendors.

89. D.

Ping is one of the most basic network commands. It helps determine connectivity and can be used to measure speed or latency.

90. C.

Traceroute is a diagnostic network command that tells us where the packet is going. This will show the route a packet takes to the destination and can show if the network is working properly.

91. A.

Address Resolution Protocol (ARP) is a command used to review the ARP table that maps an IP address to a MAC address. It only sees the local area network segment connections and is used to discover which machines are connected to your host. It can be used to monitor for ARP poisoning, which is a common spoofing or man-in-the-middle attack.

92. A.

Netstat, or "network statistics," gathers information of the system, traffic statistics, number of open connections, and number of closing or pending connections. Watching these metrics enables you to determine whether a compromise has occurred or whether it's a performance issue on a server.

93. B.

It is highly recommended to reach out to all administrators of the domains for any migration of mail and web services.

94. D.

Security Content Automation Protocol (SCAP, pronounced "ess-cap") is currently at version 1.3. SCAP is a number of open standards widely used to enumerate software and configuration issues as they pertain to security. These specifications help standardize formats used for policy compliance.

95. A.

File Integrity Monitoring (FIM) is a security technique used to secure IT infrastructure and business data. If an attacker or malicious insider generates changes to application files, operating system files, and log files, FIM can detect these changes, indicating a breach.

96. B.

With file integrity monitoring (FIM), the standard or regulation states that data must be monitored or managed so as to ensure integrity.

97. C.

The success of a sustained FIM program depends on how well it is integrated with change management. The whole purpose of FIM is to detect change, and it must hold up to the organizational needs without hampering performance.

98. A.

Some more advanced FIM solutions are a part of a host-based intrusion detection system (HIDS). As a general rule, they can detect threats in other areas, not just files.

99. B.

Agent-based file integrity can leverage software agents installed on systems needing monitoring. Agentless FIM gets up and running quickly but does not have the depth of analysis that agent-based FIM does.

100. D.

Locks secure and fasten something with the goal that only someone with a key should have access. Lock picks or skeleton keys are tools used to unlock a lock by manipulating the tumblers inside.

101. B.

Infrared (IR) cameras see at night by using light with wavelengths that are invisible to the human eye. If you need to monitor property at night, choose an IR camera.

102. A.

RFID is a tracking system that uses radio frequency. Placing tags on equipment enables you to trace who checks out the tools. And, if you have a portal-type entrance/exit reader, you'll know where these tools are, should someone need a specific tool that's checked out to another user.

103. D.

Basic RFID tags use no encryption and can be counterfeited easily. Attackers can write information and modify an existing tag or clone a tag to invalidate authenticity. By reading information from an RFID, an attacker can track the location or movement of a person or object. More advanced RFID readers send requests to the tags for identification. An attacker could use their own RFID reader and use the information for their own purposes.

104. A.

RFID is prone to virus attacks with the backend database being the main target. An RFID virus can disclose the tag data or destroy what is in the database, disrupting the service.

105. A.

Most companies use 125 kHz cards for access doors secured with electric locks. These cards have no encryption or authentication and broadcast company information when any reader is nearby, making it easy for anyone with the right equipment to replicate these cards.

106. A.

Mobile Device Management for company-owned, personally enabled (COPE) using Near Field Connection (NFC) was built for convenience, not security. All you have to do is bump, tap, or swipe against an NFC reader and the connection is valid. No login or password is necessary. NFC is concerned only with distance. Turn off NFC by default when not in use.

107. B.

eDiscovery is the collection of intangible digital data. It is different than paper information because of volume, transience, and persistence. The six stages of eDiscovery are identification, preservation, collection, processing, review, and production.

108. B.

The identification phase identifies data custodians, as well as potential data, information, documents, or records that could be relevant. To ensure that there is a complete identification of all resources, data mapping can be used to reduce complexity.

109. A.

A duty to preserve data begins when an organization anticipates litigation in the future. Care should be taken to ensure that due diligence is taken and that the data is not contaminated.

110. D.

In the collection phase, data is sent to legal for examination. The length and breadth of this data collection are determined by the identification phase.

111. C.

The official definition of this control is to actively manage, inventory, and track all hardware devices on the network so that only authorized devices are given access. Unauthorized and unmanaged devices should be prevented from gaining access.

112. D.

Many local, state, federal, and international laws, as well as industry restrictions, require that data be kept for specific periods of time.

113. B.

The format for storing the data, who has access to that data, and how that data is eventually destroyed are important to a data retention policy.

114. C.

Most often, data is recovered from hard drives, flash drives, RAID drives, and other storage media. It could be caused by physical damage or logical damage due to software updates.

115. A.

Do not save any program files or documents, because doing so makes your computer write data to the hard drive, which increases the possibility that the data you're trying to rescue will be overwritten. You should not move files or folders or reboot the machine.

116. C.

Sometimes damage is physical, and sometimes it's logical. If the machine will not boot up in its original state, follow standard procedures for removing a hard drive, and with the appropriate connection, plug it into a functioning computer to pull off files as soon as possible. If the platters inside the drive do not spin, you will need to send the hard drive to a professional company, unless you happen to have your very own clean room.

117. A.

Encryption for data at rest is a key protection against a data breach. Data at rest is stored and usually protected by a firewall or antivirus software. Defense in depth is important to data at rest and begins with encryption.

118. A.

With storage, you need security systems so strong that a break would cost potential attackers more time and effort (i.e., work factor) than the data is worth. Cost and value of data is most important—no one wants to end up with systems that are more expensive than the data's value.

119. B.

Data security means keeping it private and out of the wrong hands. Data protection is about ensuring it remains available when there is a failure.

120. D.

Network topology and subnets are not a concern to be addressed with data at rest policies and procedures.

121. C.

A growing number of organizations are choosing to store some or all of their data in the cloud. Some people argue that cloud storage is more secure than on-premise storage, but it adds complexity to storage environments and requires old dogs to learn new tricks. Often with movement to the cloud, IT personnel needs to learn how to implement cloud storage securely.

122. A.

Multifactor authentication is a method where a user is granted access only after giving more than one piece of evidence to authenticate. It could be something the user knows, is, or has.

123. C.

A direct-attached storage (DAS) system is often the cheapest option. The first problem with DAS is limited disk space, and depending on size, some servers have only two or three disk slots. This space can be consumed quickly, depending on the type of RAID deployed. The other problems with DAS are that they need to be backed up often and they cannot share data with other servers on the network. DAS is best used for operating systems.

124. C.

A storage area network (SAN) is a data network comprised of servers that connect to a centralized storage space. Storage can be easily expanded to increase data recovery. And, if the servers boot from the SAN rather than DAS, a failover server can boot from the original SAN disk, reducing downtime. It costs more, but you get more.

125. B.

Network-attached storage (NAS) offers file-sharing services over file-based protocols. The number of devices is not limited by physical limitations like port space. The performance of an NAS is based on congestion and the speed of the network.

126. C.

A data owner has administrative control over a specific data set. Some examples of a data owner are a treasurer who had administrative control and is accountable for financial data or a human resources director who has responsibility for employee data. In most enterprise organizations, the owner is not the custodian.

127. A.

The data owner is responsible for determining who has authorized access to information about certain assets in their area of control. A data owner could take this on a case-by-case basis or could define a set of rules called rule-based access control. Access is granted on the security principles of separation of duties, least privilege, and need to know.

128. C.

A system administrator is usually identified as the data custodian because of the technical expertise needed. This person has admin/sysadmin/root level of access. As a critical role, they work closely with the data owner to protect information important to the organization.

129. B.

The data owner is an administrative function, while the data custodian administers the technical control.

130. C.

Data users may come across a situation where they feel that information security is at risk. It should be reported to the appropriate authority, usually the data owner, as soon as possible.

131. A.

In no event should any access of any kind be granted to any data that is classified as sensitive without the express permission of the data owner.

132. D.

You do not want security analysts chasing irrelevant alerts down rabbit holes. Modern cyberattacks take place over a long time period, progressing through multiple stages of the kill chain. Organizations must detect attack campaigns, not isolated alerts, and you cannot do that with periodic logging.

133. D.

Patch management is expected, while unexpected software installs are not. Know your network, including what is normal and what is abnormal, and always assume you are under attack.

134. A.

While these are all good questions, the next question for mitigation should be "Can the attackers actually use what was stolen?" Attackers steal data all the time, but most of the time it is unusable due to encryption. If the data stolen is in clear text, it changes the trajectory of your disaster recovery process.

135. A.

Have every individual change their password immediately. If you were using the same password on multiple sites, change those as well. A single breached password can take down other accounts if you are reusing passwords. Just don't reuse passwords.

136. A.

Two-factor authentication (2FA), sometimes called *multifactor authentication*, is an authentication methodology where a user is granted access only after presenting two or more pieces of evidence, such as something they are, know, or have. One of the best ways to use two-factor authentication is with an application or separate device. Using 2FA with a password manager adds complexity to your defense in depth and is a great way to stop the attacker.

137. C.

Change management is extremely important with any type of transaction. With any change of account or payment recipient, trust but verify. If the account had been verified after the change or verified before payment was made, this would not have happened.

138. D.

While every company is unique, you must ensure that technical teams, legal, and public relations are all on the same page. Technical teams obviously are in charge of incident handling, legal assures compliance with the law, and public relations needs a clear corporate position to communicate to the media and the rest of the company. For example, sales will need to know what to say to customers regarding the incident but will likely get that from PR.

139. A.

Once you determine which machines were compromised, make sure that nothing was left behind that will do more damage or allow the attackers access again. Collect all evidence and logs that are appropriate, then ensure that other assets are protected against the method the attackers used to get into your organization.

140. A.

Public relations must disclose the hack. If you disclose the breach, you control the message. You can present the information correctly and reinforce your business reputation by demonstrating that you are handling the breach in a responsible way. For example, if a limited number of customers are affected, notify them in a proper and timely manner.

141. B.

A well-organized attack by skilled individuals is extremely difficult to solve with a technical investigation, but your data will be extremely helpful for detectives (i.e., authorities). They may have parts of a puzzle that you do not have access to or have established a modus operandi of hacking groups in your specific industry. Notifying the authorities is how many hacking organizations are found, by identifying certain ways of attacking or the mistakes they made.

142. C.

A hunt team is not a new concept in cybersecurity but is usually afforded only by large enterprise organizations. Hunt teams play an important part in efficiently detecting, identifying, and understanding advanced and persistent threats and correlate this data to find the bad guys.

143. A.

Mapping regulations to security metrics enables hunt team members to prove compliance quickly. If not, they have to gather, organize, and store the necessary metrics each time they need to prove compliance, which is time better spent elsewhere.

144. B.

Heuristics and behavior analysis supplement the rules with subtle and detailed interpretations of patterns of events, which are based on experience instead of a binary rule set.

145. D.

In this situation, until the evidence is presented in court, it is not necessary for the investigator to provide their credentials in the chain of custody documentation.

146. C.

Just like with physical evidence, digital evidence must have a chain of custody should you ever need to present this information in court. A technician may install a password or write blocker to reduce the risk of altering the copy of the data, and some forensic specialists will hash the drives to secure evidence.

147. A.

In criminal cases, a defendant can petition the court to exclude evidence that the prosecution obtained if someone broke the chain of custody for any reason.

148. A.

Understand what can be contained in volatile memory before you power down a machine that you believe is compromised. Use a tool that is able to quickly analyze RAM and add that data to digital evidence.

149. A.

The Internet Engineering Task Force (IETF) released guidelines for evidence collection known as the RFC 3227. This document explains the order of volatility, which is least volatile to most—archives, physical logging, disk, temporary files, routing and ARP tables, registers, and cache.

150. B.

This is incident detection and response (IDR). When you are able to learn about the different components of the attack life cycle, you become better at identifying, responding to, and remediating a threat before attackers can steal your data.

151. B.

Using dd enables you to clone a drive and flash a USB, hard disk, or any file without data loss. It is the most widely used free tool for collecting evidence. You can also use it to back up your system.

152. A.

Tcpdump is a packet analyzer utility that monitors and logs TCP/IP traffic between a computer and the network.

153. C.

On a Windows server, nbtstat displays NetBIOS over TCP/IP (NetBT) statistics. NetBIOS displays tables for both the local and remote computers. It refreshes names registered with the Windows Internet Name Service (WINS).

154. D.

When a Windows machine blue screens, it creates a memory dump or a crash dump. This file has all the computer's memory at the time of the crash. It can help diagnose problems that led to the crash in the first place.

155. A.

Using tshark helps an IT analyst capture bytes on a computer network and enables the analysis of a captured file. The more accurate the capture, the easier and faster the analysis will be.

156. A.

In forensics, when you are recovering only specific files based on headers, footers, or data structure, it is called *data carving*. Foremost was created by the USAF and can be downloaded at Sourceforge.

157. C.

In measuring the severity of an incident, the five measurable factors are scope, impact, cost, downtime, and legal ramifications.

158. A.

The scope of a breach or incident is measured in how widespread or how far the incident reached. The scope of this type of breach is minimal.

159. D.

Most organizations orchestrate their own incident classification framework and base severity on the same categories as the NIST CVE. Those categories are Critical, High, Moderate, and Low.

160. C.

You need to determine what types of records were compromised. Was it personal information with credit card data or personal information with healthcare data? Not only is each type valued differently on the Dark Web, you will be fined differently based on your compliance requirements.

161. A.

If sensitive data is encrypted properly, there can be no breach. Organizations that are the target of attackers usually face serious costs due to notification of quantitative and qualitative losses. Organizations with PII face even higher liabilities.

162. A.

After an incident, managers can evaluate the effectiveness of their response and then identify areas that need improvement, specifically, assessment, detection, notification, and evaluation. The lessons learned document details how your emergency response process can be improved.

163. D.

In an after-action report (AAR), it is time for reflection and to record what was done well and what areas need improvement.

164. C.

If the hard disk fails due to a mechanical issue, then repeated access to the drive can result in losing more data or corrupting what still exists. You should minimize access to the drive.

165. A.

Any organization that experiences a breach has the opportunity to learn from the incident. Communicating that intelligence to the organization as a whole will ensure that the risks the organization experiences are met with expertise, and that company assets, including people, are safe.

166. A.

With vulnerabilities, patch management is crucial for reducing risk. Some vulnerabilities require compensating controls, while some require removal from the organization. Either way, a reevaluation of response times, head count acquisition, and process improvement can all come from an AAR.

Chapter 4: Technical Integration of Enterprise Security

1. A.

TCP port 20 is used to transfer data, and TCP port 21 is used for control commands. The FTP server listens for a client to initiate a session on port 21 and then initiate the data connection over port 20.

2. D.

Security best practices and policies should be short—a maximum of two to three pages. Shorter policies are elaborated on with procedures, standards, and guidelines. Shorter policies are more easily understood and easier to comply with for an organization on the whole.

3. D.

The dictionary brute-force attack technique uses hundreds of likely possibilities, including real words. It cycles through them, attempting to find a legitimate password and to defeat a cipher or authentication mechanism.

4. D.

A security policy is a high-level document. A set of procedures is the opposite. Procedures are specific and precise. For example, while working for the military, the security policy said we would use port security. Procedures were how we enforced that security policy with "sticky MAC."

5. C.

Standards define the technical aspects of a security program and include any hardware/software that is required by your organization. Like procedures, standards should be detailed enough so there is no question what hardware/software should be implemented. Standards ensure consistency.

6. D.

The situation described has a security risk of data remanence. Remanence is the residual information that remains on a disk after it has been erased. The VM is unavailable, but that doesn't mean the data has been destroyed.

7. D.

Security marking uses human-readable labels. Security labeling is the use of security attributes for internal data structure inside information systems. Security marking enables organizational process-based enforcement of security policies, while labeling enables information system–based enforcement of security policies.

8. B.

A dedicated system functions at a single level of a specific classification, and all the users of that system have the same clearance and the same need to know as the system. System high mode is a single level of classification, but not everyone has the same level of need to know. Multilevel consists of multiple levels of classification and various clearance levels where not everyone has a need to know. In compartmentalized mode, everyone accessing that node has the same clearance.

9. C.

A covert channel is a type of computer attack that enables information to be leaked through existing information channels or networks using the existing structure. It has been used to steal sensitive data by using some of the space available within network packets, enabling the attacker to receive the data without leaving a data trail. A packet may have only a single bit of the covert data, making it nearly impossible to detect. The primary way of defending against covert channels is to examine source code and monitor resource usage by critical systems.

10. D.

Software developers often leave a backdoor in tools but should remove them before the software goes to market. If the backdoor is left in a product by accident, it is called a maintenance hook. A security patch is often used to remove the maintenance hook.

11. A.

Dynamic RAM is a form of storage on a motherboard that must be constantly refreshed because the stored information evaporates over time. A hard drive, ROM, and a BIOS are not as volatile as RAM and do not need refreshing over time.

12. A.

A workgroup is a prime example of privilege management where the user accounts are decentralized. The other listed options are all centralized privilege management solutions.

13. D.

Kerberos, directory services, and SAML 2.0 are all examples of single sign-on solutions. You provide your logon credentials and do not have to provide them again while in a specific environment. A workgroup is not a form of single sign-on. You have to authenticate each time to access a system.

14. D.

To prevent losing everything with just one password being exposed, enterprise-level single sign-on requires two-factor authentication, such as texting a mobile phone or using a one-time password, biometrics, or proximity card, making systems much harder to compromise.

15. A.

Standards define the technical aspects of a security program. Policies are high-level documents, while procedures are specific and include a great deal of detail.

16. C.

NIST recommends that data storage media is physically destroyed at the final stage of media life. It is also considered the best method of sanitizing data.

17. C.

Data retention is the amount of time that specific data is maintained in storage. Data stored for more time than is needed becomes a security risk to an organization.

18. A.

Data protection is the process of preventing the capture of sensitive data by those unauthorized to see or use it. Most often, encryption or cryptographic techniques are used to protect confidentiality.

19. A.

There are 10 steps in the system development life cycle, and they are ideally completed in this order: Initiation, Definition, Design, Develop, Document, Acceptance, Testing, Certification, Accreditation, and Implementation. Testing includes guidelines that determine how a system is tested.

20. D.

In the implementation phase, the system is transferred from a development-and-testing environment to production.

21. C.

Of these choices, 802.11n would provide the best speed for devices compatible with 802.11g with throughput up to 600 Mbps. Devices using the 802.11n standard transmit in both the 2.4 GHz and 5.0 GHz frequency ranges. WiMAX is based on IEEE 802.16.

22. D.

On-premise deployment solutions are the only way that an organization has complete control over the network, hardware, and software. A solution that is entirely created and deployed on-site could cost more up front than a hosted or cloud-based solution, but the local organization would have access to the system and all the data.

23. D.

Software as a service (SaaS) is a term used in cloud computing. SaaS providers use streaming services or web applications to enable users to interact with software.

24. C.

After you have established security requirements when replacing core legacy equipment, those requirements need to be escalated and communicated to all the stakeholders in the project.

25. C.

A flat network topology in a single large broadcast domain means any device sending an ARP broadcast will receive a reply. This provides potential access to every system. Network segmentation using virtual local area networks (VLANs) creates a collection of isolated networks where each network is a separate broadcast domain. If configured correctly, VLAN segmentation hinders unauthorized access to systems, giving you time to find a solution for old vulnerable protocols.

26. D.

The biggest security risk is that multiple VMs using the same transport could possibly lead to exposure.

27. D.

SOA is the architecture that enables the service to work, while the API is the service. Some concerns are that applications will run slower and need more processing power, leading to higher costs. Scalability can become an issue, and there are no industry security standards, which can lead to exposure to outside threats.

28. D.

You will want to build a centralized organization-wide access control system, bringing together multiple organizations for standardization, identity management, and authentication with the ability to repeat this with the next iteration of mergers and acquisitions.

29. D.

An enterprise service bus (ESB) is a communication system for software inside service-oriented architecture (SOA). It is a special type of client-server model focused on agility and flexibility.

30. A.

Performing a risk analysis on merging two disparate organizations together is the first thing you do. The results will feed into the interconnection policy so that you can merge the two entities securely.

31. D.

Proprietary data or intellectual property is one of the most important assets for an organization to safeguard. When doing the proper risk analysis, you must consider what would be left behind and possibly exposed in the cloud.

32. C.

Legacy is a term used to describe hardware or software that is old and for which support is not available from the vendor. For a mission-critical legacy application server, the most important policy above would be how to preserve the data on that server once it is replaced.

33. D.

SPML is a standard used for federated identity and promotes the automation of user account management operations. It presents LDAP in an XML format. SAML is XML and used for exchanging authentication/authorization and is also typically used in browsers for SSO.

34. A.

By utilizing a shared client server and storage, the goal you are working toward is increased customer data availability.

35. A.

If you place an IDS sensor somewhere in your network for intrusion detection, your end goal is important. If you want to see what threats are being aimed at your organization from the Internet, you place the IDS outside the firewall. If you want to see potentially malicious internal traffic that you have inside the perimeter of your network, you place the monitor between the firewall and internal LAN. Considering what traffic is most important, find the relevant point in the network that traffic MUST pass through to get there.

36. D.

Data provisioning and processing data in transit and at rest is the best description of the data life cycle end-to-end.

37. A.

CIS Top 20 controls is a prioritized set of best practices developed by leading security experts. The most important of these is knowing what hardware you have, what software is on it, and where it is.

38. C.

Simple Object Access Protocol (SOAP) is exactly that—simple. It is used as a messaging protocol for exchanging information via web services with disparate protocols and operating systems. This enables developers to authenticate, authorize, and communicate using Extensible Markup Language (XML).

39. A.

A global organization that collects data from customers must be concerned with data sovereignty. A learning management system (LMS) and a content management system (CMS) collect information on global students taking classes, viewing videos, and accessing files. This data is subject to the laws of the country where the data was collected. Many countries have passed various laws around the control and storage of data.

40. D.

Network segmentation enables you to increase network security by creating defense in depth. In today's threat environment, you should assume that you are always under attack and eventually will experience a breach. Network segmentation makes it much more difficult for an attacker to perpetrate an attack over your entire network, as they could with a flat network infrastructure.

41. D.

Downtime is not an option for many organizations. The best thing you can do is to be prepared for attacks. An RPO is how much data can be lost in a measured time frame, while an RTO is how long it takes to restore data from an incident. The people closest to those processes, such as business unit managers and directors, are most closely aligned to knowing what those metrics would be.

42. D.

Legal should always have a seat at the table when it comes to discussing how to control sensitive information. They should be aware of all new laws and acts that affect your business when it comes to safeguarding this resource.

43. A.

All Internet usage begins with DNS. DNS was designed in the 1980s before security was a priority. The Internet Engineering Task Force (IETF) created a solution with DNS Security Extensions (DNSSEC). DNSSEC uses digital signatures and public key cryptography on the DNS data itself, signed by the owner of the data.

44. A.

Default to the highest control for multiple data points. In this case, PHI wins with a High, integrity wins with a High, and availability is the same with a Low.

45. D.

A gap analysis assessment is a tool used to find the space between current performance and desired performance. It evaluates where you started and the actual performance and then identifies the necessary improvements to reach a goal by optimizing the allocation of resources and input.

46. A.

Transport Layer Security (TLS) is an encryption protocol intended to keep data secure when being transferred over a network. It encrypts data to ensure that eavesdroppers or other students are unable to see what you transmit, which is useful when using passwords or credit cards.

47. A.

After being hired as a subject-matter expert on network security, you must understand the business you're working with and what assets are most important to that business. For example, a bank will have different priorities than a healthcare facility.

48. D.

This rule will immediately prevent data coming or going anywhere on port 445. The others could be options, but they would take more time than you have to stop the spread immediately.

49. C.

Boundary control includes security services typically provided by devices focused on protecting a system's entry point. A firewall can be set to protect a network's border from threats originating from the Internet. You can also use routers and proxies for boundary control.

50. D.

The only answer that is a benefit to virtualization is faster provisioning and disaster recovery. Risks to virtual environments include patching, maintenance, and oversight, but the biggest is probably sprawl. It is easy to create VMs, push them out, duplicate machines, and forget about them. Once you bring them up, they could be up for weeks or months and get behind in patching, which creates a vulnerability.

51. A.

A Type 1 hypervisor is a hypervisor installed on a bare-metal server, meaning that the hypervisor is its own operating system. Type 1 hypervisors usually perform better due to the direct access to physical hardware.

52. B.

Type 2 hypervisors are applications installed on host OSs like Microsoft Windows or Linux. They are also called hosted hypervisors, because there is a host OS that translates between the OS, the VM, and the server hardware. Type 2 hypervisors are easier to deploy, but Type 1 hypervisors usually have better and faster performance.

53. D.

The best thing to do is add more disk space and employ some type of RAID configuration for speed and redundancy. With certain compliance, you need to know how long to keep the data, and if the cost is high, you must consider what type of backup medium is best for your organization. You really should not use a cloud-based backup solution unless you feel that the solution provider can completely secure your data. Sensitive financial records must have the proper security controls in place.

54. A.

A cloud-based deployment solution will probably be entirely operated and maintained by a third-party vendor. You will pay a usage fee for access to that solution but will lose some control over hardware and software.

55. C.

Infrastructure as a service (IaaS) enables a company to use hardware resources provided by a third party, including processing and networking to host varied multiple hosts.

56. B.

Software as a service (SaaS) providers use an Internet-enabled streaming service or web application to give end users access to software that would have to be installed locally or on a server. Gmail and Hotmail are examples of SaaS providers.

57. C.

One of the biggest benefits of moving virtual hosts to the cloud is elasticity. Businesses adopting this cloud computing solution can enjoy the dynamic allocation of resources to projects and workflows. It makes using the cloud efficient and cost effective.

58. A.

Using a company's stuff to build more stuff is a platform as a service (PaaS). Using programming tools and languages to develop more applications is utilizing a platform, as opposed to infrastructure or software.

59. D.

PaaS enables you to avoid the expense and complexity of having to buy and manage software licenses, application infrastructure, development tools, and other resources. You manage the applications and services that you have developed, and the cloud provider does everything else.

60. C.

Virtual desktop infrastructure (VDI) is the hosting of desktop environments on a central server. This has been called providing desktop as a service (DaaS). Thin clients are protected from unauthorized software, and data is saved in another location than the server. It uses centralized processing for better management and monitoring.

61. A.

A thin client is economical because you do not have to purchase a lot of processing power; in addition, IT support costs are negligible because there is no PC to support. There is no storage, and the server is protected through cloud management features and settings.

62. A.

A public cloud is the cloud computing model where IT services are delivered across the Internet. The defining features of public cloud solutions are elasticity and scalability for IT services at a low cost. A public cloud offers many solution choices for all types of computing requirements.

63. D.

Easy deployment and lower cost for less IT expertise can be good things.

64. B.

A private cloud is the cloud computing model where resources are located either on premise or at a vendor site, but where all resources are isolated and no other customer can use them. Private clouds are customizable to meet the needs of your business. With greater visibility comes greater control.

65. D.

Private cloud disadvantages include the expense and high total cost of ownership (TCO) as well as being difficult to scale to meet demand.

66. D.

A hybrid cloud is the cloud computing model where IT services are a mix of public and private solutions. Organizations can use a mix of both for security, performance, scalability, cost, and efficiency.

67. A.

A private cloud, public cloud, or a combination of both depends on a variety of factors, use cases, security needs, compliance, and limitations. Organizations that grow and evolve will use all three types of cloud solutions.

68. B.

A community cloud is defined by National Institute of Standards and Technology (NIST) as a collaborative effort in which infrastructure is shared between several organizations from a specific community with shared concerns. It can be managed and controlled by a group of organizations with shared interests so costs are spread over several users.

69. D.

While single tenancy is more secure due to isolation and you control access and backups, it requires more maintenance because single-tenant environments need more updates and upgrades that are managed by the customer.

70. C.

While the multitenancy cloud services would be less expensive because usage and resources are shared, they operate at maximum usage making for best efficiency. They are easier to set up because of the high volume of customers with good experience onboarding. The limitations of multitenancy are multiple access points, less control, and one tenant affecting all other tenants, so it has some risk for vulnerabilities to be exposed.

71. A.

VMs are easy to deploy, and many organizations don't follow proper procedures. This can lead to VM sprawl, which is the unplanned proliferation of VMs. Attackers can take advantage of poorly monitored resources, which create failure points, so sprawl can cause problems even if no malice is involved.

72. B.

While difficult to perpetrate, VM escape is considered a serious threat to VM security. VM escape is committed against Type 2 hypervisors. If you escape a Type 1 hypervisor, it is called hyperjacking.

73. A.

A denial of service (DoS) affects availability and can be perpetrated against on-premise assets and virtual assets as well as poorly configured cloud assets. These attacks exploit many hypervisor platforms by flooding the network with traffic and bringing operations to a halt.

74. C.

The ability to monitor VM network traffic is critical. Conventional methods will not detect VM traffic because it is controlled by internal soft switches. Hypervisors do have effective monitoring tools that should be enabled, tested, and used.

75. A.

The first priority should be to understand what data this organization has and to classify it through a data classification engine. Look for a comprehensive solution that locates and protects sensitive content on the assets uploaded to the cloud.

76. D.

Negotiating an SLA is in administrative contract guaranteeing service. It is created, not deployed to a cloud environment. You should absolutely have one that will protect the business and processes.

77. C.

Security as a service is known as SECaaS as well as SaaS. SaaS has traditionally been known as software as a service. SECaaS is applied to information security services and does not require hardware on the premises, and companies will avoid a large capital outlay. Security services can include authentication, antivirus, and anti-malware, as well as intrusion detection, incident response, and penetration testing.

78. A.

A sandbox is an environment that is used for opening files or running programs without interfering with production environments. It is used to test software as safe or unsafe. A cloud sandbox adds another layer of security as it is completely separate from your corporate network.

79. D.

CASB is mainly focused on security. Companies need visibility and access control on cloud assets, in addition to a method for data loss prevention as well as protection from malware and insider threats.

80. B.

Most enterprises use three types of provisioning. Self-provisioning is where a cloud customer fills out an online request for services with the provider. This tends to be the most expensive arrangement. Another type is provisioning in advance by signing a contract allocating a certain amount of resources per unit of time with the customer receives a discounted rate. The last type is dynamic provisioning. In this model, the customer dynamically receives the requested level of resources on an as-needed basis. When the customer needs more resources, the provider delivers them, and when the customer needs fewer resources, the provider takes some away. This model is also known as autoscaling.

81. D.

You have already made the transition from on-premise computing to cloud computing. Comprehensive cloud security should focus on all infrastructure components, servers, workstations, devices, and data. Because most attackers are after data such as healthcare records, credit card information, and intellectual property, you should prepare to answer questions regarding encryption, control, and access management.

82. D.

Your organization can avoid all these security vulnerability examples by conducting regular secure configuration assessments.

83. A.

Containers' speed, agility, and portability make them a great tool for streamlining software development.

84. D.

With containerization, benefits include reduced IT management resources, quicker application deployment, less code to move, easier-to-deploy security updates, and greatly reduced size of snapshots.

85. B.

VMs are a great choice when you are running applications that need all of the operating system's resources and functionality for running multiple programs on servers or when you have several operating systems to manage. Containers are better when you need to maximize the number of applications running on a minimal number of assets. All the other answers are reversed.

86. D.

Containers are *not* sandboxes. If an attacker gains access to a container, there is a risk of container escape. If they get access to the host, they get access to all other containers on the host, which is why security controls must be deployed on the containers as well.

87. C.

Containerization establishes a separate encrypted space on employees' mobile devices where business data is kept apart from everything else on the device. This can enable an administrator to manage what is in the container and restrict access to the corporate network.

88. D.

File integrity monitoring (FIM) exists because change is constant in your IT department. FIM monitors and detects changes in files that could indicate there has been a breach. FIM is a critical security control involving the examination of files to see when, how, and who changes a file and if those modifications are authorized. FIM is also useful to detect suspicious modifications and detect malware. It is required for certain compliance regulations like PCI-DSS.

89. B.

Platform as a service (PaaS) is the best solution for hosting databases and web servers. It provides you with a computing platform including operating systems, giving you access to hardware and software over the Internet.

90. B.

The Common Vulnerabilities and Exposures (CVE) list includes a number for identification, a description, and a public reference for all known cybersecurity vulnerabilities.

91. A.

Multifactor authentication can include two or three different factors, whereas two-factor authentication is always limited to two factors. Requiring users to authenticate with three factors is more secure, but users will expect an MFA solution to be easy to use. Remember, your end users will try to bypass your security controls if you do not make them easy to use.

92. A.

Single sign-on is an authentication solution that allows a user to log in once and have access to multiple computer systems.

93. A.

Kerberos is a single sign-on solution from Microsoft used to authenticate users once and then allow them to access the resources they are authenticated to access.

94. B.

Kerberos is a single sign-on solution that uses a ticket-granting service to provide tickets to clients to access specific network services.

95. A.

Service Provisioning Markup Language (SPML) is an automated provisioning mechanism designed to automate identity management tasks.

96. C.

A Federated Identity Management solution would allow employees from the various companies to log in once and access resources they are authenticated to access at all companies.

97. B.

Open Authorization (OAUTH) is an authorization standard that enables a user to authorize the access of their data without them sending authentication credentials.

98. A.

Simple Object Access Protocol (SOAP) is a protocol used to allow distributed web service a means of communicating in a structured format. SOAP messages are defined using XML.

99. D.

OpenID is a means of propagating identity information to different web services. For OpenID to work, the web services must have an existing trust relationship either among the web services or via a common third party.

100. D.

OAUTH does not share password information at all. OAUTH is a framework that provides access to a third-party application without providing the owner's credentials to the application.

101. D.

Accountability is the best reason to develop a logging process. When establishing a logging process, you should be aware of storage capabilities and create a log-reviewing policy that trains reviewers how to review those logs periodically.

102. A.

OAuth is an open standard that is defined by RFC. It is an authorization framework that provides third-party applications access to resources without actually sharing those credentials. SAML, SPML, and XACML are all XML-based standards developed by OASIS. SAML is used to exchange authentication and authorization information, SPML is used for federated identity single sign-on, and XACML is used to define access control policies.

103. A.

A turnstile ensures that only one authenticated person enters at a time. A turnstile is a means of physical access control and prevents tailgating, which is when an unauthorized individual attempts to follow an authorized person into a secured area.

104. A.

Remote Authentication Dial-In User Service (RADIUS) can provide authentication, authorization, and accounting (AAA) functions to users, in this case, VPN users.

105. A.

For legacy systems using Java applets, it is a client-based technology that is most likely to use a sandbox as a security mechanism. Java is an object-oriented program (OOP) that can be used to provide functionality to a website.

106. D.

Separation of duties is an access control mechanism that creates a system of checks and balances on employees with privileged access. Separation of duties requires more than one user to participate in a critical task. One person writes the check, and another person signs the check.

107. C.

A penetration test is one of the most intrusive types of vulnerability testing that will actively find and exploit weaknesses. A penetration test attempts to gain access physically and digitally without the proper authorization.

108. C.

Security Assertion Markup Language (SAML) is the best one to use for a web-based SSO environment. SAML is XML-based, which is an open standard used for authentication and authorization.

109. A.

A backdoor allows an attacker remote access to a system, enabling them to use the system like an authorized user. Some backdoors are used for business purposes, such as customer support and maintenance, but it is not a good business practice.

110. D.

Terminal Access Controller Access Control System Plus (TACACS+) is a Cisco proprietary protocol used for authentication, authorization, and accounting (AAA). RADIUS and DIAMETER do not encrypt usernames, and CHAP doesn't encrypt anything.

111. D.

Accountability is the task of reviewing logs for malicious activities. An administrator who regularly reviews server access to determine who is manipulating sensitive files is performing an accountability task.

112. A.

Decentralized access control requires more administrative overhead. Centralized access control administration does not require as much, because all the accounts are centrally located.

113. C.

Virtual desktop infrastructure (VDI) is the practice of hosting a desktop environment within a virtual machine that is hosted on a centralized server. An encrypted VDI keeps the vendor representatives out of the systems to which they should not have access.

114. D.

If the IP address 192.168.1.109 does not appear as a RADIUS client, you will need to reconfigure the server so that you receive an access request from 192.168.1.109 and you can validate the request.

115. D.

If you examine the kill chain for cybersecurity, then you know that attackers will use phishing campaigns to target insiders. Once compromised, an attacker will use privilege escalation to attempt to gain enhanced permissions across the network.

116. A.

A major drawback of Kerberos is that it can be a single point of failure. It requires availability of a central server, and if the server is down, no new users can log in.

117. C.

DNS suffers from lack of authentication of servers and, therefore, an authenticity of records. During DNS hijacking, for example, the client's configuration is changed so that DNS traffic is redirected to a rogue server that sends the client wherever the attacker wants them to go.

118. D.

IP Security (IPSec) is a suite of protocols used across an IP network providing authentication, integrity, and confidentiality. This includes Authentication Header (AH), Encapsulating Security Payloads (ESP), and Security Associations (SA), which provide the different configurations and keys used for those connections. Internet Security Association and Key Management Protocol (ISAKMP) is a component of SA and how the keys are managed and exchanged between the devices. An IPSec VPN will protect traffic being forwarded from client to server or from server to server.

119. A.

A common contextual authentication method is using a geographic location or the time of day. If a professor typically accesses their account during their planning period while in their office, any login attempt that falls outside those parameters will fail.

120. C.

If two-factor authentication (2FA) is not an option, then creating a virtual private network between your organization and the SaaS provider is the BEST option.

121. B.

Of all these answers, having a generator for backup power, intrusion protection, and strong authentication would best meet the need of protecting your customer's information.

122. D.

The best solution is to have identification and authentication carried out with a message to the customer's mobile number, which generates a one-time password to be entered into the web portal to reset passwords.

123. B.

The definition of attestation according to Merriam-Webster's dictionary is "an act or instance of proving the existence of something through evidence." The Payment Card Industry (PCI) is governed by the PCI Security Standards Council, which will certify that an organization has completed and passed or failed an audit with an attestation of compliance.

124. D.

The characters make up a hash value of the software using SHA 256. A hash is a mathematical function that provides a unique output string of characters per an input of characters. In this case, it is used to ensure that the software has not been altered during download.

125. A.

Hashing is a mathematical function used to compute a unique identifier for a particular input. You can compute the hash for the software and post it on the server along with the software. When an end user downloads the software, they can run the software through the same hash function. If the output of the hash function matches what is posted on the servers, then the software has not been altered.

126. C.

If the colleague's public key is used to encrypt the message, only the colleague's private key can decrypt it. As long as the colleague doesn't disclose their private key, only the colleague will be able to read the message.

127. D.

If the colleague's public key is used to encrypt the message, only the colleague's private key can decrypt it. Because the colleague is the only one with their private key, it ensures that only the colleague can read the message.

128. B.

If you sign a message with your private key, the only key that can decrypt it is your public key. By successfully decrypting the signature with your public key, you have proof that the message did come from you and was not altered in transit. Note: Anyone who has your public key can also read the message. Signing the message does not protect the message contents.

129. B.

Because you signed the message with your private key, only your public key will decrypt it.

130. A.

It is a digital signature, which is a process that guarantees that a message has not changed in transit. When you digitally sign a message, you hash the message and encrypt the hash using your private key. The receiver hashes the message and uses your public key to decrypt the hash sent. If they match, the message was not altered in transit and maintained integrity.

131. A.

The process will provide confidentiality via encryption, integrity of the file via the hashing process, and nonrepudiation because only the colleague's public key can decrypt the message.

132. A.

A stream cipher encrypts data bit by bit. It doesn't require as many hardware resources as other types of ciphers like block ciphers.

133. B.

RC4 is a stream cipher that encrypts data bit by bit. It doesn't require as many hardware resources and can be used on legacy what or hardware with few resources.

134. D.

The Advanced Encryption Standard (AES) is a modern symmetric block cipher ideal for encrypting large amounts of data.

135. B.

The information could be hidden from the naked eye. One means of extracting information from an organization is to hide the information in non-suspicious files such as image, music, and video files.

136. A.

The presence of unapproved software could be suspicious. Finding steganography tools on a system is a sign that information may have been extracted inappropriately. Further investigation should be performed to determine whether information was stolen.

137. C.

The stego-only analysis technique is used when only the file containing the hidden information is available. You do not have the original document or know the hidden information.

138. D.

The process of looking for hidden information in steganography data is called steganalysis.

139. A.

One technique to make it more difficult to find hidden information in a file is to encrypt the data first. When you encrypt the data, the hidden data will not appear as clear text but as random characters. This makes detection of the hidden information more difficult.

140. B.

Online Certificate Status Protocol (OCSP) is a protocol designed to quickly check individual certificates with the issuing certificate authority in real time.

141. C.

Key escrow is a means of securing cryptographic keys so a lost key can be recovered. If the key is broken up into parts, no single escrow agent has the complete key, lending to the security of the entire key.

142. C.

Certificates are managed via their serial numbers. If a certificate is revoked, the certificate's serial number is placed on the revocation list.

143. D.

You will provide the certificate authority with the public key so it can be included in the digital certificate. Private keys always stay private and are never given out to others.

144. A.

A PKI token is a hardware device used to store digital certificates and private keys. The encryption and decryption are performed on the hardware device itself.

145. B.

The Elliptic Curve Cryptography (ECC) algorithm is ideal for mobile devices because it requires less computational power to calculate, yet is considered very secure.

146. A.

Perfect Forward Secrecy is a way of protecting your asymmetric keys by only using these keys to generate temporary session keys based on your asymmetric keys. In this case, your actual key pair is never used to encrypt and decrypt the data. Also, these temporary keys are periodically changed, so if any temporary key is compromised, only the data encrypted with the temporary key is exposed. All other sessions are still secure.

147. B.

Steganographic watermarking is a way of using steganography to watermark data. In this case, the watermark is hidden in the document so that it doesn't distort the document contents but still provides a means of proving where it originated.

148. C.

Mobile devices typically have much less processing power than other computing devices, thereby requiring encryption technology that is not resource intensive.

149. C.

GNU Privacy Guard (GPG) is a free asymmetric encryption system in which the end users have to manage the keys and verify public key identities.

150. D.

You should also decide what authentication methods are used, how authentication will be implemented, and what the standard operating procedures (SOPs) are should your organization be compromised.

151. A.

After a thorough risk and needs assessment, make sure that the network security policy is part of the official company manual. In addition, ensure that all employees have security awareness training and a copy of the security policy.

152. B.

An alert from any one of these assets should trigger the network security team to take a closer look at the cause of the alert.

153. D.

By operating at the network layer, IPSec can protect data transmission in a variety of ways, giving users access to all IP-based applications. The VPN gateway and firewall are located at the perimeter of the network, and client software must be installed to use IPSec VPN if required.

154. B.

SSL VPNs grant granular access to a corporate network. A remote user can access only those applications that are important to their work. An example is access to a mailbox on an Exchange Server instance or a specific subset of URLs on the intranet.

155. A.

Anyone anywhere can log into a desktop sharing tool. A remote support session usually begins with an employee clicking a link and giving up control of a system. If this is a malicious person, you are in some serious trouble. Once they have control of the system, they can access other enterprise systems such as databases, supporting servers, and more.

156. A.

If you create a unique session key for transactions instead of relying on an encrypted session, attackers cannot gain access to data for more than one single communication between a server and a user. The benefit is increased security for both the user and the server.

157. B.

Unified communications present serious security challenges because it brings together disparate technologies. As technology becomes more complex and accessible from the public Internet, the threat increases. You must be diligent in protecting communications that are vital.

158. A.

Using a device for its intended purpose will keep your network most secure. A UC server should be protected by a firewall, which is designed to block all unknown traffic into a network and only allow traffic from trusted resources. A properly configured firewall is designed to sort through traffic, while a UC server is not.

159. C.

Do not open attachments if you cannot verify the sender.

160. A.

A shadow copy allows for manual or automatic copies of computer files to a local or remote location.

161. D.

Tracert is used to show details about the path a packet takes from where you are to where you want to be (for example, a website). Tracert allows you to diagnose the source of many problems. Ping just lets you know that the website is up or down.

162. A.

When a UC server is updated, it is important to follow the best practices for updating. Make sure you know what has changed and how the update impacts the rest of your environment; back up the system first and perform the update during a proper maintenance window.

163. C.

Social engineering is manipulating people to give up information. A social engineering attack can be an email from a friend or another trusted source that contains a compelling story or pretext. The danger of social engineering with collaboration tools is that an end user's guard is down because these are co-workers they can trust, which makes it easy to extract information.

164. D.

Replacement cost is the cost to replace the property on the same premises with other assets of comparable material and quality for the same purpose.

165. A.

The classification of data almost always is used for confidentiality. Once you classify data, you will know to what extent you need to provide access, encryption, etc., on that specific piece of data.

166. C.

A nondisclosure agreement (NDA) is a legal document that restricts what can be shared by either party.

167. A.

A distributed denial of service (DDOS) is an attack performed through a multitude of systems on a single target. A website, or in this case, VoIP, receives a massive amount of incoming data in the form of messages, requests, or calls. All of this incoming data forces the site, or service, to shut down and deny the service to customers and users.

168. A.

Not all vendors offer secure data center environments with multiple power sources and remote backups. Some cut costs and pass that risk on to you, the customer. This risk can knock you out of compliance if there is equipment failure for any reason.

169. D.

The cipher lock on the server room door is physical security as opposed to technical controls.

170. C.

A standard hardening practice is to turn off any unused services. If a feature is not used, do not enable it. If you use the UC server for voice, video, and instant messaging but not email, then turn off the email functionality. There will be less protocol traffic, and the server will do less work.

171. C.

Privileged users can compromise sensitive data. Evaluate how flexible the tool's levels of user access are and evaluate if there are security risks at each level. The right collaboration tool should permit administrators to set up controls around user visibility and terminate access rights for an account that is suspected to be compromised.

172. A.

The best answer here is to use strict password guidelines. Require users to change their passwords and use a device-based recovery tool rather than common passwords like their mother's maiden name. Every attacker worth their salt has an account at Ancestry.com.

173. B.

The best way to protect against these summaries being leaked outside of your email setup is to use a summary page instead.

174. A.

Attackers get creative and can piece together the name of your organization and randomly try different collaboration tools to try to find a way into your organization. Change the `mycompanyname.appname.com` to something more random to obfuscate the login portal.

175. A.

The major question that you should ask the vendor is what level of encryption they offer, and if the tools encryption is comprehensive. If it is not compliant with HIPAA or HITECH, you could be open to major regulatory non-compliance risk.

176. C.

The best programs today have some of the best people in the security world working 24/7 to identify and prevent issues. Make sure that your vendor has the necessary support for your team to be successful, and consider training to help minimize adoption problems.

177. A.

The management of your application requires end-to-end monitoring, so a connection from your location to the cloud environment is the best way to have great control over and visibility into attacks that threaten your environment.

178. A.

You can configure various security-related settings under Group Policy within Active Directory, such as the ones mentioned in the question.

179. B.

You could use Group Policy within Active Directory to configure lockout durations for unsuccessful login attempts. By locking out an account that is under attack for 10 minutes, it can greatly increase the time it takes for the attacker to be successful using a brute-force attack. Shibboleth is a SSO technology that can use the WAYF - "where are you from" service.

180. A.

Identity proofing is the process of verifying someone's identity based on information provided by a trusted authority. A driver's license is a form of identification provided by a trusted authority, in this case the government.

181. A.

Using the classic technique of acquiring credentials, attackers gain access to the collaboration account and send legitimate-looking URLs to team members. You have social awareness training for employees regarding email, but you have to teach them that there are other ways that attackers can get into your network.

182. C.

The padlock in the URL field indicates that TLS or SSL is used to encrypt the data.

183. B.

Secure Shell (SSH) encrypts the data sent to the network equipment. The other options send data in clear text.

184. D.

Using a RADIUS solution would provide an authentication, authorization, and account (AAA) function that will allow credentials to be easily managed from a central location while also providing login tracking. Using common usernames and passwords would prevent tracking login activity per user. Having unique usernames and passwords on each device will be difficult to manage, as each device needs to be modified as credentials are changed.

185. A.

For these requirements, the ability to audit event logs that include source address and time stamps is most critical.

186. C.

While SSL does encrypt data, TLS is the latest and most secure means of securing web-based communications today.

187. B.

A known vulnerability should always be managed by patching or installing compensating controls so that the vulnerability cannot be exploited.

188. D.

Whitelisting programs will prevent the user from downloading and installing programs that were not on the whitelist. This prevents unknown and untested software programs from being installed on a system.

189. D.

Of the options available, creating a corporate policy that specifies employees are not to divulge corporate information on social media sites, and the consequences of doing so, is a great first step. The next step is to train the employees on the policy and the importance of not divulging such information.

190. A.

A digital signature provides a means of verifying that an email originated from a particular user and that the email has not been altered. The term nonrepudiation describes the result of the user signing the email, but not the technology used.

Chapter 5: Research, Development, and Collaboration

1. A.

A best practice can be described as a procedure that is accepted or prescribed as being most correct. The results it produces are better than other means because it has become a standard way of doing things. In 1995, one of the first vulnerability assessment tools, known as Security Admin Tool for Analyzing Networks (SATAN), was shared with the community and at first was widely disparaged. Today, the Center for Internet Security (CIS) recommends constantly scanning for vulnerabilities as number 3 of the top 20 controls.

2. B.

Due care is using reasonable care to protect the interests of your enterprise. Due diligence is the actual practice of specific activities that maintain due care. If proper due care is not taken, you open the organization up to legal liability.

3. C.

Due diligence has the meaning of "required carefulness." Due diligence is exercising informed care that is expected of reasonable people. Performing this kind of process ensures that the proper information is systematically and deliberately protected.

4. A.

A best practice provides as much security as possible, while balancing other factors such as cost, usability, and scalability.

5. D.

Fiscal responsibility is essential for budgets and decision-making when it comes to spending. It is not fiscally responsible for any organization to spend money it doesn't have or to spend more money on an asset than that asset is worth.

6. A.

The National Institute of Standards and Technologies (NIST) is part of the U.S. Department of Commerce. NIST promotes innovation and industrial competition by advancing science and supporting advanced technologies including cybersecurity.

7. A.

PCI-DSS best practices were collectively created in 2006 by American Express, Discover, Visa, Mastercard, and JDB International for *any* organization, regardless of size or number of transactions, that accepts, transmits, or stores any cardholder data. These best practices improve the security posture of an organization and safeguard cardholder information. You can find PCI-DSS best practices at www.pcicomplianceguide.org.

8. B.

All merchants fall into one of four levels based on transaction volume over a 12-month period. Transaction volume is based on the number of credit, debit, or prepaid cards from a business. Merchant level 1 processes more than 6 million transactions annually, whereas merchants at level 4 process 20,000 or less. Any merchant that suffers a breach resulting in data compromise may be escalated to a higher level.

9. A.

A method of authentication is utilizing hardware but in a new way. We used licensing and tokens in the past, but putting the authentication into hardware is especially important for the Internet of Things (IoT). Good authentication requires three things from users: what they know, who they are, and what they have. The device itself becomes what they have. This way, the network ensures that the entity trying to gain access is something that should have access.

10. B.

Using analytics to trigger a red flag to system administrators for a user behaving badly or outside the parameters of normal behavior is called user behavior analytics (UBA). Using big data by taking a baseline over a certain period of time of any access outside of their normal baseline triggers an alert. This way, you're able to differentiate between legitimate activity and illegitimate activity.

11. A.

By using encryption and tokenization, you can be assured that even if data is stolen, it cannot be sold. It can also help move data securely around a large enterprise, and analytics can be performed on the data, which reduces risk and is required by certain compliance regulations such as PCI, PII, and PHI.

12. C.

You need to know where this malicious behavior is coming from. Instead of looking at users, machine learning looks at the entity. With proper business analytics and developments in machine-learning models, we know that a specific data center behaves a certain way. Any anomalous behavior should trigger an alert.

13. D.

More approaches to security are being created in and for the cloud and are continuing to evolve. Some cloud-hosting organizations, like Amazon, have programs of certified data centers including above-average data center security. The provider will be responsible for building physical security into their facility.

14. C.

The RFC system was invented in 1969 and have become the official documents of Internet specifications and communication protocols, procedures, and events. These static documents from the technology community are authored by engineers and computer scientists and shape the workings of the Internet and Internet-connected systems. Not all RFCs are standards, they can also be classified as Informational, Best Practice, and Historic. For more information, you can visit `rfc-editor.org`.

15. D.

Cyberthreat intelligence is extremely beneficial to every organization. However, of those listed, it is least beneficial to your marketing plan. Properly applied, it can provide insight into cyberthreats, enabling faster response as well as resource allocation.

16. B.

Strategic cyber intelligence informs decision-makers on long-term issues and overall intent. Operational cyber intelligence guides support and response operations and usually comes as a forensic report. Tactical intelligence assesses real-time events and supports day-to-day operations.

17. A.

All four of these are threat models. However, spoofing identity, tampering with data, repudiation, information disclosure, denial of service, and elevation of privilege (STRIDE) was developed in 1999 by Microsoft. These steps help systematically determine how an attacker uses a threat against you. PASTA is a seven-step risk assessment model, and TRIKE is used for security auditing. VAST enables you to scale the threat model across an entire ecosystem and SDLC and gives actionable output.

18. B.

An unintended flaw left in software or in an operating system where there is no patch or fix is called a zero-day vulnerability. These vulnerabilities open an organization up to exploitation should they be found by cybercriminals. The term *zero-day* refers to a software vulnerability without a fix. Once the vulnerability is made public, the vendor has to work quickly to fix the issue. If it is used against an organization before the fix or patch is made available, it is known as a zero-day attack.

19. D.

A security awareness program is vital to establish safe and effective personal online security habits. This should not only be done for compliance, but should become a best practice after you have strategic operations in place.

20. A.

As an organization, you should reserve your brand on all social media channels. This enables you to reach across different channels, making it easier to do business. However, do not ignore accounts that you stopped using or don't use often. Idle social media accounts can be used fraudulently against you and could send false information, damaging your business.

21. B.

Even when you lock down your social media accounts, you must beware of third-party applications that integrate with big social networks. Attackers gained access to Forbes' Twitter account through a third-party app called Twitter Counter, which is used for analysis.

22. A.

Your organization needs to think carefully about who needs to have posting permission as well as passwords to social media accounts. Limiting access is the best way to keep them secure.

23. D.

The latest threats on social media would be in your social media training. Your social media policy should be easy to understand, and training will give employees a chance to engage, ask questions, and review latest threats on social media and discuss if the social media policy needs updating.

24. A.

By appropriating an organization's specific hashtag, bots can distribute spam or malicious links that will appear in an organization's circle. Trend-jack is similar in that attackers will pick the tops trends of the day to disseminate the attack, making a "social media watering hole" and planting the payload where the potential users are gathering.

25. B.

Most social networks are monitored for malicious activity. A post that is instantly reposted by the thousands is a clear indicator that there is malicious activity. The original posting account is banned and is called the martyr bot. The original account sacrifices itself to spread the attack.

26. A.

Social media companies update privacy settings regularly, which can impact your account and give you more control over how data is gathered and used. You should also perform a scan of who has access to your social media platforms as well as publishing rights. Any employee who does not work for your company needs their access suspended.

27. A.

Cybercriminals can penetrate your systems and make your sensors show fake results. You can fail to notice alarms and miss an opportunity to solve a problem before irreversible damage happens. Attackers can fabricate data and use it against you. This attack is thwarted with fraud detection.

28. B.

If an outsider has access to the mappings to storage options, they can change those settings or add new ones. It can ruin all data processes when attackers make mappers produce inadequate lists of key/value pairs, which will make the data faulty. It could also give an attacker access to sensitive data.

29. A.

A data warehouse will be used to grant users access to what they have a right to see. Granting access is difficult, so for a medical research facility only the medical information gets copied to a separate data warehouse and is provided to a specific user group.

30. A.

Data provenance is a big data security concern. Unauthorized changes in metadata lead to the wrong dataset, which makes it nearly impossible to find the correct information. Untraceable data sources can be a huge impediment to finding security breaches as well as any fake data that has been injected into real data.

31. D.

A hazard of machine learning is model drift. Machines learn for themselves, and it's impossible to figure out how they learned and why decisions were made. It is, therefore, difficult to prevent undesirable outcomes in advance or to trace them to correct them afterward.

32. A.

Most security vendors are moving away from signature-based systems used to detect malware to machine learning systems that try to interpret actions and events and learn from a variety of inputs about what is safe and what is not.

33. C.

This actually happened. A casino in North America detected a ransomware attack that used the network-attached fish tank as a point of entry. The attack was spotted due to machine learning algorithms that detected the intrusion, and no damage was done.

34. A.

Many organizations today are using AI and machine learning to triage threats so workers can focus on critical attacks. Machines can handle the repetitive work so that you can free up time to deal with strategic issues such as modernizing infrastructure.

35. B.

A computer emergency response team (CERT) is an expert group that handles incidents. CERT is also a training organization for FEMA that trains volunteers for emergency preparedness. The name computer emergency response team comes from Carnegie Mellon University (CMU). CMU can certify organizations that are building a computer security incident response team (CSIRT).

36. C.

The SDLC has several steps beginning with initiation. This is where the idea develops and includes documenting objectives and answering questions.

37. D.

After initiation and planning, the next step is to research and evaluate how the system functions, see how it fits end-user needs, and include any future functionality that might not exist in the first iteration.

38. A.

After a project has been initiated and function requirements and system design specifications are completed, then comes the development phase of the life cycle. During development, the creation of system source code, including decisions on methodology, is decided on. Source code is tested and analyzed for security, and after this phase everything is documented.

39. C.

After all controls are documented, an independent third party should be testing for functionality and security. Doing so will verify that the system meets all specifications that were documented up to this point in the system development life cycle.

40. B.

Certification is the process where a certifying officer compares the system against a set of functional and security standards. Accreditation is the process by which management approves the system for implementation. Even if a system is certified, it might not be accredited by management.

41. D.

Implementation is the phase where a system is transferred from a development environment to a production environment ready for end users.

42. A.

Once a system is in production, the post-installation phase in which the system is used in production is called operations and maintenance support. The system is monitored for weaknesses and vulnerabilities that did not appear during development. The systems data backup and restore procedures are also tested. If changes need to be made, it enters the phase of revision and system replacement.

43. B.

The accreditation process is where the system is accepted by the data owner, even if it has not been certified. Accreditation is different than certification, which means that a system has been tested by an authorized body and proven to fit the security requirements of the data owner.

44. B.

Licensing is not a phase in the SDLC, and you are not responsible for this process.

45. B.

The waterfall method of software development begins with long planning phases and design with a very rigid path through a set of phases. Waterfall is a common methodology for large projects.

46. C.

Agile software development has been in use since 2001, when the waterfall methodology was too strict and rigid. Agile emphasizes teamwork and feedback, which changes the direction of the software. There are two major types of agile methods: Scrum and Kanban. Scrum defines roles and events, whereas Kanban is simple but has a lot of flexibility.

47. A.

Fuzzing is a technique used in software testing that uses invalid data or random input called fuzz. It is done to discover implementation bugs in the software.

48. D.

A spiral software development process is beneficial because of risk management; development is fast, and there is always room for feedback. It is not advisable if it's a small project because it's known to be expensive. There is more documentation with the spiral model because it has intermediate phases that require it. To be effective, the model has to be followed precisely.

49. A.

A web application security plan should outline your organization's goals and contain a checklist based on infrastructure, individuals in the organization who are involved in maintaining web application security, and cost.

50. C.

The application performs authentication, so you would be checking for the appropriate vulnerability for this process. Privilege escalation is the only vulnerability that has anything to do with authentication.

51. B.

An application that uses a large amount of data, especially when done with an HTML editor, is at high risk of injection attacks if proper prevention measures are not enforced.

52. A.

You test for different things at different stages of the web application development cycle. With static application security testing (SAST), the tester has access to the framework and design and will test from the inside out. SAST doesn't need the application to be deployed. Because the scan can be executed early in the SDLC, it can find problems sooner.

53. C.

You test for different things at different stages of the web application development cycle. With dynamic application security testing (DAST), the tester has no knowledge of the technology or framework. DAST tests from the outside in, which represents what an attacker would do. DAST does not check source code. It analyzes by executing the application itself. Unfortunately, DAST must be done at the end of the SDLC when you actually have an application to test, and therefore, the vulnerabilities will be more expensive to fix.

54. B.

A critical application would be externally facing and have customer information that needs protecting. These applications would need to be managed and tested first because they would be targeted by attackers. Serious applications may be internal or external and have sensitive information. Normal applications would be at the bottom of the list and would be included in tests only after critical and serious applications are fully tested.

55. A.

Categorizing applications by importance and then categorizing vulnerabilities can take considerable time. You want to test for the most threatening vulnerabilities as quickly as possible.

56. A.

NX is an abbreviation for "no execute," which is a bit used in a CPU that keeps storage and instructions separate. Some companies use proprietary acronyms so they can market security features. For example, Intel calls it XD, which means execute disable. AMD calls it EVP, for enhanced virus protection.

57. C.

In a buffer overflow attack, an attacker knows where the code for a certain function accepts input. The attacker feeds more information into that spot and can include a malicious payload. Major operating systems today support Address Space Layout Randomization (ASLR). ASLR randomizes the locations of different portions of the code. Basically, ASLR turns this attack into buffer overflow "whack-a-mole" where the attacker has to properly guess the location of the address space.

58. B.

When development merges with operations, it is called DevOps. The collaboration between developers and operations requires an agile model, which follows a flow of information between coders and users. More recently, DevOps has turned into SecDevOps, where security is integrated into the flow of information.

59. B.

Code that is useful for only a short time period and is used for a unique reason can be called low-quality code. On the other hand, if you have built code and intend to use it for years for multiple applications, it is called high-quality code.

60. D.

Many teams find that this is an economical and streamlined way to work because errors are identified and handled quickly. It lets a team bring software to production faster than other approaches.

61. A.

Versioning is a way to control software so that everyone knows the latest and greatest version. Major revisions of software require the first number to change (i.e., 1.0 to 2.0). Minor revisions would increase from, for example, 1.7 to 1.8.

62. D.

A security requirements traceability matrix (SRTM) is documentation used for technical projects that call for security to be included in testing. This matrix is used to make sure there is accountability for all processes. Each row in the spreadsheet is a new requirement, so it's easy to view and compare the tests needed.

63. A.

When doing unit testing, you test individual modules, or programs, to see whether the module is accepting input properly and whether it provides the right output to the next part of the program.

64. C.

A peer review is sometimes called a code review. You inspect all the code to make sure that it works as it's supposed to and that all security and business needs are met, but it can take a long time to perform. The time and effort can result in delays that may outweigh the benefits.

65. A.

Most attackers are going after vertical privilege escalation, in which a lower privilege user or application accesses functions reserved for a higher privileged one. Smart attackers also use horizontal privilege escalation in which a normal user accesses certain functions from another normal user. A wealth of information can be stolen with horizontal privilege escalation, which is rarely monitored.

66. D.

I had to. Anyway, cookies are not always designed to store sensitive data. In fact, some cookies that are used with the checkbox Remember Me function may hold usernames and passwords in Base64, which can be reverse engineered on several websites.

67. B.

Vulnerability management software has grown extremely sophisticated. A tool like Rapid7's Nexpose can scan your environment and give you a treasure trove of information, including the IP, OS, hostname, number of vulnerabilities, and their CVSS scores. What vulnerability management software cannot do is natively add your business context and how important those assets are to your business. That can come only from the business.

68. A.

Without an accurate inventory of systems, software, versions, locations, addresses, and data, it is nearly impossible to assess the priority of a real-time security alert.

69. A.

First, you would be surprised how many organizations name their servers with the operating system and department they are provisioned for. If we were doing a penetration test, we would assume that this server was a Microsoft Server 2016 machine with HR information being processed on it. This information enabled an attacker to tie all these findings together with a common inventory that contains all the details in the above question. Having an accurate inventory is extremely useful in creating a risk management program. (And, you should never name an asset so that the purpose or operating system can be determined from its hostname.)

70. B.

You can use Nmap detect to detect OS vendor, generation, and device type. Nmap probes the target with TCP and UDP packets and examines OS specifics like initial sequence numbers (ISNs), IP identifier, timestamps, explicit congestion notifications (ECNs), and window sizes. Every operating system has distinctive responses to these probes, which results in an OS fingerprint.

71. A.

In the United States alone, there are more than half a million cybersecurity job openings with an average base salary of $96,000, according to CyberSeek. The lack of skilled professionals is incredibly important, and we must expand the talent pool.

72. A.

Most experts agree that a rise in misconfiguration because of a lack of experience and education will lead to more breaches of cloud environments.

73. A.

Leveraging machine learning and innovating artificial intelligence will help find and respond to threats. Unfortunately, as with every tool, attackers are using this technology as well. In the future, we will see new machine learning malware and AI spear fishing that increases the length and breadth of cyberattacks.

74. D.

Organizations today must reduce their IoT attack surface, increase the attack surfaces they monitor, and attempt to reduce false positive alerts that often affect IoT devices.

75. D.

Achieving security collaboration objectives while preserving fundamental properties is done with a voluntary bottom-up self-organization, which is the "think globally, act locally" solution.

76. D.

A successful sales organization requires marketing, enablement, and product training to build trust and for the customer to see value in the tools that you are selling.

77. A.

There is no one-size-fits-all method for communicating up to stakeholders and down to staff. Independent review has proven successful. As someone tasked to communicate with upper management or department heads, you take your findings and share that information.

78. B.

A structured review is another successful approach to communicating security and collaborating on risk. All findings are openly discussed with all appropriate people at the table. This is a more formal review than the independent review.

79. D.

The modified Delphi collaboration methodology enables you to find consensus among groups with anonymity. It is similar to the structured review, but instead of discussion, responses are written for future review.

80. A.

You may be asked for your technical expertise to create policies that need updating or processes that need modifying. If any part of the security requirements is dependent on people, your organization must be aware of how security works and should not attempt to circumvent those controls.

81. A.

Programmers are driven by a different set of requirements than security professionals. Programmers must make it work so a product can be sold, while security must make it safe so no one gets attacked. It is rare to find a programmer with a security background, or a security professional who can program. Programmers are given a list of requirements that may be just a small piece of the puzzle, so understanding how the entire puzzle will be seen by the user may not be well communicated.

82. A.

Personally, I have been told by network engineers, "I can ping it. It isn't my problem." The objective of these roles is different. Dev builds, Sec protects, and Ops keeps it running. Sometimes, these roles will have conflicts, so it requires great communication between the three to accomplish an organization's goals.

83. D.

One common employee control is least privilege. If you don't need information to perform your job, you shouldn't have access to that information.

84. A.

A background check should be conducted on any candidate that you are bringing into your organization. Credentials need to be validated, and positions and experience verified. This way you have the right person in the right position.

85. A.

Anyone in a financial role at an organization who refuses to take time off can be suspect. They may not want anyone else to uncover their malfeasance while they are out of the office.

86. A.

Job rotation is vital to prevent a single point of failure. By rotating employees periodically, you have a backup in case of an emergency.

87. A.

Dual control ensures separation of duties and prevents theft or misappropriation of information. This is usually found in high-risk areas.

88. C.

An important document to have new employees sign is a nondisclosure agreement (NDA). NDAs protect organizations from the leak of sensitive information, preserving confidentiality.

89. C.

A stakeholder is any person, or group of people, who has a direct or indirect stake in an organization. They could consist of employees, consultants, users, or managers.

90. B.

A preventative control would try to keep something from happening. If something did happen, then you would want to layer a detective control on top of the preventative one so that you have visibility that it happened, and you can quickly correct the problem. An example of a preventative control would be a firewall or fence. An example of a detective control would be auditing or an intrusion detection system.

91. A.

The three-tiered approach consists of a brainstorming session, evaluating the ideas that come out of the brainstorming session, and then deciding which solution is best. More than one solution can work in a situation, but you will want to think about things such as cost and complexity. Doing so will help you work these security controls into the budget and timeline.

92. A.

After an incident, the team should recommend technology, policy, governance, and training changes so that the incident does not happen again. Understanding the lessons learned will enable information to be shared across the company and added to existing security policy and procedures.

93. A.

GRC stands for governance, risk, and compliance. A good GRC strategy leads to better decision-making, stronger IT investments, the elimination of silos, and reduced fragmentation. Governance ensures that activities align with business goals. Risk ensures that any risk associated with an activity supports the business goals. Compliance ensures that all activities meet laws and that regulations are used and secured properly. ITIL, PMI, and CRMA are certifications you can attain in GRC.

94. D.

Upper management needs to be kept informed of all things related to security so that they can make the best security policy decisions as well as administrative, technical, and physical controls. In turn, they should be seen and heard supporting security measures put in place by the organization.

95. D.

Administrative controls consist of security awareness training and password policies. Technical control examples involve encryption and firewalls. Physical controls include gates and guards.

96. B.

An SSL VPN will encrypt; data remains in your data center, and users have the same programs on the virtual workstation image.

97. A.

As a technical project manager, you are responsible for the entire process from beginning to end—from customer input to audit review.

98. A.

Laws and regulations differ from country to country. Opening offices in other countries will make those offices fall under different jurisdictions.

99. D.

The database is in a secure network with limited access. It is probably compliant and inaccessible to most attackers. The best answer is inappropriate administrator access.

100. A.

The only way to combat all three of those concerns is with robust security awareness training for all employees.

101. B.

HIPAA is one of the strictest compliance regulations. Having access to confidential information on a personal device is not only bad practice but could lead to fines if, or when, patient records are lost.

102. D.

Security awareness training should focus on customer data that is gathered, used, and shared in the organization; and how it is protected and why. When employees understand compliance and regulations as well as the ramifications of not following policy, it drives faster and more complete adoption.

103. C.

Asset management is the most likely use case for configuration management software (CMS). A CMS is used to ensure that configurations are deployed on new systems and are maintained in their secure state. It can also be used for compliance, standardization, change control, and license management.

104. A.

It is extremely important to have senior management fully accept and endorse the security policy. Otherwise, it can be difficult to implement disciplinary action against employees who violate the policy.

105. A.

Details and procedures should not be in your security policy. A security policy should be agile enough to change with technology and not have to be edited with every software update or hardware refresh.

106. B.

A procedure would be step-by-step instructions. A standard defines the technical aspects of your program, in addition to any hardware or software that is required.

107. C.

A comprehensive program will have policies, procedures, standards, and baselines. Guidelines are optional and provide helpful information for employees. They are considered discretionary because you should follow them, but it is not required.

Chapter 6: Practice Test 1

1. B.

The main difference between Type 1 and Type 2 hypervisors is that Type 1 runs on bare metal and Type 2 runs in an operating system.

2. C.

A vulnerability assessment would be the best option to look for known vulnerabilities in an operating system, software, or a web application.

3. D.

Bob writes the check. Alice signs the check. This is called dual control. It prevents one person from having too much control and prevents fraud. If Bob and Alice decide to work together to defraud an organization, it is called collusion.

4. A.

The security triad is often referred to as the CIA triad. Verification is not a part of the triad.

5. D.

Spam is junk email, spim is junk instant messages.

6. C.

Terminal Access Controller Access Control Server (TACACS+) is a security protocol used to handle authentication, authorization, and accounting. It was developed by Cisco to handle growing security needs.

7. B.

Encryption as a whole is used for confidentiality. Symmetric encryption is specifically used for privacy as well as authentication. The biggest issue with symmetric encryption is key distribution.

8. A.

To make sure they have the right person in the right job, an organization should do a background check and call references.

9. B.

Encryption is the process by which you take clear text and convert it to ciphertext using different algorithms.

10. D.

Created by Ron Rivest in 1987, RC4 is one of the most widely used streaming ciphers and is used in popular protocols like SSL. However, it is no longer considered secure, so careful consideration should be taken if you do use it. DES, 3DES, AES, and Blowfish are all block ciphers.

11. D.

Broadcasting is useful in the Address Resolution Protocol (ARP) and the Dynamic Host Configuration Protocol (DHCP). ARP uses broadcasting to map MAC addresses to IP addresses. DHCP uses broadcasting to reach the server for dynamically assigning IP addresses to hosts on your network.

12. A.

Metasploit is the premier penetration testing tool, created by HD Moore and owned by Rapid7. By default, payloads created in Metasploit use TCP port 4444.

13. C.

Enterprise architecture is the practice of organizing and documenting IT assets so that they can be strategically managed, expanded, and budgeted.

14. A.

Least privilege is the practice of limiting access to the level an employee needs to get their job done. For example, an administrator does not need the ability to open email in a browser on a critical server while signed in as an administrator. That can be dangerous.

15. D.

ASLR is a security technique that implements memory protection by randomly mixing memory addresses. This makes an attack more challenging because the address of the required code is unknown.

16. A.

A virtual desktop infrastructure (VDI) is a centralized solution that enables a server to interface with the end user through a host system.

17. A.

Classful routing classifies IPv4 addresses that start with 0.0.0.0 to 127.255.255.255 as a Class A address. The first 8 bits, or the first octet, denote the network portion, and the last three octets belong to the host portion. There are several reserved spaces within the Class A network space to include 127.x.x.x, which is reserved for loopback addressing.

18. B.

DNS uses port 53 for both TCP and UDP. TCP is used for DNS zone transfers, and UDP is for DNS queries.

19. D.

A digital signature is a mathematical process that verifies the authenticity of messages and documents. It enables a message to be received from a known sender and with the belief that it was not altered in transit. A digital signature is a hash value that is encrypted with the private key of a sender.

20. B.

Scalability, accessibility, and decreased cost are all advantages of cloud computing.

21. C.

The tool has completed an OS fingerprint with the result of Microsoft Windows Server 2016.

22. C.

Job rotation is a security tenet that provides for cross-training as well as detecting fraud. It also decreases the negative effect if someone leaves the organization.

23. D.

Logical unit numbering (LUN) is an authorization process that makes a LUN available to a select number of hosts.

24. B.

If Internet Message Access Protocol (IMAP) is being used, the message received is not stored on the local device but on the server. Post Office Protocol (POP3) will attempt to download the email to the local device.

25. A.

If a company has heavily invested in software and that company goes out of business, it would be beneficial to have access to the proprietary software code.

26. C.

According to RFC 5905, Network Time Protocol (NTP) version 4 is used to synchronize system clocks among a set of distributed time servers and clients.

27. A.

When a certificate expires, it should be added to the certificate revocation list (CRL).

28. C.

A router is most closely associated with access control lists (ACLs). An ACL is the basic firewall control to either allow or disallow traffic into a network.

29. D.

Vishing is an attack where a scammer fakes the caller ID so they appear to be coming from a trusted source.

30. B.

A cross-site request forgery (CSRF) is an attack that forces an end user to execute actions in a web application that they are currently authenticating. As an administrator, CSRF can compromise an entire web application.

31. D.

In the United States, it is illegal to discriminate against a job applicant based on race, color, religion, sex, age, national origin, or disability.

32. D.

The best time to terminate an employee's access to company assets and network devices is at the time of termination.

33. D.

Network-attached storage (NAS) is the target for read and write operations. While configuring the NAS, you have an option of enabling NFS or SMB. NFS and SMB are network protocols at the application layer used for accessing files over the network.

34. A.

Voice over IP (VoIP) is more susceptible to power outages than the traditional Plain Old Telephone Systems (POTS). Loss of power means the entire system fails.

35. B.

In the hierarchy of documentation, policy documentation is the highest tier, defining who, what, and why regarding an overall security posture of an organization.

36. A.

A cookie maintains the session state of a user while in a browser.

37. C.

Kali, formerly known as Backtrack, is an operating system built as a Linux distribution, oftentimes bootable. Kali Linux is available in 32-bit, 64-bit, and ARM, as well as several specialized builds for hardware platforms including Windows.

38. B.

Denial of service (DoS) and distributed denial of service (DDoS) are attacks that do not give unauthorized access but rather block legitimate users from access.

39. D.

When a user belongs to a large number of security groups, it becomes difficult to authenticate. This is because the ticket Kerberos builds is not large enough to contain all of the user's group memberships.

40. D.

A wildcard certificate is a public key certificate that can be used with multiple subdomains of a domain. A wildcard certificate can be cheaper and more convenient to manage than owning a certificate for every subdomain.

41. B.

A service-level agreement offers precisely measured statements such as "There will be fewer than 50 lost man hours per year due to computer maintenance." The operational level agreement (OLA) states what the functional IT group will need to do in relation to each other to support the SLA. For example, an OLA may state, "The server team will do patching of the servers every Friday at 5 p.m."

42. C.

A storage-attached network (SAN) will appear to the client OS as a local disk or volume. It can be formatted and used locally as a backup drive or file storage.

43. A.

Information is sent across the Internet in packets. Packets are sent at regular intervals. The set amount of time it takes to reach their destination is latency. Jitter is the fluctuation of latency over time.

44. C.

A baseline is the document that defines a minimum level of security needed for an organization.

45. D.

In April 2014, the North American Registry for Internet numbers announced it had reached the last phase of its IPv4 countdown plan. There are no more IPv4 addresses. IPv4 works with a 32-bit decimal address, whereas IPv6 works with a 128-bit hexadecimal address. There are four billion IPv4 addresses. There are 340 undecillion IPv6 addresses.

46. A.

By default, LDAP communication between client and server is not encrypted. This means it would be possible to capture traffic and view the information between client and server, which can be dangerous when transmitting usernames and passwords. LDAPS adds encryption.

47. B.

The main drawback of symmetric encryption is that everyone engaged has to exchange the key used to encrypt the data before they can decrypt it.

48. D.

The software is likely very different. Policy documentation would state that vulnerability management would be done. Procedures would list the step-by-step procedures and processes that you take to run the new software.

49. B.

IEEE 802.1q is the networking standard that supports virtual LANs.

50. A.

An application programming interface (API) is a tool that can allow two applications to talk to each other.

51. C.

Layer 2 Tunneling Protocol is used to support virtual private networks. It does not provide encryption, so it is often implemented with IPSec.

52. B.

According to ISO 27001, senior management is responsible for the content in a security policy. The intent of involving upper management in the security program is to ensure that governance is aligned with framework. It ensures the intended outcome of a security program.

53. A.

A honeypot would be a detective control function and a technical control type. Control functions include preventative, detective, and corrective functions. Control types are physical, technical, and administrative.

54. C.

The best example of fault tolerance for hardware would have an identical server running in parallel. Fault-tolerant systems use backup components that automatically take the place of failed components, ensuring no loss of service.

55. D.

Formal logic, or mathematical logic, is based on propositions or Booleans that can be true or false. These are combined with conditions that are the foundation of how computers make decisions.

56. C.

IMAP can be used as a replacement to POP3. It can be beneficial for mobile users because of folder management, remote mail, and the ability to sign in from multiple mobile devices. SMTP is used to send mail; IMAP and POP3 are used to receive mail.

57. B.

DNSSEC does not protect against DNS kiting or tasting. DNS kiting, or tasting, is a practice where someone registers, cancels, and registers the domain again, all within a grace period. Income can be earned from the site because the site is functional, but you don't have to pay to register the site.

58. A.

An asymmetric encryption algorithm has easier key exchange and management but needs a bigger key than a symmetric algorithm to have the same work factor.

59. D.

There must be a permit statement on an ACL. Otherwise, all deny statements will add to the implicit deny all, and nothing is permitted.

60. A.

Simple Object Access Protocol (SOAP) uses XML so that it can be neutral among web services. It can run on Windows, Mac, and Linux, and allows clients to use web services and get responses independent of platform or language.

61. D.

Chain of custody must be followed, should evidence need to be admitted in a court of law. Chain of custody indicates the collection, control, transfer, protection, and analysis of the evidence. It is important to maintain the chain of custody to preserve integrity and to prevent contamination.

62. D.

A business continuity and incident response plan is an administrative control type.

63. D.

Regression testing happens after software is changed to make sure the program works as intended.

64. A.

By teaching all employees when they are hired and then annually, you hope to prevent breaches, events, or incidents in the future. It is a preventative control.

65. B.

Hypertext Transfer Protocol (HTTP) typically runs over port 80.

66. B.

The A record is the most basic type of DNS record. It is used to correlate a domain with an IP address.

67. D.

SHA-512 is one of the strongest encryption algorithms used today. Authored by the NSA, it has 128 bits with 80 rounds. The other two secure hashes used today are RIPEMD-320 and Whirlpool.

68. D.

Extensible Access Control Markup Language (XACML) has architecture and a processing model that helps evaluate access requests according to rules placed in policies.

69. C.

Organizations still use Information Technology Security Evaluation Criteria (ITSEC). ITSEC uses the terminology target of evaluation (ToE) and has seven evaluation levels. Prior to ITSEC being developed in Europe, TCSEC was created by the U.S. Defense Department, is better known as the "orange book," and was more stringent than ITSEC.

70. D.

Encrypted packets are not processed by most intrusion detection devices. Other potential issues with NIDS include high-speed network data overload, tuning difficulties, and signature development lag time.

71. C.

An extended ACL allows you to permit or deny traffic from specific IP addresses to a specific destination IP address and port. With an extended access list, you can match information such as source and destination IP addresses, port numbers, and type of protocol. DES is an encryption algorithm, not a network-based protocol.

72. D.

You do not want to experience the same incident again. After you have completed all the steps in an incident response process, you bring all stakeholders together to list the lessons learned so that history does not repeat itself.

73. A.

SNMP version 3 (SNMPv3) adds encryption and authentication, which can be used together or separately.

74. B.

Telnet is a protocol used to establish a connection to TCP port 23. It is blocked because there is no built-in security and should be avoided because of eavesdropping. Usernames and passwords are sent in the clear.

75. D.

UDP is connectionless, so there will not be a sequence number.

76. B.

A service level agreement (SLA) is the agreement between parties that lists the level of support that your company will receive from the provider.

77. D.

Audit logs would be a detective control function and an administrative control type.

78. B.

A scytale was a simple tool used by the Spartans to perform a cipher. It was made by wrapping a long thin strip of leather around a piece of wood of a certain diameter.

79. A.

The intent of Bell–LaPadula is to protect the confidentiality of information for an organization.

80. D.

PPTP is one of the oldest protocols and enables hosts to set up a connection between two endpoints. Remote Access Service (RAS) is a service, not a protocol. L2TP is the best option. L2TP is a VPN protocol that is paired with IPSec to provide encryption and authentication for traffic that passes through the connection.

81. D.

A smartphone with location enabled will capture the coordinates of the user while taking a picture.

82. A.

An information security audit is performed to ensure that the protections you have placed on information systems are working as expected.

83. C.

Having a corporate policy regarding digital and physical data destruction is important to protect against sensitive data being found in the garbage.

84. D.

If you want to use the drive again after removing all data, then perform a seven-pass drive wipe at the bit level. Degaussing will ruin the drive and make it inoperable. Emptying the recycle bin or microwaving the drive will not actually remove any data.

85. B.

The formula to use would be SLE = AV × EF. $15,000 × .20 = $3,000.

86. D.

A partnership is a type of business where two or more individuals share potential profits as well as risk.

87. B.

A TPM chip is technology designed to provide hardware-based encryption.

88. A.

The three major security clearances for national security positions are Confidential, Secret, and Top Secret.

89. B.

The General Data Protection Regulation (GDPR) is a legal framework that sets guidelines for the collection and processing of personal information for all people who live in the European Union (EU).

90. D.

Resource management is not a threat to a manufacturing organization.

91. B.

Applying, cataloging, scheduling, and implementing change are all part of the Change Control process. Changes should be made in the most organized manner possible.

Chapter 7: Practice Test 2

1. A.

Procedures will be the most granular document with step-by-step instructions.

2. C.

Modified Delphi is a group technique used to bring mutual agreement by soliciting feedback and using anonymous questionnaires to further discussion.

3. C.

Outsourcing is when a company obtains goods or services from an outside supplier. In this example, a company may save money by outsourcing the call center rather than hiring new employees.

4. A.

TLS protocol uses asymmetric encryption for key exchange, such as Diffie–Hellman and a symmetric algorithm like AES for data encryption.

5. C.

Canonical Name (CNAME) records are used to alias one name to another.

6. A.

Testing starts once the coding is finished. The software is tested thoroughly, and any defects found are returned to developers for correcting. Testing is done until the customer is satisfied.

7. D.

Smartphones can pick up on infrared light. Most smartphone cameras can see the illuminating light from IR cameras.

8. D.

Brewer and Nash is the security model for organizations that need to mitigate conflicts of interest. It is also called the Chinese Wall.

9. D.

When using the cloud, it is difficult to know where your data is stored. The company you are using may be incorporated in the United States with server farms in Brazil. Many companies outsource to reduce costs.

10. D.

Quantitative data can be expressed as numbers. If you can measure it, it is a quantity.

11. C.

Input fields in web applications can be vulnerable to SQL injection. An attacker can use SQL commands in the input field in a way to change the statement executed on the server. Running the command shown executes the following SQL query: SELECT id FROM users WHERE username='username' AND password='password' OR 1=1;. Because OR 1=1 will always test true, the attacker will gain access to the account with the passed username in the field.

12. A.

The Security Account Manager (SAM) is a database file in Windows located on your system at C:\Windows\System32\config. They are also stored in the registry at HKEY_LOCAL_MACHINE\SAM.

13. C.

Security mechanisms should prevent unauthorized access and usage of data and functions. These preventive measures are circumvented by attackers finding new vulnerabilities and security gaps.

14. C.

An enterprise risk management (ERM) team identifies risk and adopts risk management best practices to either avoid, accept, transfer, or limit risk. Insurance is an example of risk transference.

15. B.

ALE is calculated by taking the asset value (AV) times the exposure factor (EF) times the annual rate of occurrence (ARO). In this scenario the ALE is $10,000 × 10% × 1.

16. A.

Using public WiFi can be dangerous, but it would not be as important in this policy-making situation.

17. B.

The Security Content Automation Protocol (SCAP) is used for standardizing automated vulnerability management, measurement, and policy compliance.

18. C.

Containerization is a standardized unit for development and deployment. It is a stand-alone lightweight instance of software that includes code, system tools, libraries, and settings. The two most popular containerization tools are Docker and Kubernetes.

19. C.

Senior management is responsible for setting goals, initiating analysis, and making sure the proper people and resources are assigned and available during risk analysis.

20. D.

Sideloading is a term that refers to transferring a file between two local devices without using the Internet. A file can be transferred using WiFi, Bluetooth, or USB. Sideloading can also describe installing applications on Android devices that do not reside in the Play store.

21. A.

In data storage, a hash function is a function that, when given a key, generates an address in the database table. This system uses a combination of numbers and letters to arrange data.

22. B.

Most developers will provide a hash for files to be downloaded from their site to make sure that the file is not corrupted during download or tampered with.

23. B.

According to RFC 2845, Transaction Signature (TSIG) is used to authenticate updates to a dynamic DNS database. It can also be used to protect zone transfers.

24. B.

Tethering is sharing connectivity from one device that is connected to the Internet with other devices.

25. D.

The Biba model focuses on integrity. The three goals are to prevent data modification by anyone unauthorized, to prevent unauthorized modification by anyone authorized, and to maintain consistency.

26. C.

Vector-oriented security is an approach in layering defense mechanisms to protect valuable information and data. Vector-oriented security focuses on common attack vectors like permanently disabling USB ports so they cannot be used.

27. C.

Public classification means that it can be released and freely distributed. FOUO means For Official Use Only. Secret and Unclassified are governmental information classifications.

28. A.

A hardware security module (HSM) is a physical device that is used to manage keys for strong authentication. It is usually an external device that plugs into a network server or a plug-in card.

29. D.

Public relations would be a qualitative control because it does not seek a numerical or mathematical statistic. Qualitative is subjective and deals with words and meaning.

30. D.

Data in transit is more vulnerable than data at rest. Data in transit has a greater risk that it will end up compromised. The keys to securing data in transit are to control access as tightly as possible, use authentication, and be able to track suspicious behavior and threats.

31. A.

The risk has been evaluated and management decided that the benefits outweigh the risk.

32. D.

Financial loss would be the threat combined with a vulnerability, which is better described as an impact or result to the organization.

33. D.

Electronic Data Interchange (EDI) is the computer-to-computer exchange of business documentation in a standard electronic format. EDI can cut down on cost, increase processing speed, and reduce errors if implemented correctly. The exchange of EDI documents is usually between business partners.

34. A.

There are many ways to protect personally identifiable information (PII). Use encryption, strong passwords, MFA, and backups. You will also want to have policy in place that dictates how long to keep personal information and how often to update systems, and to always use a secure wireless network when working with PII.

35. B.

The principle of least privilege is the practice of limiting the access rights of users to the minimum to get their job done. This reduces the risk of attackers gaining access to systems and compromising critical systems.

36. C.

Snort is an open-source, free, and lightweight network intrusion detection system for both Windows and Linux that detects any new threats to a network.

37. D.

When taking the CASP+, you should be comfortable using a tool like Network Mapper (Nmap). Of the options listed, -sL and -sn are both used for host discovery. -sU and -sT are used for UDP and TCP, respectively. TCP uses a three-way handshake to establish a reliable connection.

38. C.

DES is a symmetric encryption algorithm and uses a single shared key.

39. B.

Windows utilizes BitLocker on computers that have a Trusted Platform Module (TPM) chip on the motherboard for full disk encryption.

40. C.

A heuristic antivirus application examines the code and searches for specific commands or instructions that would not normally be found in an application. A behavioral detection antivirus program watches the operating system, looking for anything suspicious or out of the normal range of behavior.

41. B.

A hash function returns a fixed output for variable input. There is a chance that different inputs can produce the same hash output. If this occurs, it is referred to as a collision. Separate chaining is a collision resolution technique that works by creating a linked list to the place where the collision occurred. The new key generated is inserted into the linked list.

42. A.

.pcap files are data files created by Wireshark. The NIC is in promiscuous mode on a system using Wireshark default settings. In a .pcap file, you will see the time, source/destination IP, protocol, and length of the data traversing your network.

43. D.

InSSIDer is a tool created by Metageeks. It is a spectrum analyzer that will assist an administrator in determining areas of interference, signal strength, and coverage.

44. B.

Remote Desktop Connection will allow a user to authenticate and have access to all programs, files, and network resources on a system.

45. B.

A virtual private network (VPN) is a tool to protect privacy and security on the Internet. VPN securely connects two computers with an encrypted tunnel to transfer data between a remote user and a corporate network.

46. D.

The CLI command to flush and reset the cached contents of DNS is ipconfig / flushdns.

47. A.

Netstat will display active TCP connections. With certain options, it can also display listening ports, statistics, and the IP routing table.

48. C.

The show running-config command is the configuration in the router's memory. You will see IP addresses, interfaces, passwords, protocols, and other settings.

49. A.

A directional WiFi antenna is not going to boost any signal—it directs the energy from the transmitter. You can adjust a directional antenna's signal gain and angle to provide the specific range you need. You do not want unauthorized personnel in the parking lot able to use your corporate guest WiFi.

50. D.

Using the cloud is a trade. You gain speed, performance, and cost, but you lose control over the security processes.

51. B.

Procmon in sysinternals is a powerful tool that combines Filemon and Regmon. Process Monitor will give insight to the Windows registries, filesystems, and processes.

52. B.

Get-FileHash '.\Confidential.xls' -Algorithm SHA1 uses the Get-FileHash cmdlet to compute the hash value for the Confidential Excel file. When you press Enter and give it a moment to compute, you will see the hash value.

53. A.

These are four of my favorite hacking tools that are free and available on the Internet. Go to www.l0phtcrack.com, download these tools, and remember to use your powers for good.

54. A.

The default option for privileged users is -sS. This is a TCP SYN scan. Nmap will send a SYN packet, as if you were going to open a real connection, and you wait for a response. If you get a SYN/ACK back, the port is open. A RST means the port is closed.

55. C.

John the Ripper is a fast password cracker. It is free and open-source.

56. A.

PuTTY is a free implementation of a versatile terminal program. It supports SSH and Telnet as well as raw socket connections.

57. B.

Phishing is when an attacker sends fraudulent emails that attempt to trick the recipient into divulging sensitive information or downloading malware. Smishing is using text messages instead of email.

58. A.

A security incident and event manager (SIEM) is a tool that pulls in data from many sources and correlates information based on time and location.

59. C.

A standard should make a policy meaningful and effective. It will include one or more accepted specifications for hardware, software, or behavior.

60. C.

A buffer overflow condition happens when a program attempts to put more data in a buffer than it was designed for. It can corrupt data, crash a program, or sometimes cause the execution of malicious code.

61. B.

Trojans present themselves as one thing, when in reality they are something else.

62. A.

Simple Mail Transfer Protocol (SMTP) will send mail. POP3 and IMAP receive email.

63. B.

A nondisclosure agreement (NDA) is a legal contract between two parties. This document is usually a confidentiality agreement where parties agree not to disclose the information listed in the agreement.

64. A.

A mandatory vacation has a fraud deterrent purpose similar to job rotation. The vacation time allows a full, unhampered investigation into all suspicious shenanigans.

65. A.

This is similar to the macro virus that was named the Melissa virus. When a user opens a document or spreadsheet containing the virus, it sends email to the first 50 people in their address book. Not all macro viruses are detected by antivirus software. Use caution when opening email attachments.

66. C.

There are many advantages of using Group Policy over Local Policy. They include adding systems to a domain so that you can oversee security, computer settings, and registry modification.

67. B.

Of all these, a password is typically the easiest to compromise. A password is a string of characters associated with a username. Users will create passwords that are easy to remember. Some of the most commonly used passwords are still 123456, password, and qwerty.

68. B.

With asset tracking, you can ensure that a terminated employee returns their company laptop containing sensitive data. Asset tracking databases will determine the location of a given piece of equipment or data.

69. A.

Steganography can be used to create hidden information in images. The binary bit weight increases in significance from right to left with the rightmost bit equal to 1. A legitimate use of steganography is to hide digital signatures called watermarks for copyright protection.

70. B.

Pretty Good Privacy (PGP) can be used to encrypt mail, files, and drives. It is used to provide confidentiality, integrity, and nonrepudiation. Confidentiality provides encryption, integrity with a hash, and nonrepudiation with a digital signature. S/MIME is used for email, and L2TP is not used with disk drives.

71. C.

Synchronizing time across a network uses Network Time Protocol (NTP). An NTP client listens for a broadcast from an NTP server, and the NTP client adjusts its time. For certain authentication methodologies like Kerberos, NTP is a must for the process to work properly.

72. B.

A warm site would be the best option. A cold site would take much longer than your maximum tolerable downtime (MTD) would allow, and a hot site is extremely expensive. A warm site usually has equipment and power but no data, but could be operational within the MTD.

73. D.

To allow only hosts from mycompany.net to access the intranet, you need to allow the mycompany.net ACL rule. ACLs usually follow specific to general pattern matching, so the last rule in the ACL is the most general.

74. D.

Solid-state drives are different from magnetic drives because there are no moving parts. A quick or full format deletes only the filesystem and does not delete the data. Degaussing ruins any hard drive, and it cannot be reused. To securely erase data from a flash-based solid-state drive, you should use the software the manufacturer provided.

75. C.

A honeypot will attract malicious users. Administrators then are able to use that information to protect legitimate assets. The location of the honeypot, as well as the services running on it and the data it contains, will determine what kind of attacks it will be vulnerable to. A honeynet is an entire network set up to attract attackers, not just a single system. A botnet is a collection of compromised computers called zombies and is controlled by a zombie master.

76. A.

Objectives and key results (OKR) are goals set to align and drive the best results. The only proactive layer in this list is running a vulnerability scan with Nesses or Nexpose and fixing the broken things. All the others are reactive to either a breach, an auditor, or results of resource allocation.

77. B.

The Ring model is a method of using four ringed layers that use system calls to communicate with the CPU. The innermost ring, known as Ring 0, is the most trusted kernel layer. Ring 1 contains OS components that are not the kernel, Ring 2 contains device drivers, and the outermost, least trusted layer, Ring 3, contains users.

78. C.

You need to configure a switched port analyzer (SPAN) if you want to monitor traffic passing through a switch. These ports are used for sniffing traffic or connecting an IDS. An IDS is used to detect malicious traffic, but it cannot monitor all the traffic unless it is connected to a promiscuous mode port.

79. A.

The body of data that is gathered by event logging is called an audit trail. Audit trails allow a security professional to build a timeline of events and actions that happened on a system to prove that an individual or entity is responsible for malicious activity.

80. D.

Offshoring medical imaging records would be dangerous. Having a third party in another country performing business-critical functions can violate HIPAA. As a provider, you must ensure that the foreign company who is providing storage services takes the proper steps to protect the data.

81. D.

Redundant array of independent disks (RAID) 10 provides striping for a set of mirrored disks. RAID 1 is encapsulated within RAID 0, providing fault tolerance and increased performance. If one disk is lost, the mirrored set can take its place.

82. C.

Virtual memory is a memory protection and management technique that maps hardware memory to an application. This enables more than one application to access the same information from the same memory address, instead of having each application load its own copy of a library into memory.

83. C.

A recovery point objective (RPO) indicates the amount of data loss or system unavailability measured in units of time that a business can endure. The RPO can help decide how often systems should be backed up.

84. C.

Data mining is the process of searching for specific patterns in large volumes of data. This can be used to draw conclusions about consumer behavior or a compromised credit card.

85. B.

Baselining is a configuration management task that involves taking a snapshot of a system's security configuration at a specific moment in time. That snapshot can be compared to a past snapshot, or a future snapshot, to determine what security changes have been made.

86. A.

Revoke! Of the choices listed, you should revoke the key to prevent unauthorized access. After the key has been revoked, you can then recover the data using a master decryption key or by recovering the revoked key. After data is recovered, encrypt with a new replacement key and give the new key to the user.

87. D.

Hardening a system so it provides only the required functionality is the best way to mitigate any zero-day issues an organization may have. A zero-day vulnerability has no fix. Hardening the system involves removing any services or applications that are not required.

88. C.

Backing up data is the role of a data custodian. The data custodian is usually responsible for data backups, network and endpoint security, systems maintenance, as well as disaster recovery. The data owner makes high-level security decisions, and the data custodian carries them out.

89. B.

You estimate four laptops each quarter will fail, costing $1,000 each. Therefore, $1,000 is the single loss expectancy (SLE).

90. A.

A proxy firewall is also known as an application-level gateway firewall. It is used primarily to hide the source of a network connection by terminating the connection and initiating a new connection. This allows you to hide the true source of the traffic.

Index

S

X

Z

Comprehensive Online Learning Environment

Register to gain one year of FREE access after activation to the online interactive learning environment and test bank to help you study for your CASP+ certification exam—included with your purchase of this book!

The online test bank includes the following:

- **Practice Test Questions** to reinforce what you learned
- **Bonus Practice Exam** to test your knowledge of the material

Go to http://www.wiley.com/go/sybextestprep to register and gain access to this interactive online learning environment and test bank with study tools.

Register and Access the Online Test Bank

To register your book and get access to the online test bank, follow these steps:

1. Go to bit.ly/SybexTest.
2. Select your book from the list.
3. Complete the required registration information, including answering the security verification to prove book ownership. You will be emailed a PIN code.
4. Follow the directions in the email or go to https://www.wiley.com/go/sybextestprep.
5. Enter the PIN code you received and click the "Activate PIN" button.
6. On the Create an Account or Login page, enter your username and password, and click Login. A "Thank you for activating your PIN!" message will appear. If you don't have an account already, create a new account.
7. Click the "Go to My Account" button to add your new book to the My Products page.

Comprehensive Online Learning Environment

Register to gain one year of FREE access after activation to the online interactive learning environment and test bank to help you study for your CASP+ certification exam—included with your purchase of this book!

The online test bank includes the following:

- **Practice Test Questions** to reinforce what you've learned
- **Bonus Practice Exam** to test your knowledge of the material

Go to http://www.wiley.com/go/sybextestprep to register and gain access to this comprehensive study tool package.

Register and Access the Online Test Bank

To register your book and get access to the online test bank, follow these steps:

1. Go to bit.ly/SybexTest.
2. Select your book from the list.
3. Complete the required registration information, including answering the security verification to prove book ownership. You will be emailed a PIN code.
4. Follow the directions in the email or go to https://www.wiley.com/go/sybextestprep.
5. Enter the PIN code you received and click the "Activate PIN" button.
6. On the Create an Account or Login page, enter your username and password, and click Login. A "Thank you for activating your PIN!" message will appear. If you don't have an account already, create a new account.
7. Click the "Go to My Account" button to add your new book to the My Products page.